Removing the emperor's clothes

Australia and tobacco plain packaging

Simon Chapman and Becky Freeman

SYDNEY UNIVERSITY PRESS

First published by Sydney University Press
© Simon Chapman and Becky Freeman 2014
© Sydney University Press 2014

Sydney University Press
Fisher Library F03
University of Sydney NSW 2006
AUSTRALIA
Email: sup.info@sydney.edu.au
sydney.edu.au/sup

National Library of Australia Cataloguing-in-Publication Data

Creator:	Chapman, Simon, 1951 - author.
Title:	Removing the emperor's clothes : Australia and tobacco plain packaging / Simon Chapman and Becky Freeman.
ISBN:	9781743323977 (paperback)
	9781743323984 (ebook : epub)
	9781743323991 (ebook : Kindle)
	9781743324295 (ebook : PDF)
Notes:	Includes bibliographical references and index.
Subjects:	Tobacco use--Australia--Prevention.
	Tobacco package labels--Australia.
	Advertising--Tobacco--Australia.
	Tobacco jars and boxes--Australia.
Other Authors/	
Contributors:	Freeman, Becky, author.
Dewey Number:	362.2960994

Cover design by Miguel Yamin

To Nicola Roxon, former Australian Health Minister and Attorney General; to her staff, and the executive and staff of the Australian Department of Health; and to all our colleagues with sincere thanks for your inspiring leadership, resilience and determination in making public health history and saving many, uncountable lives from tobacco-caused disease.

Contents

Foreword

The plain packaging story has attracted public attention in a way even its most ardent supporters would have found hard to credit at the outset.

At its simplest, the story is one of the public good against commercial evil – governments and health authorities introducing an evidence-based measure in the face of ferocious opposition from a lethal and discredited, but still powerful industry. But the story has much more than this. It has heroes and villains, political chicanery, legal cases in the High Court and international tribunals, global companies promoting their claims through front groups, research versus junk science, attempts to distract and disrupt the processes of government, smear campaigns, shadowy lobbyists, battles for media hearts and headlines, and dire warnings about Chinese criminal gangs.

While most of the tobacco industry's claims and predictions have been duly discredited, its greatest concern – the domino effect – has been justified. Once even one country with a population of 23 million showed that plain packaging could be implemented, others would see it as something feasible. It is clearly now only a matter of time before, like tobacco advertising bans and measures to protect non-smokers from passive smoking, plain packaging is introduced in other countries – always of course opposed by the tobacco industry with ever-increasing desperation.

Nobody is better placed to tell the story than Simon Chapman and his colleague and co-author Becky Freeman, and they do so with a splendidly readable mix of information, anecdote, science, passion and humour. They take us from the origins of plain packaging through to all the processes and political activity that led to its introduction, while also providing thorough analyses of both the science around packaging and the tobacco industry's own internal and external positions, machinations and skullduggery.

As they emphasise, plain packaging was not intended as a single magic bullet to end all smoking overnight; rather it is the next and most logical step in a comprehensive approach to end tobacco promotion and to reduce smoking over time, with a special focus on children and young people. But as they also note, the international tobacco industry's frenetic and aggressive response – more ferocious than any of us can remember over any issue in several decades – provides ample confirmation of the importance the tobacco companies attach to their capacity to promote through packaging to adults and children alike.

So what have we learned from the plain packaging story?

First and foremost, we have learned that this powerful and ruthless industry can be defeated, even on an issue that it clearly sees as being of fundamental importance for its long-term survival.

Second, political leadership and integrity can trump cynical commercial interest. The authors rightly laud Nicola Roxon, Australia's pioneering health minister and attorney general, to whom they dedicate their book. She saw prevention as a priority, recognised the importance of further action on tobacco, implemented comprehensive approaches, backed plain packaging – and drove it through, despite immense and often vicious industry opposition. Legislation cannot happen without legislators: for me, as for Chapman and Freeman, Nicola Roxon is simply the best and most courageous minister for prevention Australia has seen. As they further point out, the legislation went through with cross-party backing, since confirmed by the incoming Coalition government: credit is properly paid to the then Opposition for treating this as a health issue rather than a political football, and to some of its MPs, notably Dr Mal Washer, for their staunch support.

Third, tobacco companies are increasingly, in the Australian vernacular, 'on the nose'. Their lies and deceptions over decades have created an environment in which media, politicians and the community simply do not believe what they say. Their lack of credibility is compounded by increasing difficulty in finding anyone willing to be associated with them, or even people of high calibre who want to work for an industry whose products kill one in two regular users. One must wonder if some of the industry's remarkable own goals (such as blatantly ridiculous assertions about illicit sales, or expecting that 'astroturfing' would not be exposed) would have occurred in earlier decades when they had smarter, classier leaders and executives.

Fourth, public health coalitions can work well and cohesively towards a common goal. The coalition in support of plain packaging was both organised and instinctive, with wonderful support not only from core tobacco control groups, but also a wide range of health and community organisations. It is not surprising that those working in other areas of public health look to tobacco control as an advocacy model.

Fifth, sound research and a strong evidence base underpin both good public health policy and effective advocacy. Australia has been blessed with outstanding tobacco researchers for many years; the authors rightly identify Melanie Wakefield and Michelle Scollo as stellar researchers who live in the real world and understand its needs, while maintaining a constant focus on academic rigour and integrity.

As an author, Simon Chapman is inevitably constrained in describing to the full his own massive contributions. Simon has, of course, created a unique niche – he is not only an outstanding and creative advocate, teacher, editor, prolific author and media commentator, but also a leading researcher who has made many important contributions to tobacco control literature over many years. It was Simon who proposed plain packaging as a major recommendation for the Australian National Preventative Health Taskforce after work he and others had done in this area; he was a crucial figure in the activity that led to its implementation; he has tirelessly pursued and exposed the industry's deceitful counter-arguments; and he deserves even further credit for following up with this book, as well as so much other invaluable work in tobacco control. His example should inspire other public health academics to understand that the roles of researcher and campaigner can be combined to exceptional effect.

Sixth, while this battle has been won, it is a battle in a war that began 64 years ago with the *BMJ* (1) and *JAMA* (2) reports by Doll and Hill and Wynder and Graham demonstrating the lethal consequences of smoking beyond any doubt. The global battle will continue as long as there is a commercial tobacco industry, and as long as its leaders – board members and chief executives – remain personally untouched by the literally millions of deaths that their actions have caused. In Australia, the battle must continue, to avoid complacency and to ensure that governments support the continuing action that is needed to complement plain packaging.

So while this book tells a great story, it is also an important text for any who are interested in how good public health policy is developed and implemented, or whoe are interested in the art and science of public health advocacy. There should be no illusions about the obstacles entailed in taking on massive global industries. Chapman and Freeman offer encouragement that, given persistence, good science, research-based recommendations, skilled advocacy and perhaps above all, politicians with integrity, the public good can indeed prevail.

Mike Daube AO
Professor of Health Policy
Curtin University
President, Australian Council on Smoking and Health (ACOSH)

Abbreviations

AAR	Alliance of Australian Retailers
ABC	Australian Broadcasting Corporation
ACCC	Australian Competition and Consumer Commission
AIHW	Australian Institute of Health and Welfare
ALEC	American Legislative Exchange Council
AMA	Australian Medical Association
APEC	Asia-Pacific Economic cooperation
ARA	Australian Retailers Association
ASH	Action on Smoking and Health
BAT	British American Tobacco
BATA	British American Tobacco Australasia (and Australia)
BATCO	British American Tobacco Company
BIT	Bilateral Investment Treaty
BUGA UP	Billboard utilising graffitists against unhealthy promotion
CPI	consumer price index
DFAT	Department of Foreign Affairs and Trade

FCTC   Framework Convention on Tobacco Control

FOI   freedom of information

GATT   General Agreement on Tariff and Trade

IP   intellectual property

IPA   Institute of Public Affairs

ISDS   Investor-State Dispute Settlement

ITC   International Tobacco Control

MCDS   Ministerial Council on Drug Strategy

NARGA   National Association of Retail Grocers of Australia

NDSHS   National Drug Strategy Household Survey

NGO   non-government organisation

NHMRC   National Health and Medical Research Council

PEG   percutaneous endoscopic gastrostomy

PMA   Philip Morris Asia

PML   Philip Morris Limited

PR   public relations

PWC   PriceWaterhouseCoopers

RJR   RJ Reynolds

TBT   Technical Barriers to Trade

TPP   Trans-Pacific Partnership

TRIPS   Trade-Related Aspects of Intellectual Property

WHO   World Health Organization

WIPO   World Intellectual Property Organization

WTO   World Trade Organization

Introduction

Since 1 December 2012 all tobacco products sold in Australia – cigarettes, hand-rolling tobacco, cigars and pipe tobacco – have been required to be sold in standard 'plain' packs. The only features of the pack that now differentiate one brand from another are the mandatory brand and 'variant' names (for example *Dunhill* – the brand name – and *Premier Red* – a variant of the *Dunhill* brand). The tobacco manufacturing and importing companies are required to comply with graphic health warning legislation, put their name and address on the side of the pack, and have a unique bar code, which means nothing to any smoker. Other than these differences, all packs look the same, aside from the variations induced by having one of 14 graphic health warnings.

But there is nothing plain about Australia's plain packs. They are anything but plain white or drab boxes. The plain packaging legislation was accompanied by new regulations about cigarette pack warnings requiring that the graphic (picture) warnings that had appeared on all Australian packs since 2006 be increased to 75% of the front of the pack. The size of the combined text and graphic warning must take up 90% of the back of the pack.

World first

Australia's plain packaging legislation was the first time anywhere in the world that a government had mandated what the entire appearance of packaging for *any* product must look like. There are many categories of consumer goods where governments require mandatory inclusions on packaging or apply standards to the products themselves. Ingredient labelling on foods, warning labels on dangerous household or garden products like cleaning agents, pesticides or flammable goods, and pharmaceutical product information about dosage and contra-indications, are all examples where such requirements are common. Many governments also require that certain consumer goods must meet safety standards and that advertising claims for them should not be misleading.

But nowhere has there been any example of the entire packaging of a product been prescribed. The Australian legislation was therefore globally historic, unique and made the statement that tobacco products were, in every respect, *exceptional* items of commerce.

Australia joined the front line of global tobacco control 30 years ago when it became one of the first nations to start banning tobacco advertising (direct advertising of cigarettes was banned on radio and television from September 1976). Since that time, successive Australian governments at state and federal levels have incrementally progressed their commitment toward a comprehensive approach to tobacco control. Components of Australia's approaches to tobacco control include the following:[1]

- Taxing tobacco to increase its cost to smokers or potential smokers, thereby putting a brake on consumption and stimulating cessation. After Norway, Australia has the most expensive cigarettes in the world. (3)
- Mass reach anti-smoking media campaigns, well-funded in Australia by most global standards. (4)
- Smokefree workplace and public spaces legislation which prevents smoking inside all public places including all forms of public trans-

---

1 The best single reference for very detailed information on all aspects of tobacco control in Australia is www.tobaccoinaustralia.org.

port, restaurants, cafes, bars and pubs, theatres, cinemas, public halls and, increasingly, sports stadiums and some outdoor dining areas.

- Large, graphic pack warnings.
- Bans on the retail display and point-of-sale promotion of tobacco products.
- A prohibition on the use of the deceptive cigarette descriptors 'light' and 'mild' (5)
- Limits on duty-free imports (only 50 cigarettes) per adult.
- Government subsidy of evidence-based smoking cessation medications and Quitline funding.
- Specific focus programs such as the *Tackling Indigenous smoking* initiative.

Plain packaging is the latest change in a long series of encroachments onto the pack that commenced with the first tiny warning at the base of packs that appeared from 1973. The tobacco industry strongly resisted all of these in Australia, as elsewhere around the world. A British American Tobacco (BAT) official wrote to its German branch office in 1978: 'Obviously the group policy should be to avoid health warnings on all tobacco products for just as long as we can.' Over the next decades Big Tobacco sought to defeat, dilute and delay even the most modest changes to pack warnings (see a history of this in Australia here (6)).

The industry threw everything it could at the effort to stop plain packaging: millions of dollars in hysterical TV and other advertising, a forlorn High Court challenge that was rejected by all but one of the seven judges, intense public relations activity, a conga-line of melodramatic political threats and bluster from industry allies, including often obscure US trade and commerce groups. The slippery slope metaphor was given its biggest ever workout: life as we know it would surely soon collapse entirely into dreary North Korean conformity when anything posing even the smallest risk to health was treated in the same way as tobacco.

Between us, we have worked in tobacco control for a combined total of 50 years, as researchers and advocates for policy change in several different countries. Neither of us ever experienced anything remotely as intense and as sustained as the tobacco industry's push back against the impending introduction of plain packaging. As we discuss in the final chapter, plain packaging has already begun to spread to other nations.

Because the stakes are so large and the potential impacts so devastating to the tobacco industry, we would expect similar resistance there to such developments. This is already happening in Great Britain, Ireland and New Zealand, using a template that was tried and failed miserably in Australia.

There is probably no more telling illustration of how much the tobacco industry fears plain packaging than a comment made to a parliamentary committee in August 2011 by the chief executive of British American Tobacco Australia (BATA), David Crow. Crow almost begged the politicians to keep on raising tobacco tax instead of introducing plain packs. He said:

> What I do believe is that . . . if the objective is to reduce consumption then you would move towards areas which have been evidence-based not only in this country but in others around the world – things like education, which have been proven to work and have been the focus of many studies across the world. They have been proven to work very, very well. We have great examples in this country not only on tobacco but on things like skin cancer and drink driving laws, where they have changed consumer behaviour. We have seen that being effective not only here but elsewhere. *There should be more, more and more on that.* We need uniformity on pricing; we need to get pricing right and excise regimes right. *We understand that the price going up when the excise goes up reduces consumption. We saw that last year very effectively with the increase in excise. There was a 25 per cent increase in the excise and we saw the volumes go down by about 10.2 per cent; there was about a 10.2 per cent reduction in the industry last year in Australia.* So there are ways of achieving the objectives that do not infringe on the property rights, do not breach the laws and the international commitments and do not mean that the Australian government would have to compensate people. (7) [our emphases]

Paul Grogan, head of advocacy for Cancer Council Australia, was incredulous at Crow's candour here, in underscoring the sheer desperation of the industry to offer up even another significant tax rise in lieu of plain packs:

I was at a hearing where he was fronting the industry presentation and he effectively said 'we need to increase tobacco excise'. And I was thinking, really great! Because we know that really works. That really struck a chord with a few members of the committee who were informed enough to know that [tax] really does work. So they were saying 'how desperate is this guy, if he's putting up as an alternative something that has been proven to work over 30 years of evidence? Maybe this thing [plain packaging] will work even better'. It was a very strange kind of desperation.

Why plain packs?

Why is tobacco so 'like no other product' that it warrants this treatment? Globally, tobacco claims more than five million deaths a year. Many smokers suffer for years from wretched diseases like emphysema which eventually makes taking a few steps a major effort. Thousands of previously private internal tobacco industry documents read like recipe books from crack cocaine labs, detailing how the cigarette can be better engineered as a nicotine delivery device to 'make it harder for existing smokers to leave the product'. (8)

Lung cancer is a disease that was rarely seen before the mid-1930s. (9) Thanks to cheap cigarettes that flowed from the mechanisation of cigarette manufacture, today lung cancer is the world's leading cause of cancer death, way ahead of breast, prostate and all other cancers which often attract massive community and political support. Lung cancer in males has been falling every year in Australia since 1982, and female lung cancer rates will probably never reach even half the heights experienced by men (Figure 1), thanks to successive governments taking incremental action to curtail the industry since 1973 when health warnings first appeared. By 2004, the male lung cancer rate had fallen to that last seen in 1963. In 50 years from now, lung cancer may once again be 'history'.

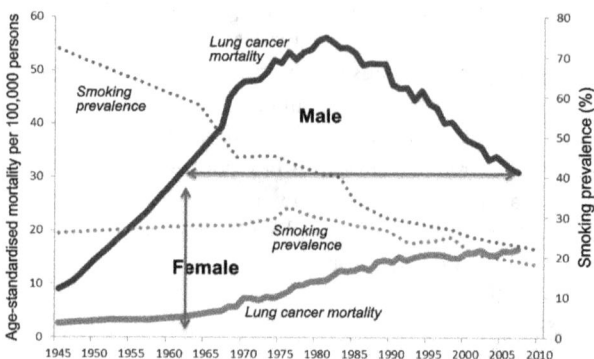

Figure 1 Male lung cancer rates per 100,000 as low as they were in 1963. Source: Australian Institute of Health and Welfare National Mortality Database

The Soviet dictator Joseph Stalin famously said that 'a single death is a tragedy, a million deaths is a statistic'. And in tobacco control, there are statistics to die for. Tobacco caused about 100 million deaths last century. But a projected one billion people will die from tobacco-caused disease this century if present trends continue. (10)

The average smoker takes 12.7 puffs per cigarette. (11) A person who starts smoking at age 15, and smokes 20 cigarettes a day for 40 years, will baste the delicate pink linings of their mouth, throat and lungs with a cocktail of 69 carcinogens (12) some 3,710,940 times by the time they reach just 55 years of age.

Half of long-term smokers die early from a tobacco-caused disease, taking an average of 10 years off the normal life expectancy. (13) Consider the case of former Beatle George Harrison, who died of lung cancer at just 58. At the time of his death, British life expectancy for men was 75 years. So he lost 17 years that we can assume he might otherwise have lived. If we assume Harrison started smoking late – at 18 years – he smoked for 40 years. A cigarette takes about six minutes to smoke. So for every cigarette that Harrison smoked, he lost more than five times the time it took to smoke them all, off his normal life expectancy (14).

On and on it goes. But even stratospheric statistics on tobacco deaths have become banal for many. (10) People rationalise that life's a jungle of risks, and that feeling fine or seeing longevity in a relative who smokes means that they are bulletproof. People cling to self-exempting beliefs (15, 16) such as that air pollution causes most lung cancer, or that putting on some weight if you quit is more dangerous than smoking.

What is so often missing from these reflections about smoking is any real appreciation of the suffering and greatly diminished quality of life in the years that people can spend living with smoking caused disease.

On many occasions across our careers we have received unsolicited letters, calls and email from people living with tobacco-caused disease. Two in particular stand out.

An articulate 52-year-old woman called me a few years ago. Give the 'smoking kills' line a rest, she urged:

I've smoked for 30 years. I have emphysema. I am virtually housebound. I get exhausted walking more than a few metres. I have urinary incontinence, and because I can't move quickly to the toilet, I wet myself and smell. I can't bear the embarrassment, so I stay isolated at home. Smoking has ruined my life. You should start telling people about the living hell smoking causes while you're still alive, not just that it kills you.

Then early this year, amid publicity on the 50th anniversary of the first historic United States Surgeon General's report on smoking, an amazingly brave woman, Karen, wrote to me about her experiences with cancer of the mouth. Smoking tobacco causes around 70% of oral cancer in men, and around 55% in women. (17) In 2009, 3031 Australian were diagnosed with various head and neck cancers, and in 2010, 1045 died. (18)

Here are Karen's words, used with her permission.

Karen's story

This cancer is brutal! Treatments are cruel! Daily for six to eight weeks during radiotherapy treatments our head and face is covered with a tight mask and bolted to a slab while radiotherapy is blasted at our mouth, teeth, jaw, face and neck. Damage during and after this treatment is horrendous. Many of us will never speak clearly, swallow or function normally again.

Patients endure tracheotomies inserted in their wind pipe because we cannot breathe naturally through our mouth and nose due to swelling and other side effects.

Many people are left with PEG [percutaneous endoscopic gastrostomy] feeding tubes shoved in their stomach for the rest of their lives because they will never swallow normal food via their mouth again. I had a PEG tube for three and a half years. A tube hanging from our stomach is sickening and depressing. Think about never eating another meal or swallowing again! You can't imagine the never ending physical and emotional hell this particular disease causes.

I was diagnosed in 2007 at 46 years of age. Yes, I smoked for several years. I have endured 12 surgeries since 2007 trying to improve my quality of life.

Almost all my entire tongue, lower jaw, gums and beautiful teeth have been removed and reconstructed because of treatments to remove cancer. Bone was taken from my hip to reconstruct my jaw. Normal function is gone. Permanently. My perfect face is now disfigured.

I have not sat down to a normal meal with friends or family in almost seven years. Those pleasures of socialising, eating at restaurants and dinner parties that everyone regularly attends are history for us. I struggle to control saliva because of oral cavity nerve damage and facial trauma. Sometimes I dribble when I try to speak. I will never kiss again.

My life has been destroyed by this cancer, as has many other wonderful people around Australia. We lose our careers. Relationships fall apart.

We can't make appointments over the telephone or ask for something over a counter. No one can understand us! We write down questions during appointments because we can't speak and doctors don't understand what we're saying. That doesn't work! This is frustrating, humiliating and extremely upsetting.

The aftermath from this disease is debilitating and permanent. Dental issues are painful and relentless, yet the previous federal government abolished the Enhanced Care Dental Scheme. This is shameful!

We can't just pick up from where we left off. We can't 'do coffee' with friends and chat about our issues like most other cancer patients because we can't speak or drink as normal. We can't cover our mouth with a piece of clothing and get on with it. Our face is our identity!

Many smokers say things like 'oh well, I'm going to die anyway' or 'I could get hit by a bus tomorrow'. Well, from my experience I can honestly say dying immediately would be much easier than the long slow suffering this disease puts patients through. In 2007 while in hospital I had a cardiac arrest because the tracheotomy blocked. Once resuscitated, little did I know I had years and years of pain, ongoing treatments and loss of normal function ahead of me! It's devastating!

My lower face and mouth has been cut and shut many times. My neck/throat has been dissected twice ear to ear. It's been a long difficult road! I've undergone six surgeries in the past three years trying to improve mouth function and facial appearance. More than likely there's a few more down the track. I have a wonderful plastic surgeon who genuinely cares!

Karen's hopes are for more resources to be given to care and support for people in her situation. We hope her story stimulates far greater attention to the impact of cancer on people's lives.

But with so much potential for head and neck cancers to be prevented, we hope too that her unforgettable words will be passed along to anyone still smoking. It is stories like Karen's which explain why tobacco control is so important.

Plain packaging is the latest strategy in a suite of policies and awareness campaigns that have been driving smoking down in nations like Australia over the past three to four decades. It is difficult to over-state the global importance of Australia's leadership: the new tobacco packaging law makes an exceptional statement about tobacco, lifting it into a league above all other health risks.

There is one parallel: prescribed drugs, which are designed to save lives and enhance health, but are heavily restricted because of misuse concerns. Unlike cigarettes, antibiotics, oral contraceptives and cholesterol-controlling drugs are not sold in pretty, highly market-re-searched boxes, but in plain packs with the name and dosage instruc-tions.

The tobacco industry has been stripped of its ability to call its car-cinogenic products 'mild' or 'light'; banished from all above-the-line advertising and all sponsorship; told by all major political parties in Australia, except the Nationals and Liberal Democrats, that its polit-ical donations are unwanted; uniquely excluded from giving research money to universities; rejected as an investment option by an increas-ing number of superannuation funds; (19) and ensconced in the pub-lic's mind as the index case example of corporate mendacity.

The new Australian pack law sets a catastrophic precedent for the global tobacco industry because it rips the very heart out of its ability to dress the pack to make a killing. Tobacco packaging is now devoid of any graphic feature – including colours and special scripts on the cigarette itself – that conveys any associations other than harm. Just as no Australian aged 22 or under has today ever seen a football match sponsored by tobacco or a cigarette advertisement in any Australian publication or on television, the next generation of kids will grow up having no sense of what the totally image-driven difference is between Brand X or Brand Y, and how they might select a brand to distract from some aspect of a fragile personality. The new law has effectively put an end to this lethal corporate pied piper's promotional tune that has led many millions to early deaths. The emperor of cancer now has no clothes in Australia.

In public health and medicine, we venerate milestones like public sanitation, the discovery of anaesthesia, the introduction of vaccina-tion, and the development of antibiotics and contraception. With chronic diseases like cancer, heart and respiratory disease dominating global disease profiles, governments with the courage to tackle corpo-rations whose goals are antithetical to public health deserve a similar place in history. This law, combined with the significant tax rises, is as big as it gets.

We have written this book principally for those in other countries wanting to make the best case for plain packaging and to defend it from the inevitable attacks that will follow. We also wanted to produce a history of how such a major step in the history of tobacco control occurred, how it was resisted and how it prevailed. So often, such histories in public health exist as oral histories only, so we wanted to capture as much of it as we could.

Acknowledgements

Simon wrote most of the book, with Becky writing Chapter 3. So where the book uses the first person ('I') this refers to Simon. In 2013, we and Mike Daube were invited by the World Health Organization's regional office for the Western Pacific to write a shortened version of a publication which shares some main goals of this book. Some sections of this book draw on early drafts of that publication, generally in expanded form.

We are grateful to Nicola Roxon, the Australian health minister from December 2007 till December 2011, and then attorney general until February 2013; her chief of staff Dr Angela Pratt; Professor Mike Daube who chaired the Tobacco Committee of the National Preventative Health Taskforce; and several closely involved informants who preferred to remain anonymous, for giving us their time for interviews and many follow-up queries. Michelle Scollo has our special thanks for her fastidious responses to many queries. Several long-time colleagues and friends, including some public servants, who were members of a government taskforce set up to advise on legal attacks on the plain packaging legislation were unable to speak with us about any matters germane to that role because of legally binding confidentiality agreements they had signed. There may one day be another book that will describe that chapter of the story of plain packaging in Australia.

Thanks to Sydney University Press, and especially our editor Agata Mrva-Montoya for her encouragement and enormous efficiency.

I would also like to thank the Rockefeller Foundation for giving me a full month's residency in April 2014 at the Rockefeller's Villa Serbelloni at Bellagio, Italy, to complete the book. For 29 glorious days I wrote for up to eight hours a day in a tranquil study overlooking the twin lakes of Lago di Lecco and Lago di Como. It was a writer's paradise.

1
Early advocacy for plain packs

The idea that governments might require all tobacco products to be sold in so-called plain, standardised or generic packs, devoid of any element or feature that might contribute to their attractiveness or allure to smokers or future smokers, can be traced back to Canada in the mid-1980s. Dr Gerry Karr appears to be the first person to have formally proposed the idea in a motion presented at a Canadian Medical Association annual general meeting in June 1986, (20) and David Sweanor, a Canadian tobacco control activist, was recommending it to politicians in 1988. (21) Over the next decade, the proposal received some attention from researchers and advocates in Australia (David Hill and Ron Borland and colleagues) (22), New Zealand (Park Beede, Rob Lawson, Mike Shepherd and Michael Carr-Gregg, (23–26) and a considerable amount of attention in Canada (27, 28).

Carr-Gregg, who headed up a coalition of tobacco control groups in New Zealand, told us he had been told about plain packaging by David Sweanor. The coalition soon promoted the idea to a parliamentary committee sitting and Carr-Gregg says: 'I remember the expression on the industry's face when we outlined this at a select committee – they looked apoplectic! One of them rushed out of the room (presumably to phone head office of BAT [British American Tobacco]). I don't think they saw that coming!'

The vanguard New Zealand government's Toxic Substances Board 1989 report (29) endorsed a proposal by Murray Laugesen, representing the Coalition Against Tobacco Advertising and Promotion, that cigarettes be sold only in white packs with black text and no colours or logos. This recommendation was not taken up by the government, but the momentum had begun.

In 1990 the conference resolutions at the Seventh World Conference on Tobacco or Health in Perth included one submitted by Canadian advocate Gar Mahood stating:

> Generic packaging: given the importance of package designs in promoting tobacco products, this Conference endorses the concept of mandatory generic packaging of all tobacco products, and urges all countries to include generic packaging in their tobacco control legislation. (30)

A similar resolution was passed at the 1994 world conference in Buenos Aires.

A BATCO fax from 1994 summed up these early beginnings, concluding prophetically with 'the rest is history' (Figure 1.1).

Early Australian interest

In 1992, the Australian Ministerial Council on Drug Strategy (MCDS) comprising health, police and justice ministers from all eight states and territories, considered a report commissioned by the MCDS Tobacco Taskforce, chaired by Mike Daube. (22) This report recommended that 'regulations be extended to cover the colours, design and wording of the entire exterior of the pack'. The MCDS report proposed large new warnings and asked for a report on plain packaging. While new, stronger warnings were mandated on all packs from January 1995, the idea of plain packaging did not progress. At that stage the ministers were only prepared to move in a staged process to larger, stronger warnings.

A memo from WD & HO Wills (the BAT company then trading in Australia) noted:

> Mike Daube's influence as chairman of the Tobacco Taskforce reviewing pack labelling in 1991 was a crucial first step in a wider

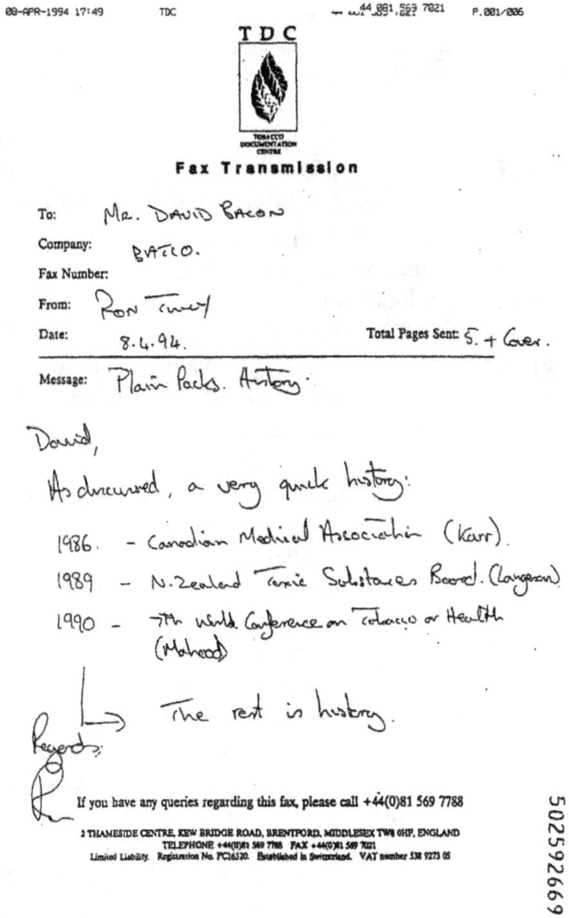

08-APR-1994 17:49 TDC 44 081 569 7021 P.001/006

TDC

TOBACCO DOCUMENTATION CENTRE

Fax Transmission

To: Mr. David Bacon

Company: BATCO.

Fax Number:

From: Ron Tully

Date: 8.4.94. Total Pages Sent: 5. + Cover.

Message: Plain Packs. History.

David,

As discussed, a very quick history:

1986. - Canadian Medical Association (Kerr).

1989 - N. Zealand Toxic Substances Board. (Laugesen)

1990 - 7th World Conference on Tobacco or Health (Mahood)

→ The rest is history.

Regards,

R

If you have any queries regarding this fax, please call +44(0)81 569 7788

2 THAMESIDE CENTRE, KEW BRIDGE ROAD, BRENTFORD, MIDDLESEX TW8 0HF, ENGLAND
TELEPHONE +44(0)81 569 7788 FAX +44(0)81 569 7021
Limited Liability. Registration No. FC16520. Established in Switzerland. VAT number 538 9273 05

502592669

Figure 1.1 BATCO summary of plain packaging developments, 1993. A 70 page dossier of these various early papers was prepared for a BATCO meeting held in September 1993 (31) where those attending considered how they might derail this early momentum.

agenda, which, of course, culminated in the CBRC [Centre for Behavioural Research in Cancer] Report in 1992. (32)

Daube returned to the plain packaging agenda 17 years later, when he chaired the National Preventative Health Taskforce Tobacco Committee (see pp 18).

In 1993, Cancer Council Australia's national cancer prevention policy included a recommendation for plain packs. This recommendation was maintained in all six subsequent updates of the policy.

In December 1994, Western Australia's health minister, Peter Foss, called for the introduction of plain packaging (33) and the Australian Medical Association lobbied for it in 1995. (34)

In September 1997, the Australian government responded to a Senate committee's recommendation that plain packaging be considered. While not committing in any way to the policy, its careful wording did not close the door on the possibility:

> In response to the mounting interest in generic packaging, the Commonwealth obtained advice from the attorney general's department on the legal and constitutional barriers to generic packaging. This advice indicates that the Commonwealth does possess powers under the constitution to introduce such packaging but that any attempt to use these powers to introduce further tobacco control legislation needs to be considered in the context of the increasingly critical attention being focused on the necessity, appropriateness, justification and basis for regulation by such bodies as the Office of Regulatory Review, the High Court and Senate standing committees. In addition, further regulation needs to be considered in the context of Australia's international obligations regarding free trade under the General Agreement on Tariff and Trade (GATT), and our obligations under international covenants such as the Paris Convention for the Protection of Industrial Property, and the agreement on Trade-Related Aspects of Intellectual Property Rights (TRIPS). (35)

As we will see in Chapter 6, the High Court of Australia roundly rejected tobacco companies' constitutional arguments in 2012 and much legal scholarship has challenged expressed concerns about Australia's international treaty obligations. (36) However tobacco industry commentary in other countries, and a subsequent withdrawal from an early attempt to introduce such legislation by the Canadian government, may have influenced Australian political thinking at the time. Responding to the Australian Medical Association's calls for plain packaging, a spokesperson for the then Labor health minister Carmen Lawrence is reported to have said plain packs 'would breach constitutional requirement for free trade. We would have to buy the tobacco companies' trademarks, and that would cost us hundreds of millions of dollars.' (34)

Canadian campaign

In the mid-1990s, Canada went further than any nation and considered introducing plain packaging legislation, with Health Canada commissioning a thumping 427 page expert review. (27) The then Canadian Prime Minister Jean Chrétien had announced in February 1994 a significant rollback of tobacco taxes, after increased tobacco smuggling into Canada occurred via Native American reservations on the US-Canada border. (37) To counter concerns about the impact this would have on the health of Canadians, he promised several compensatory measures, including consideration of plain packaging of cigarettes. Within weeks of this announcement, the Canadian House of Commons Standing Committee on Health launched public hearings into the possible impact and effects of plain packaging.

The tobacco industry responded by launching a coordinated campaign that focused on framing plain packaging as an intellectual property issue; countering health agency research with industry-sponsored expertise (an edited book was produced by the long-time tobacco industry consultant, the late John Luik; (38)) and creating a public debate designed to weaken public support. The tobacco companies Philip Morris and RJ Reynolds worked with former US trade representative Carla Hills and former deputy trade representative Julius Katz to tell the Canadian government that plain packaging would be an 'unlawful expropriation' of their trademark rights and that 'the compensation claims of affected foreign trademark holders would be staggering, amounting to hundreds of millions of dollars.' (39)

The tobacco industry decided to fight plain packaging on trade grounds. Arguments focused on intellectual property agreements governed by the World Intellectual Property Organization (WIPO) and the investment protection contained in the North American Free Trade Agreement. Despite being told repeatedly by WIPO that its analysis was flawed, (40) the industry persisted in telling the government and the media that plain packaging would be contrary to intellectual property protections. Following the industry's misrepresentation of international trade law, a newly appointed Canadian health minister dropped plain packaging. By 1995, plain packaging was no longer on the policy radar in Canada due to the success of the tobacco industry's campaign, coupled with a Canadian Supreme Court ruling against provisions of the *Tobacco Products Control Act* on advertising and promotion.

However, as two slides from an internal industry presentation show (Figure 1.2), from at least 1994 the tobacco industry was well aware that international trade treaties and conventions provided it with 'little protection', 'little support' and 'little joy' in defeating plain packaging. Its success in framing plain packaging as being incompatible with these treaties and conventions was a triumph of public relations spin over sophisticated legal understanding of what those treaties would have allowed. The spin had succeeded.

Plain pack group

Examining
Treaties & conventions
Industry bodies
   All with trade mark protection interest
GATT/TRIPS

Findings

**Current conventions & treaties afford
little protection
GATT/TRIPS little joy
Other industry groupings little support
Domestic political solutions needed**

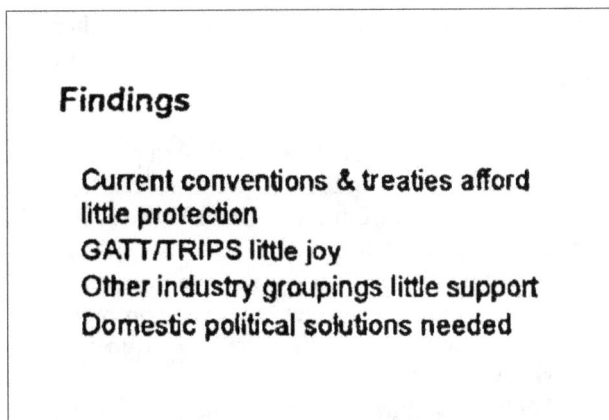

Figure 1.2 Tobacco industry knowledge of legal impediments in
opposing plain packaging, 1990s. Source:
http://legacy.library.ucsf.edu/tid/hpp34a99

Canadians Rob Cunningham and Ken Kyle published a summary of
the case for plain packaging in 1995. (41) Physicians for a Smoke-free
Canada have written a detailed account of why Canada did not adopt
plain packaging in the 1990s, some 20 years ago. (39) Their report reviews internal tobacco industry documents from the period that have
since come as a result of settlements of legal actions in the United
States, and traces the tobacco industry campaign to ensure that plain
packaging reforms would not succeed.

The new millennium

The failure of New Zealand, Canada and Australia to progress in the
1990s may have temporarily taken the wind out of the sails of advocacy
for plain packs. But the concept had taken firm root and was never far
from the surface of future possibilities in global tobacco control circles.
Two papers on the importance of packaging in the tobacco advertising
and promotional mix (42, 43) were published early in the new millen-
nium by Australian researcher Melanie Wakefield's group, and a case
study of tobacco packaging was published in the legal literature in 2004

by Melbourne lawyer Benn McGrady. It explored whether the TRIPS agreement 'creates a positive right to use a trademark,' concluding that it did not. (44)

In May 2003, the World Health Assembly, the parliament of the World Health Association, adopted the world's first global health treaty, the Framework Convention on Tobacco Control (FCTC). As of April 2014, 178 nations (as well the European Union) have ratified the treaty and have thereby become 'Parties' to it.

Recommendations on plain packaging were included in guidelines on packaging and labelling and on advertising and promotion that were adopted at the 3rd Conference of the Parties, held in Durban, South Africa, in November 2008. (45)

Clause 46 of the guidelines for implementation of article 11, *Guidelines on packaging and labelling of tobacco products*, states:

Plain packaging
Parties should consider adopting measures to restrict or prohibit the use of logos, colours, brand images or promotional information on packaging other than brand names and product names displayed in a standard colour and font style (plain packaging). This may increase the noticeability and effectiveness of health warnings and messages, prevent the package from detracting attention from them, and address industry package design techniques that may suggest that some products are less harmful than others. (46)

And article 13, *Guidelines on tobacco advertising, promotion and sponsorship* (47) states:

16. The effect of advertising or promotion on packaging can be eliminated by requiring plain packaging: black and white or two other contrasting colours, as prescribed by national authorities; nothing other than a brand name, a product name and/or manufacturer's name, contact details and the quantity of product in the packaging, without any logos or other features apart from health warnings, tax stamps and other government-mandated information or markings; prescribed font style and size; and standardized shape, size and materials. There should be no advertising or promotion inside or attached to the package or on individual cigarettes or other tobacco products.

17. If plain packaging is not yet mandated, the restriction should cover as many as possible of the design features that make tobacco products more attractive to consumers such as animal or other figures, 'fun' phrases, coloured cigarette papers, attractive smells, novelty or seasonal packs.

Recommendation

Packaging and product design are important elements of advertising and promotion. Parties should consider adopting plain packaging requirements to eliminate the effects of advertising or promotion on packaging. Packaging, individual cigarettes or other tobacco products should carry no advertising or promotion, including design features that make products attractive.

In 2005, Cancer Research UK called for the implementation of plain packaging for tobacco products, allowing for only the brand name, the health warning and any other mandatory consumer information to appear on such packs. After studying tobacco company documents, Cancer Research UK concluded plain packaging was 'the next step in breaking the links between the tobacco industry and its consumers'. (48)

In 2006, Canadian lawyer Eric Le Gresley presented on the legal considerations relevant to plain packaging to a global audience at the 13th World Conference on Tobacco or Health in Washington DC.

Timely review

In August 2007, we were part of a research team working on a three-year National Health and Medical Research Council (NHMRC) grant examining various options for 'the future of tobacco control'. (49) Being a very advanced nation in global tobacco control, Australia had fully implemented almost all of the planks of a comprehensive tobacco control policy platform. But smoking prevalence remained at just under one in five adults, and our project sought to focus on some of the less developed or more contentious issues where Australia (and indeed most nations) had not advanced very far. Our group published papers on issues as diverse as regulating the retail environment, (50) genetic testing for susceptibility to smoking, (51) harm reduction (52) and, later, smoker licensing. (53)

Plain packaging was one such issue, and along with Matthew Rimmer, a legal scholar in intellectual property from the Australian National University, we published an online review, (54) later peer-reviewed, (10) on the concept of plain packaging and the evidence and arguments for it.

Researchers are often asked to nominate papers they have produced which they believe have been influential in 'real world' settings. This was one such paper. Our review was cited by numerous other researchers who went on to conduct experiments that clearly demonstrated that removing the design elements of packaging sharply reduced product appeal and increased consumer attention to health warnings—see Chapter 2. Our review has been steadily cited by other researchers (Google Scholar shows 111 citations by October 2014, easily the most for any paper yet published on plain packaging) but by far the most important outcome was the timing of its publication and the role it played in shaping the wording of the background and recommendation on plain packaging in the reports of Australia's National Preventative Health Taskforce (see pp 18).

In May 2008 Scotland's *Smoking Prevention Action Plan* (55) committed its government to consider moving towards plain packaging of tobacco products, in conjunction with the British government and other devolved administrations.

The British government followed suit, releasing a *Consultation on the future of tobacco control,* (56) where it sought reactions from stakeholders and the public on measures that included plain packaging.

In June 2008, the Cancer Council of Western Australia included a question about plain packaging among 21 other tobacco control policy related questions as part of a post-campaign evaluation survey of 408 smokers and non-smokers in metropolitan and non-metropolitan areas. They asked: 'To what extent are you in favour or against each of the following measures?' The statement given was: 'Selling tobacco products in plain packaging, with only the brand name and health warnings.'

Combining those who were in favour or strongly in favour, 87% of non-smokers, 67% of recent quitters and 45% of smokers were in favour. Among smokers, only 13% were against, with the remainder having no opinion.

In 2011, the Australian public continued to be supportive of the proposal, with 72% of the community supporting the idea in an April 2011 Victorian survey, notwithstanding heavy industry spending on advertising and public relations. (57)

Industry awareness of the approaching storm

From at least 2007, there were signs that the tobacco industry was well aware that the plain packaging issue was about to awaken from its short siesta. Morgan Stanley advised investors:

> In our opinion, [after taxation] the other two regulatory environment changes that concern the industry the most are homogenous packaging and below-the-counter sales. Both would significantly restrict the industry's ability to promote their products. (58)

In September 2008, Adam Spielman, a tobacco analyst at Citigroup, was interviewed by the trade magazine *Tobacco Journal International*. (59) Spielman was in no doubt as to how important it would be to the industry to stop plain packaging, saying:

> If the proposal is carried out, it would reduce the brand equity of cigarettes massively. In my opinion, more than half the brand impact is in the design of the cigarette packet, as opposed to the name of the particular brand. As the industry's profits depend on some consumers paying a premium of as much as GBP 1.50 (EUR 1.90) for certain brands, anything that weakens this will dramatically reduce profitability. In terms of market shares, you would expect an even more rapid trend of downtrading. Over time, I think the proposal would result in a very severe reduction in the industry's profit.

Spielman noted with some prescience that plain packaging in the UK was 'unlikely in the next year or two. On a five- or ten-year view, then I think it is certainly possible.' He continued:

> It is important to remember that every anti-tobacco proposal that has been consulted on by the UK government in the last 10 years has

been implemented. In addition, the industry has little hope in appealing to natural justice – no politician has any incentive to support it.

Spielman returned to the issue in 2010, writing:

The most important issue is plain packaging, but there is no advance here. We have always said that, for investors, the no 1 regulatory issue is plain (or generic) packaging: we believe greying out all packs would lead to rapid downtrading. (60)

In a video review, Euromonitor's tobacco analyst Don Hedley described plain packaging as the mother of all battles that would be faced by the tobacco industry. (61) Two tobacco industry trade magazines, *Tobacco Journal International* (April 2008) and *Tobacco Reporter* (November 2012) ran cover stories on plain packaging (see Figures 1.3 and 1.4). The *Tobacco Journal International* cover warned 'plain packaging can kill your business'. Actually, this was the whole point, or as Homer Simpson might have put it: 'D'oh!' Effective tobacco control unavoidably means reduced sales of tobacco.

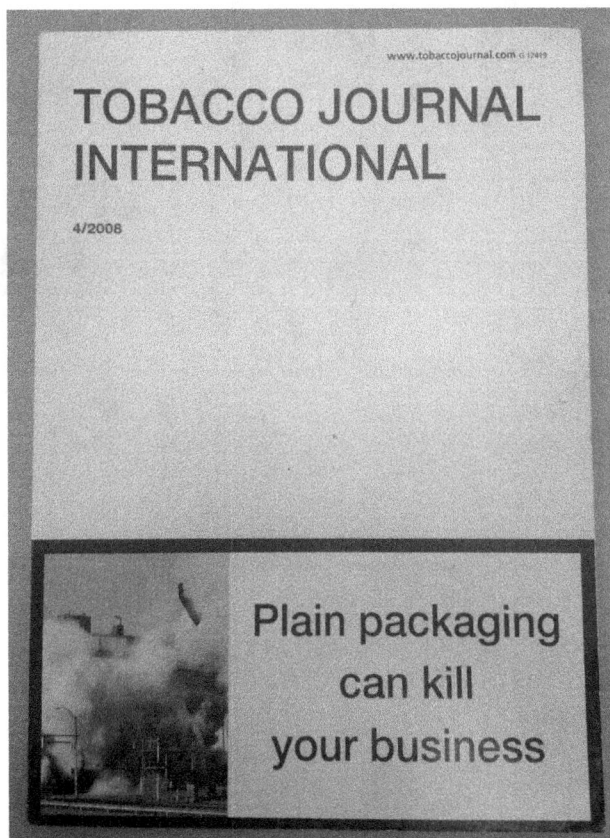

Figure 1.3 Cover of trade journal Tobacco Journal International, April 2008

tobaccoreporter

November 2012   vs $6

■■■
Alternative solutions
Coping with plain
packaging
Page 52

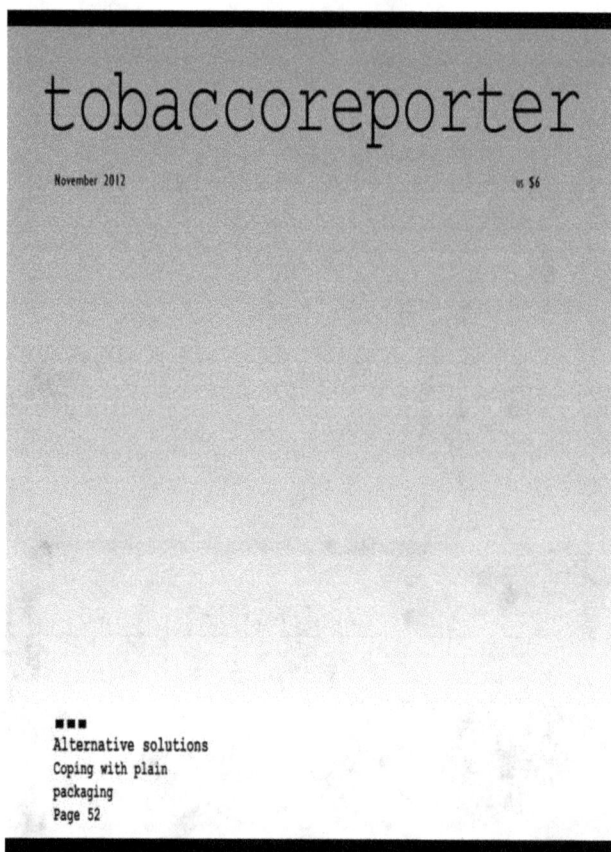

Figure 1.4 Cover of trade journal Tobacco Reporter, November 2012

2
Prevention on a new government's agenda

It is commonly said that conservative governments have ideological antibodies to preventive health policy, particularly when it comes to anything regulatory. The conventional wisdom is that they are comfortable with funding education and information campaigns, but almost congenitally leery of anything regulatory. However, this characterisation is difficult to sustain when it comes to tobacco control.

From the early 1980s on, various state governments from both sides of politics had run sporadic mass reach campaigns commencing in New South Wales (62) and Western Australia (63) and implemented state and territory-level legislative measures.

But the conservative Coalition government under prime minister John Howard (1996–2007) changed that, introducing at least three very important, sustained initiatives that were anything but signs of a tobacco-friendly party.

As health minister Michael Wooldridge (1996–2001) ensured unprecedented levels of funding for Australia's first national tobacco control campaign, which commenced in June 1997. Australian government funding was in excess of $7m over two years, with another $2m being spent by state governments. Funding for the national campaign was maintained and increased throughout the Howard era and continued during the Labor government years. Funding for tobacco control programs in Australia increased from 26 cents per adult in 1996 to 55 cents per adult in 1998 and continued at 49 cents per adult from 2001.[1]

Table 2.1: Recent health ministers and prime ministers, Australia

Health minister	Prime minister	Party	Duration
Tony Abbott	John Howard	Coalition	Oct'03 – Dec'07
Nicola Roxon	Kevin Rudd	Labor	Dec'07 – Jun'10
	Julia Gillard		Jun'10 – Dec'11
Tanya Plibersek	Julia Gillard		Dec'11 – Jul'13
	Kevin Rudd		Jul'13 – Sept'13
Peter Dutton	Tony Abbott	Coalition	Sept'13 on

In 1999, after several years of extensive lobbying by health groups using magnificent, detailed reports prepared by Michelle Scollo for the Cancer Council Australia, the Coalition government switched from levying excise and customs duty on cigarettes on a weight basis to a per stick basis. Over the ensuing years, this had a dramatic effect on increasing the retail price of tobacco, while also increasing government revenue. With price being the single most important determinant of consumption, this decision could never be construed as the act of a government or party which was soft on tobacco contro.

Also during this time, the Coalition government followed Canada to be one of the first nations to require graphic health warnings on all tobacco packs (announced in 2003, with regulations adopted in July 2004 and fully implemented from March 2006). This was in the face of strident tobacco industry opposition, and so again an action incompatible with the idea of a government soft on tobacco control. Tony Abbott, later prime minister, was health minister in the Coalition government at that time.

The newly elected Labor government brimmed with enthusiasm about health policy reform. While in Opposition, Kevin Rudd had made a point of emphasising that prevention would be promoted as a

1   See http://tiny.cc/1seqox

major platform of health policy reform (see http://www.youtube.com/watch?v=PwON8dc9zw4).

Rudd's health minister was lawyer Nicola Roxon, who held a Labor seat in Melbourne's socially disadvantaged inner west. Roxon had been in parliament since 1998 and Rudd had appointed her as shadow health minister in December 2006. She rapidly developed a reputation within health and medical circles as a highly intelligent, population-focused, big picture politician. ABC-TV's *Australian Story*, broadcast a 30 minute portrait of Roxon, including her reflections on her decision to support plain packaging (see http://www.abc.net.au/austory/specials/kickingthehabit/default.htm) and *The Age* (64) and the *Australian Financial Review* (65) newspapers ran lengthy portraits.

Her chief of staff from mid-2008 was Dr Angela Pratt, who had done her doctoral research on political debates surrounding Indigenous rights since the 1970s, before spending several years as a researcher specialising in health policy in the Canberra Parliamentary Library. The two formed a formidable team, complemented by staffers Chris Picton (later to be Nicola Roxon's chief of staff when she became Attorney General), Chris Altis and, later, Angela Koutoulas. These staff were frequently in contact with key individuals in the public health and research communities seeking advice and information, and at different times urging that we might ramp up public discussion of particular aspects of the plain packs proposal.

Angela Pratt recalled the last year of Labor being in Opposition:

It was the year before an election so we wanted to carve out an agenda in health that distinguished us from the Government. . . . I see that year of Opposition as laying the groundwork for all of the things in this area that came after. In particular in that year of Opposition, the Labor Party released a policy paper which was all about putting prevention at the centre of the health debate. In that paper we proposed establishing the Prevention Taskforce as well as doing a few other things to put preventive health on the political agenda and very much on Labor's health agenda. We also thought of it as a Labor agenda in that the people who are most predominantly affected by preventable illness, including preventable illness caused by tobacco smoke, are people in lower socioeconomic groups. So it was in a sense a new take on an old-fashioned Labor issue, in that it was trying to look after the people who are most disadvantaged by the problem. We saw that as an area that the previous government had neglected.

Within two months of taking government, Rudd convened the *Australia 2020 Summit*, which saw 1000 Australian leaders in 10 policy areas converge on Canberra in April to engage in a two day 'future vision' exercise for the country. Prevention is a word that featured often in the Summit's report across a number of fields. It was a theme in health policy that would continue throughout the life of the two terms Labor was in power.

In 2008, with 50 or so others from the health sector around Australia, I was invited to a briefing in Canberra by Roxon. Just as Rudd had emphasised in his public speeches, her presentation started with, and dwelt on prevention, not in its usual role as a Cinderella-like policy confection to be sprinkled on the 'real' meat and potatoes of health policy like hospital crises and expensive drug subsidies, destined to turn into a neglected pumpkin after any midnight of fiscal restraint, but as a *primary* consideration. Here was a rare government health minister sending direct and forceful signals that chronic disease prevention was to be taken seriously. To most in the room, Roxon seemed to 'get it', to understand the enormous potential for a population-focused approach to public health to achieve major and lasting reductions in mortality and social costs, and wide-scale improvements in health and quality of life. There was palpable excitement in the room that prevention might at last be elevated in health policy reform.

The National Preventative Health Taskforce

In April 2009, the new government lost no time in getting prevention further on to the policy agenda by announcing the establishment of a National Preventative Health Taskforce to develop a framework and recommendations for national action on prevention, focusing in the first instance on three leading areas – obesity, tobacco and alcohol. While a few were mildly irritated by it being called 'preventative' instead of the more felicitous 'preventive', the establishment of a peak national committee focused entirely on prevention was seen as the opening of a massive door of opportunity.

Mike Daube, who after the now-retired Nigel Gray and David Hill (both former directors of the Cancer Council Victoria) has a longer track record in tobacco control than anyone in Australia, was appointed to the Taskforce as both deputy chair, and as chair of its tobacco committee. The Taskforce was chaired by the widely respected Professor Rob Moodie. The members of the committee advising the taskforce on tobacco control were Viki Briggs (an Indigenous specialist in tobacco control), Dr Christine Connors (a public health doctor from the Northern Territory), Mike Daube, Dr Shaun Larkin (managing director of the health insurance company HCF), Kate Purcell (a highly experienced tobacco control specialist from NSW), Dr Lyn Roberts (CEO of the National Heart Foundation), Denise Sullivan (another highly experienced public health specialist from Western Australia), Professor Melanie Wakefield (arguably the world's leading researcher on mass reach campaign evaluation in tobacco control) and me. Michelle Scollo, former director of Quit Victoria and to many, the most encyclopaedic and astute person in Australian tobacco control, was appointed as the official writer for the committee.

Daube said that the invitations to sit on the taskforce came directly from the minister's office:

Absolutely from the minister's office. I'm sure with some advice from the department and I think particularly having people like Rob [Moodie, the chair], myself and Lyn Roberts on there sent out a very strong signal about what this was to be about – this wasn't just to be about 'popular' prevention. This was to be about coming up with significant recommendations that would make a difference.

My view was that this was a chance of a lifetime, the one chance you get in a lifetime. You've got a terrific minister. You've got a powerful commission taskforce. You have the best committee you could find. So let's go for it.

So that's the message I tried to send out to the committee and the superb secretariat. It was our chance to produce the best report that you could do.

On the first day the tobacco committee met, Daube emphasised to us that his brief had been to convene a committee who should be in no doubt that the government wanted recommendations that would really make a difference. Roxon backed this in an interview, saying:

> The only real riding instructions that I can recall having to reiterate quite often was to not give us one all-or-nothing recommendation, but to give us a cascading range of options, but not to be scared about what was included in those options.

We all agreed that we should prepare a report and give recommendations that reflected world's best practice in tobacco control. In one meeting after a lengthy discussion about where Australia was at the time and where it might go, we took turns to propose sometimes bold, but always evidence-based recommendations. One of these was a substantial increased tobacco tax: two lots of 25%. A 25% increase was introduced within 24 hours of its announcement in April 2010. A 2013 Treasury paper shows that this increase reduced apparent consumption of duct tobacco products by 11%, nearly twice the 6% that had been predicted. (66) In 2013, a further four annual 12.5% increases were announced and later adopted by the incoming Coalition government. Tobacco taxes were to rise 75% over seven years, on top of the routine rises reflecting changes in the consumer price index. Labor had introduced this, and the Coalition supported it.

Having been closely involved with plain packaging in the months before the committee's formation through our review of industry documents and tobacco trade literature, (67) when it came to my turn in the committee, I recommended plain packaging, which was unanimously supported.

Three National Preventative Health Taskforce committees each produced an initial paper in December 2008. (68) The tobacco discussion paper included consideration of a wide range of policy initiatives, including plain packaging. Following its release there was an extensive period, until April 2009, for consultation and public submissions. Some 400 submissions were received. (69)

It was noteworthy that notwithstanding a very broad range of issues and options considered in the discussion paper, 43 of the 142 pages of responses from the major tobacco companies active in Australia (BAT, Philip Morris, Imperial Tobacco) were devoted to opposing plain packaging.

Mike Daube's instincts saw this as extremely telling:

> Nearly a third of their responses were on plain packaging. So we thought wow, we're onto something here. We thought it was going to be good. We didn't realise it could be that important and I don't think they could have been more helpful in showing us where the main game was for them.

Early media interest

In April, ABC TV's program *Lateline* ran a lengthy item on the possibility that Australia would pick up the plain packaging baton dropped by Canada in the mid-1990s. I had recommended to *Lateline*'s reporter Peter Lloyd that Canadian researcher Cynthia Callard would be the ideal person to interview.

Callard emphasised that the earlier decisions byCanada and Australia to not pursue plain packing had nothing to do with the strength of the legal case made against the move, but said everything about the success of the tobacco industry's bluff at the time. (70) She said:

> Well, they did that because the whole legal and trade world is a bit behind a black curtain. It is not like the scientific world, where things are published and data are shared. They could come in and tell governments that they had a good case, that they had legal opinions that told them they had a good case, that their trademarks could be protected.
>
> Now we knew that this was unlikely to be the case because the key issue is that you can own a trademark, but it doesn't give you the right to use it. The only thing that ownership gives you is the right to stop other people from using it, and what we now know as a result of . . . documents that were released as a result of US court actions, is that the tobacco companies had gone to their own lawyers, they had gone to the international agencies like WIPO that govern trademarks, they had surveyed all of the trade agreements they could find and they came to an internal conclusion that they had no case.

But instead of telling governments, well, we were wrong, they paid people to publish books that provided contrary evidence and they just played a good game of chicken.

Sadly, governments blinked and they caved. The Canadian government first and then the Australian government. What we hope now is that with this stronger evidence of exactly the nature of the industry bluffing, that the trade departments will be more supportive of the health ministries to bring in plain packaging.

The taskforce's final report, delivered to the health minister on 30 June and released in September 2009, contained a recommendation on plain packaging as part of a comprehensive approach: 'Mandate plain packaging of cigarettes and increase the required size of graphic health warnings to take up at least 90% of the front and 100% of the back of the pack.' (68)

The report elaborated:

Plain packaging would prohibit brand imagery, colours, corporate logos and trademarks, permitting manufacturers only to print the brand name in a mandated size, font and place, in addition to required health warnings and other legally mandated product information such as toxic constituents, tax paid seals or package contents. A standard cardboard texture would be mandatory, and the size and shape of the package and cellophane wrapper would also be prescribed. (67) A detailed analysis of current marketing practices suggests that plain packaging would also need to encompass pack interiors and the cigarette itself, given the potential for manufacturers to use colours, bandings and markings, and different length and gauges to make cigarettes more 'interesting' and appealing. Any use of perfuming, incorporation of audio chips or affixing of 'onserts' would also need to be banned.

The legislative announcement

Nearly eight months passed until 29 April 2010, when prime minister Kevin Rudd and health minister Nicola Roxon made the historic announcement that Australia would mandate plain packaging from July

2012, (71) along with a 25% tax increase and a range of further initiatives on tobacco.

Over those eight months, some committee members had written opinion page articles and otherwise commented on the importance of plain packaging, but none of us had received any feedback or indication from the government or the bureaucracy as to which recommendations might be selected for adoption. The proposed legislation was first announced at a press conference held by the two, although late night television broke the news the night before.

Several of us had been called by Roxon's office about 6pm that night, because a television station had got wind of the imminent announcement. For those closely involved, that phone call was one of those occasions like always remembering where you were when a big news incident occurs. I picked up the phone at home and Angela Pratt, Roxon's chief of staff said deadpan: 'I thought you might like to know that we'll be announcing in the morning that we'll be introducing plain packaging.'

Daube, as chair, had been briefed a few days earlier.

I was going into a lecture and the mobile rang and I looked at it and thought do I take this call? Oh, who knows? So I took it and there was a voice on the other end saying 'Nicola Roxon here.' So I thought well, maybe it was good idea to take the call and she says 'Mike, you can't tell anyone but we're going with the tax and we're going with plain packaging'. It was so hard to keep the widest grin you've ever seen off my face when I walked in to do that lecture.

From that moment, some of us working in population-focused tobacco control in Australia did little else for the next four years. We concentrated our efforts to ensure the announced bill would be passed, then defended it from industry-motivated attempts to discredit its impact.

I asked Pratt about how the plain packaging proposal was received by Rudd. She said:

He was very supportive. I clearly remember being in the meeting when the idea was first put to him when we were discussing how to respond to all of the tobacco recommendations from the prevention taskforce – taxation, packaging, social marketing and other things.

The idea was put to him and he said, 'yes, let's go for it. I like it, let's go for it.' It's a simple idea at its heart with a compelling logic which the PM [prime minister] got right away.

Rohan Greenland, lobbyist at the Heart Foundation, recalls that his then CEO, Lyn Roberts, and the CEO of the Cancer Council Australia, Ian Olver, had met with Rudd well before the announcement. Plain packaging was not discussed, but the two presented Rudd with data on the widespread support for tobacco control in the community, and assured him that any policy advances on tobacco would be very well received. They sensed he was very receptive.

So what is plain packaging and what aspects of packaging are addressed in the Australian law?

'Plain' packaging (sometimes called 'generic' or 'standardised' packaging) is the term given to Australia's pioneering national legislation (72) which requires all tobacco products (cigarettes, roll-your-own tobacco, pipe tobacco and cigars) to be sold in prescribed packaging. All packaging for every brand is identical, except for the brand and variant names and the name of each brand's manufacturer, which still enable each brand to be clearly identified. Here are the essential features of plain cigarette packaging.

- The brand name must appear on the front of the box in a standard size and font.
- The name of any brand variant must also appear immediately below the brand name, also in a standard font.
- All remaining surfaces must be in the colour 'drab dark brown'.
- 75% of the front of the pack must show one of 14 prescribed graphic (pictorial) health warnings. (73) These 14 warnings are required to be rotated according to a particular pattern across the years, so that each 24 months after the 1 December implementation date, each of the 14 different warnings will have been evenly distributed across all tobacco stock. The same graphic warning must also appear on the back of the pack in smaller size, along with the relevant accompanying textual warning. The size of the combined graphic and text warning on the back of the pack is 90% of the surface area.
- On the top of the pack (both back and front), the matching textual warning must appear.

- The number of cigarettes in the pack must be shown in the bottom right-hand front corner.
- The Quitline phone number must appear on the back of the pack.
- All writing in all the above matters must conform to standard, specified fonts which is the same for all brands.
- The left hand side of the box must show another textual warning.
- The box shape, wrap, and colour of all cigarettes must conform to prescribed standards, the same for all brands.

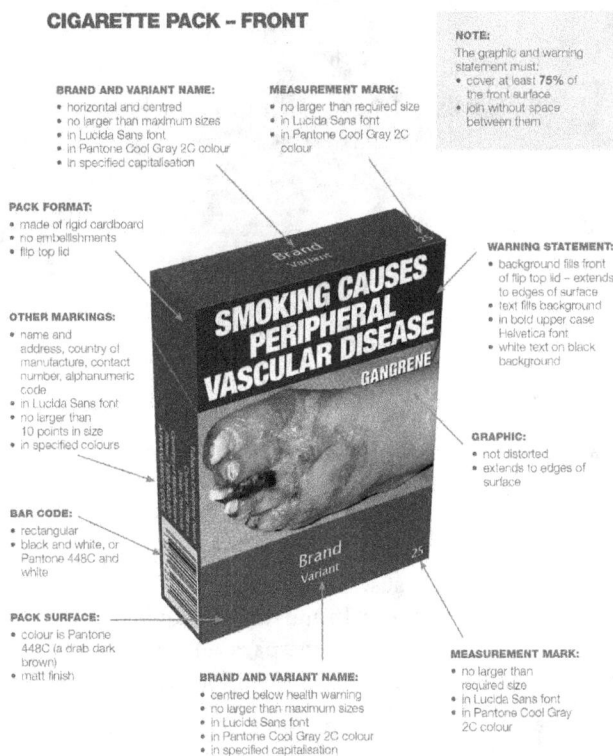

CIGARETTE PACK – FRONT

NOTE:
The graphic and warning statement must:
- cover at least **75%** of the front surface
- join without space between them

BRAND AND VARIANT NAME:
- horizontal and centred
- no larger than maximum sizes
- in Lucida Sans font
- in Pantone Cool Gray 2C colour
- in specified capitalisation

MEASUREMENT MARK:
- no larger than required size
- in Lucida Sans font
- in Pantone Cool Gray 2C colour

PACK FORMAT:
- made of rigid cardboard
- no embellishments
- flip top lid

OTHER MARKINGS:
- name and address, country of manufacture, contact number, alphanumeric code
- in Lucida Sans font
- no larger than 10 points in size
- in specified colours

BAR CODE:
- rectangular
- black and white, or Pantone 448C and white

PACK SURFACE:
- colour is Pantone 448C (a drab dark brown)
- matt finish

SMOKING CAUSES PERIPHERAL VASCULAR DISEASE
GANGRENE

Brand Variant

Brand Variant

WARNING STATEMENT:
- background fills front of flip top lid – extends to edges of surface
- text fills background
- in bold upper case Helvetica font
- white text on black background

GRAPHIC:
- not distorted
- extends to edges of surface

MEASUREMENT MARK:
- no larger than required size
- in Lucida Sans font
- in Pantone Cool Gray 2C colour

BRAND AND VARIANT NAME:
- centred below health warning
- no larger than maximum sizes
- in Lucida Sans font
- in Pantone Cool Gray 2C colour
- in specified capitalisation

Figure 2.1 Australia's plain cigarette pack specifications. Source: http://tiny.cc/3xeqox

CIGARETTE PACK – BACK

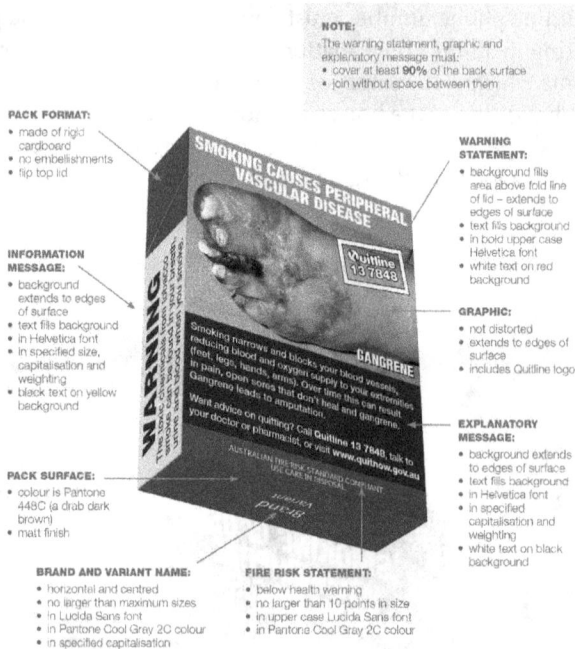

NOTE:
The warning statement, graphic and explanatory message must:
* cover at least **90%** of the back surface
* join without space between them

PACK FORMAT:
* made of rigid cardboard
* no embellishments
* flip top lid

INFORMATION MESSAGE:
* background extends to edges of surface
* text fills background
* in Helvetica font
* in specified size, capitalisation and weighting
* black text on yellow background

PACK SURFACE:
* colour is Pantone 448C (a drab dark brown)
* matt finish

WARNING STATEMENT:
* background fills area above fold line of lid – extends to edges of surface
* text fills background
* in bold upper case Helvetica font
* white text on red background

GRAPHIC:
* not distorted
* extends to edges of surface
* includes Quitline logo

EXPLANATORY MESSAGE:
* background extends to edges of surface
* text fills background
* in Helvetica font
* in specified capitalisation and weighting
* white text on black background

BRAND AND VARIANT NAME:
* horizontal and centred
* no larger than maximum sizes
* in Lucida Sans font
* in Pantone Cool Gray 2C colour
* in specified capitalisation

FIRE RISK STATEMENT:
* below health warning
* no larger than 10 points in size
* in upper case Lucida Sans font
* in Pantone Cool Gray 2C colour

Figure 2.2 Australia's plain cigarette pack specifications. Source: http://tiny.cc/3xeqox

Australia's plain packs are therefore far from being just 'plain' boxes. They are fully coloured because the boxes must all carry a large graphic health warning, front and rear. In moving to require the health warnings to cover 75% of the front of the pack and 90% of the rear, Australian warnings had set the standard then for the largest in the world, ahead of Uruguay (80% front and back) and Canada (75% front and back).

The goals of plain packaging

The Australian government implemented plain packaging as part of its long-standing policy commitment to end all forms of tobacco advertising and promotion within its control. The path toward ending tobacco advertising had commenced in September 1976 when the then Fraser-led Liberal government enacted legislation, first proposed by the previous Whitlam Labor government, and banned directadvertising on cigarettes on television and radio. Over the next 16 years, successive Labor and Coalition governments both federally and at state level had incrementally enacted further extensions of tobacco advertising bans in different media (cinema, outdoor, point-of-sale), culminating in the Tobacco Advertising Prohibition Act of 1992 (74) which ended all tobacco sponsorship in sport and in cultural settings. The WHO's FCTC, ratified by Australia in December 2003, locked Australia into a list of nations today numbering 178 (75) which are legally obligated to ban all forms of tobacco advertising and promotion.

This background is central to an appreciation of why the Australian government enacted plain packaging legislation: packaging is indisputably a form of product promotion (see Chapter 3). Indeed, the 2014 Chantler Report (76) noted that 'Japan Tobacco International responded to the decision to introduce tobacco plain packaging in Australia by attempting to sue the Australian government for taking possession of its mobile 'billboard'.

Plain packaging was also designed to maximise the impact of the graphic health warnings on future and current smokers and to reduce the ability of the pack to mislead consumers.

Australia's plain packaging Act describes the objectives of the legislation as:

(1) (a) to improve public health by:
(i) discouraging people from taking up smoking, or using tobacco products; and
(ii) encouraging people to give up smoking, and to stop using tobacco products; and
(iii) discouraging people who have given up smoking, or who have stopped using tobacco products, from relapsing; and

(iv) reducing people's exposure to smoke from tobacco products; and
(b) to give effect to certain obligations that Australia has as a party to the Convention on Tobacco Control.
(2) It is the intention of the Parliament to contribute to achieving the objects in subsection (1) by regulating the retail packaging and appearance of tobacco products in order to:
(a) reduce the appeal of tobacco products to consumers; and
(b) increase the effectiveness of health warnings on the retail packaging of tobacco products; and
(c) reduce the ability of the retail packaging of tobacco products to mislead consumers about the harmful effects of smoking or using tobacco products.

As we will discuss in Chapter 7, the precise wording of these objectives is of utmost importance to questions on evaluation of the impact of the policy.

Prevention as the primary goal

In announcing the government's intention to introduce plain packaging, Nicola Roxon emphasised from the outset that the leading goal of the legislation was one of prevention of uptake among young people. She said:

> And of course we're targeting people who have not yet started, and that's the key to this plain packaging announcement – to make sure we make it less attractive for people to experiment with tobacco in the first place. (77)

Paul Grogan from the Cancer Council Australia saw this emphasis as critical to the success in getting multi-party support during the many months ahead of the passing of the legislation:

> In years of government relations work, I've never met a parliamentarian or advisor of any political persuasion who opposed the idea of protecting young people from tobacco addiction. The fact that the

rationale and much of the evidence for plain packaging was about preventing take-up and benefiting children and young adults made it easier to promote to parliamentarians from a range of backgrounds.

The final 'look' of plain packaging

The way Australia's plain packs appear was not the whim of some influential bureaucrat or committee. No one simply declared: 'let's have them look this way!' Instead, almost every facet of their appearance was subject to extensive market research testing. The Department of Health and Ageing established an expert advisory group of Australian and international tobacco control researchers and stakeholders to advise on plain packaging design. They oversaw comprehensive consumer research which would inform the way that plain packaging would actually look. (78)

Six studies were conducted to optimise the plain packaging design and the impact of revised graphic health warnings, which would change at the same time the packs were introduced. The studies are detailed in Table 2.2 below. The results of this work, together with an existing body of experimental evidence on the effects of plain packaging on consumer purchase preferences, led to the final plain packaging design. The full results of the consumer research can be found in a highly detailed report on the health department website (79): http://tiny.cc/2vfqox. Key findings and recommendations of the market research combined with the experimental research include: (78, 79)

Plain packaging colour: A dark olive brown colour emerged as the best candidate for plain packaging. Consumers found cigarette packages in this colour to be less appealing, to contain cigarettes that were perceived to be more harmful to health, of lower quality, and to make it harder to quit smoking. Additionally, this colour was not at all similar to any existing cigarette brand and failed to generate any positive associations for consumers. While a dark brown coloured pack also tested well on these elements, it elicited unintended positive associations such as reminding consumers of chocolate and creating feelings of luxury and warmth.

The official name of the colour chosen for surfaces of the pack not occupied by health warnings is Pantone 448G. Initially people, including Roxon, referred to it as 'olive green'. The Australian Olive Association was not happy, with its chief executive saying Roxon:

> ... referred to it as 'disgusting' olive green, so it hasn't been very favourable. To associate any food with cigarettes is a thoughtless thing to do, especially one that's had a very good reputation as being a healthy product. You could have called it 'drab green' or 'khaki green' or, better still, not used green at all. (80)

It was a fair cop: the colour can much more accurately be described as 'dark drab brown'.

Pack size and shape

Innovative packaging shape, size and opening can create strong associations which contribute to appeal and brand personality. Cigarette packs are therefore required to be a standard rectangular shape with a standard flip-top opening. The size is also limited, ranging from a minimum based on standard packs of 20 cigarettes to a maximum based on a standard pack of 50 cigarettes.

Font and font size for brand name

Testing revealed that a 14 point font size was the smallest size that maintained legibility of the brand name, when read at a distance of one metre. The Lucida Sans font type was found in testing to be easier to read than Arial. Ensuring brand name legibility addressed a key concern raised by retailers that plain packs would lead to retailer confusion and slowed or incorrect purchases by consumers.

Design of graphic health warnings (size and layout)

Larger front-of-pack graphic health warnings were more noticeable, easier to understand, prompted a stronger reaction to 'stop and think' and conveyed the seriousness of health risks. Additionally, larger warnings reduced the overall appeal and perception of the quality of the packaging. A graphic health warning covering 75% of the front of the pack elicited the highest noticeability, message comprehension and dissuasive effect on appeal.

Table 2.2: Summary of studies on pack appearance

Study	Description	Objectives	Methodology
Study 1	Consumer perceptions of branding appeal, attractiveness and smoking harm	To understand the impact of current brand and packaging design (brand, colour, finish, pack size) on appeal, attractiveness and perceived harm amongst current smokers	Eighteen face-to-face group clinics including a self-completion questionnaire and group discussion among (n=122) at least weekly smokers aged 18–64 years old
Study 2	Consumer perceptions of plain pack colour	To identify a shortlist of potential plain packaging colours	Online survey among (n=409) at least weekly smokers aged 18–65 years old
Study 3	Legibility of brand names on plain packs for retailers	To identify the optimal combination of design elements (font size, font colour) for legibility and ease of identification amongst potential retailers	Face-to-face interviews with (n=10) respondents aged 40 years old and older
Study 4	Consumer perceptions of plain pack colour with brand elements	To shortlist plain packaging colours that minimised brand impact	Online survey among (n=455) at least weekly smokers aged 18–64 years old
Study 5 (Face-to-face)	Consumer appraisal of plain packs with new health warnings using prototype packs	To identify the optimal plain packaging designs in combination with the new front-of-pack graphic health warnings	Twenty face-to-face group clinics including a self-completion questionnaire and short group discussion among (n=193) at least weekly smokers aged 16–64 years old

Study	Description	Objectives	Methodology
Study 5 (Online)	Consumer appraisal of different graphic health warning sizes and layouts on pack	To identify the optimal plain packaging designs in combination with the new front-of-pack graphic health warnings	Online survey among (n=409) at least weekly smokers aged 18–64 years old
Study 6 (Online)	Consumer appraisal of different graphic health warning sizes and layouts on pack – Testing 75% GHW layout	To identify the optimal plain packaging designs in combination with the new front-of-pack graphic health warnings	Online survey among (n=205) at least weekly smokers aged 18–64 years old

Cigarettes, too

The inclusion of brand names and other design embellishments on the cigarettes themselves is associated with level of appeal and perceived brand personalities. It is less appreciated that Australia's legislation also standardised the look of cigarettes, not just the packs in which they are sold. In the past, tobacco companies have introduced different colours and bandings on cigarette wrappers (the paper in a cigarette) to make them look more appealing and interesting (See Figures 2.3 and 2.4). Like packs, cigarettes are used in branding and marketing. Accordingly, the regulations accompanying Australia's new law contain very important provisions which specify that the appearance of cigarettes is also governed by the Act (see Table 2.2). Cigarette stick appearance is limited to either plain white, or plain white with an 'imitation cork' filter tip. No branding, other colours or design features are permitted.

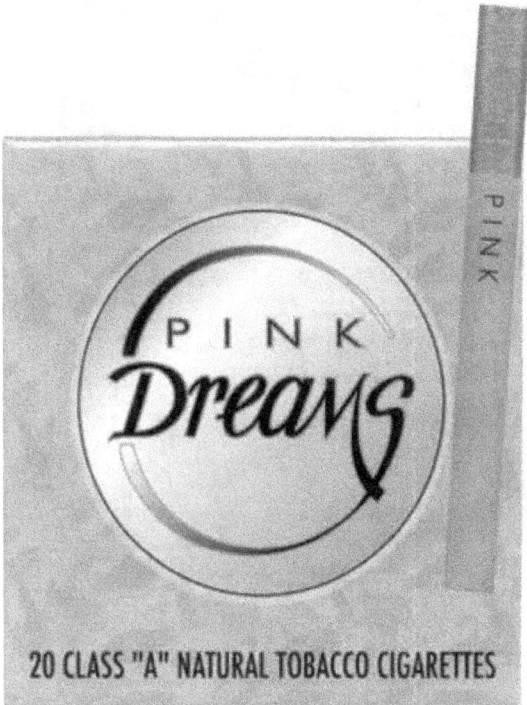

Figure 2.3 Pink Dream cigarettes. Source: http://tiny.cc/
v0fqox

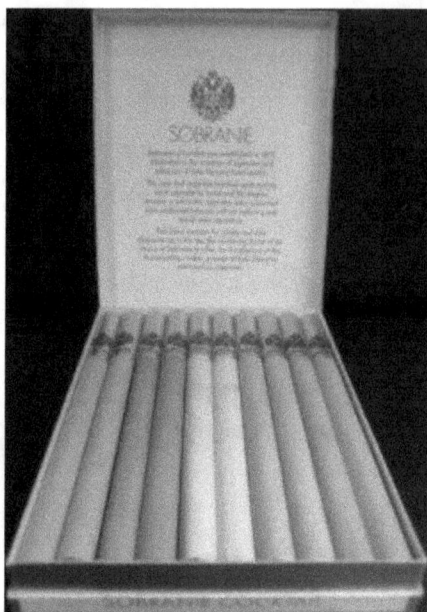

Figure 2.4 Sobranie cigarettes. Source:
http://cigarettezoom.com/cigarettes-manufac-
turers/

3

Why the industry cares so much about packaging – the silent salesman

Packaging design is a major way of differentiating and promoting brands, being particularly important in homogenous consumer products such as cigarettes where, like bottled water, few objective differences exist. (81) Marketing literature routinely highlights the critical role played by pack design in the overall marketing mix, emphasising that the 'product package is the communication life-blood of the firm', the 'silent salesman' that reaches out to customers, (82) and that packaging 'act[s] as a promotional tool in its own right.' (83)

Colours and typeface have long been known to elicit particular responses in consumers, often shaped by strong social and cultural forces.[1] Imagery and symbols also exert powerful effects, linking desirable attributes with particular brands. Cigarette packaging conveys this crucial sense of brand identity through logos, colours, fonts, pictures, packaging materials and shapes. For example, the world's most popular cigarette brand, *Marlboro*, (84) can readily be identified through its iconic red chevron (see Figure 3.1). The powerful association of the bold colour red with *Marlboro* is embodied in Philip Morris International's continued multi-million dollar sponsorship of the Ferrari

---

1 Portions of Chapter 2 are drawn from: Freeman B, Chapman S and Rimmer M. Review: the case for the plain packaging of tobacco products. Addiction 2008;103:580–90. and Scollo, M and Freeman B. Packaging as Promotion. Tobacco in Australia. 2012. Available from: http://tinyurl.com/nf44zrv

Formula 1 racing team, despite the fact that neither the official logo nor brand name appears on the red race car (see Figure 3.2). In 2013, the *Marlboro* brand was estimated to be worth $US69 billion, making it the eighth most valuable brand in the world, just behind *Microsoft* and *Coca-Cola*. (85)

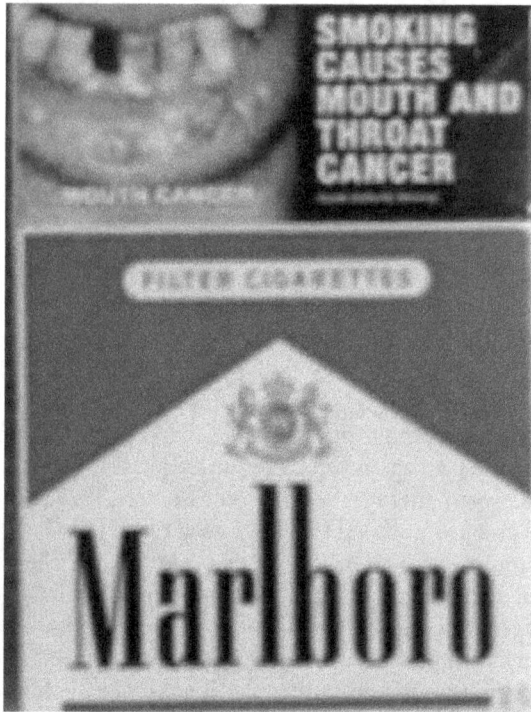

Figure 3.1 The Marlboro brand as it appeared in Australia prior to the plain packaging reforms. Source: Becky Freeman private collection

Figure 3.2 The 2014 Scuderia Ferrari Formula 1 car. Source: Official Scuderia Ferrari Formula 1 team website http://tiny.cc/n7fqox

The importance of packaging in promoting tobacco use

The tobacco industry has always claimed that it has no interest in attracting new, non-smoking customers but is interested only in stimulating brand-switching among current smokers and in maintaining brand loyalty in current customers. Notwithstanding the commercial absurdity of any industry professing disinterest in attracting new recruits to its products, this position has been comprehensively undermined by a multitude of revelations from internal industry documents that candidly acknowledge the vital importance of attracting new smokers (predominantly youth). (86–93)

These internal documents confirm that companies have invested heavily in pack design in order to communicate specific messages to specific demographic groups including young people. (43, 91) In the early 1990s a presenter addressing marketing staff at Philip Morris remarked that smokers: 'are ready for change' and 'once exposed to innovative [packaging] especially young adults see their current packaging as dated and boring'. (94) The presenter said packs aimed at younger women should be 'slick, sleek, flashy, glittery, shiny, silky, bold'. (94) In designing tobacco packs, the tobacco industry counts among potential purchasers those already smoking the brand, those smoking other brands and those not yet smoking but who might be persuaded to take it up.

If, as the tobacco industry contends, cigarette pack design is primarily intended to convey important consumer information, then very few facts are being shared with smokers. Tobacco packaging has historically carried very little 'information'. Internationally, apart from showing the brand and variant names, the manufacturer's name, the number of cigarettes in the pack (all required components under plain packaging laws) and, in some countries, nicotine and tar levels, cigarette packs rarely contain any other information. Furthermore, misleading on-pack descriptors like 'light' or 'mild' are now restricted in several jurisdictions. Cigarette packaging then plays an essential role in differentiating one product from another. The industry has long known that different brands of similar cigarettes are often indistinguishable to smokers. As an industry document from 1979 explained, 'one of every two smokers is not able to distinguish in blind (masked) tests between similar cigarettes.' (95)

In 1975, the government of Norway introduced what was then the world's most comprehensive ban on tobacco advertising. Yet a 2003 study conducted with young adult Norwegian smokers aged 18–23 (born five to 10 years after the ban) highlights how the tobacco industry continued to market to this demographic through persuasive cigarette pack design. This study showed that cigarette brands and cigarette package designs gave meaning to personal characteristics, to social identity and to positions in status hierarchies. In the young smokers' accounts, brands appeared to add 'an extra dimension to the social meaning of smoking in their daily life.' (96) With the increasing prevalence of tobacco advertising and sponsorship bans throughout the world, the pack has fast become the most important promotional vehicle for reaching potential and current smokers. (43, 97–102)

Several nations have now banned the open display of tobacco products in retail locations. Point-of-sale displays have been found to be highly visible and persuasive forms of promotion.

Power walls and counter top displays are highly visible and eye-catching. They present an unavoidable and unfortunate spill of promotional imagery and product reminders to vulnerable consumers including young people, former smokers . . . and smokers of all ages who are trying to quit. (103)

With removal of point-of-sale as an opportunity for promotion, BAT and Philip Morris (104) have predicted that, in the future, pack design alone will drive brand imagery. Unless governments impose complete restrictions on packaging design, bans on the retail display of tobacco will encourage a further shift in industry investment towards innovative pack design, with the pack functioning as the only remaining vehicle for product promotion. The industry trade journal Tobacco Journal International states it best:

> When most media advertising is illegal and even promotion at point of sale is under threat, the pack itself is the last chance saloon for tobacco company brand managers to sell their products to the smoking public. (105)

Pack design can not only communicate the 'personality' of a cigarette brand to the smoker, but smokers can project these characteristics by handling and displaying the package throughout their daily routines. (43) Once again the tobacco sector provides the most succinct summary as to why this is so essential:

> Today, with restrictions in advertising, when the pack is seen in the hands of the right person, it is surely the best product placement that a cigarette company can get for free. This personal appeal is a major aspect driving cigarette packaging design. An attractive pack is something smokers want to be seen with. (106)

Just as designer clothing, accessories and cars serve as social cues to style, status, values and character, so too can cigarette packs signify a range of attributes about users. As 'badge products' cigarettes can reinforce the characteristics conjured by brand image. (43, 107–110) This behaviour not only affects the single consumer, but also exerts a powerful effect on their friends, associates and even casual contacts. Consumer theory and research has demonstrated that incidental brand encounters (ICBEs) powerfully affect buying patterns in ways in which the consumer is not fully aware. A series of four studies by Ferraro,

Bettmand and Chartrand published in the *Journal for Consumer Research* in 2008 found that repeated exposure to simulated ICBEs:

> ... increases choice of the focal brand among people not aware of the brand exposure, that perceptual fluency underlies these effects and these effects are moderated by perceivers' automatic responses to the type of user observed with the brand. (111)

Minimising the effect of health warnings

The other important goal of packaging design that is unique to tobacco products is to use the pack to obscure, downplay and minimise government-mandated health warnings. Again, the industry is refreshingly candid about this challenge.

> Tobacco product packaging is a paradox in paper and cardboard. Like any [fast moving consumer good], a cigarette pack aims to attract the eye, display the brand to advantage, and generally look cool. However, the difference between tobacco and other industries is that, in looking at the packaging, the consumer is also looking at a health warning. One might forgive a pack designer coming to the conclusion that the less a consumer looks at a cigarette pack, the better. But packaging developments demonstrate a different mindset, with tobacco product manufacturers competing with their rivals just as fiercely as confectionery and soap manufacturers. (105)

This effect is reflected in the results of plain pack research that shows consistently that pack brand imagery distracts from and reduces the impact of health warnings. Students have been found to have an enhanced ability to recall tobacco health warnings on plain packs than on branded packs. (23, 28) Health warnings printed on plain packs are seen as being more serious than the exact same warnings printed on branded packs. These findings suggest that positive brand imagery diffuses the overall impact of health warnings. (112) For example, in 2010 a *Benson and Hedges superslims* cigarette pack from Canada incorporated the required graphic health warning so that the pack appeared to be reminiscent of a digital music player (see Figure 3.3). The small size of the *superslims* pack also significantly reduced the size of the graphic health warning (as warnings were then required to be 50% of the surface area of the front of the pack, not a specific size) potentially further reducing its impact.

Figure 3.3 Comparison of Benson and Hedges superslims cigarette packaging to a digital music player. Source: Becky Freeman private collection

Other packaging designers have confirmed that branding elements on packs are essential for differentiating brands, even in the face of graphic health warnings:

Although the warnings, graphic or otherwise, cannot be said to enhance the aesthetics of the pack, they function separately from the branding in communication terms. Because they are on all packs, they do not differentiate one brand from another, whereas the branding device, colours and other elements of the identity enable consumers to readily recognise their chosen brands. (106)

Subverting bans on light and mild descriptors

The industry has also found that packaging design is a useful way to work around legislation meant to protect consumers from misleading product descriptors. In nations where the deceptive descriptors 'light' and 'mild' have been banned, manufacturers have used packaging innovations to subvert the intent of those bans (113) where different colour gradations and intensities are used to perpetuate smokers' understanding that a brand is allegedly lower or higher yielding.[14] For example, Derby cigarettes in Brazil substituted red for full strength cigarettes, blue for mild, and silver for light (see Figure 3.4). (114)

Cigarette packaging as a key aspect of marketing

Several insightful and illustrative statements have been made by industry insiders about how influential brand and package design is in the repetitive, daily ritual of carrying, opening and displaying cigarette packs. The recurring and ingrained use of cigarettes is reflected in the physical properties of the packages themselves.

If you smoke, a cigarette pack is one of the few things you use regularly that makes a statement about you. A cigarette pack is the only thing you take out of your pocket 20 times a day and lay out for everyone to see. That's a lot different than buying your soap powder in generic packaging. (115)

Packaging styles convey an essential advertising image: Packaging design, structure, and graphics play an integral part in brand image, which, along with tradition, plays a heavy role in tobacco sales. Handled an average of 20 or more times a day, cigarettes are carried in pockets and purses, and displayed on counters, bars, desks,

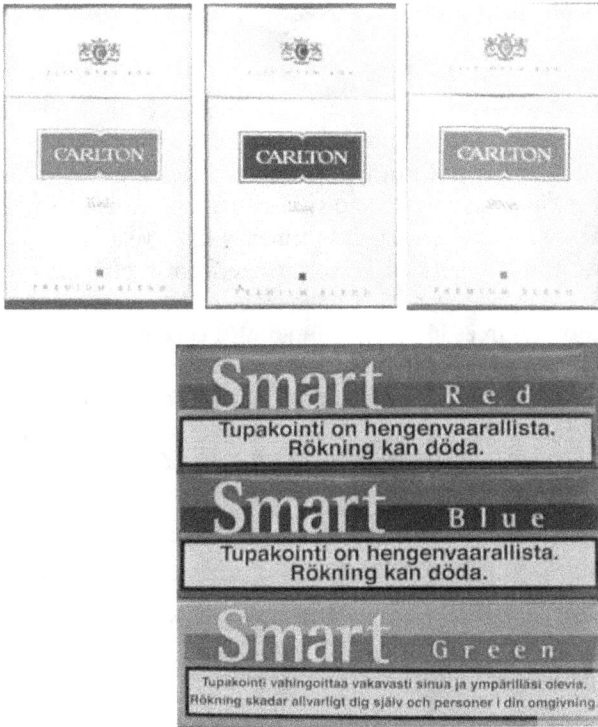

Figure 3.4 Brazil: cigarette manufacturers substituted red for full strength cigarettes, blue for mild, and silver for light. Source: http://www.smoke-free.ca/pdf_1/Endingthedeception-2005.pdf

and coffee tables. Brands display an image in the same way as clothing, car, and restaurant choices. (116)

When we offered them *Marlboros* at half price – in generic brown boxes – only 21% were interested, even though we assured them that each package was fresh, had been sealed at the factory and was identical (except for the different packaging) to what they normally bought at their local, tobacconist or cigarette machine. How to account for the difference? Simple. Smokers put their cigarettes in and out of their pockets 20 to 25 times a day. The package makes a statement. The consumer is expressing how he wants to be seen by others. (117)

The tobacco industry, and its service providers such as printing and packaging companies and advertising agencies, offer unique and telling insights into the myriad of opportunities that packaging presents to reinvigorate flagging brands and sell everything 'old as new again'. Any naivety in assuming a package is primarily to serve as a safe container for goods is swiftly refuted by this quote from a packaging industry consultant, who said that: 'Packaging is the embodiment of all the time, money and resources invested in building a consumer packaged good.' (118) It should be no surprise that the tobacco industry is fiercely protective of this investment, and is constantly seeking to improve pack design.

The tobacco industry trade magazine, *World Tobacco*, contains numerous examples of appeals to manufacturers to use packaging as an advertising vehicle. (98, 99, 102, 119–121) Manufacturers were advised:

> If your brand can no longer shout from billboards, let alone from the cinema screen or the pages of a glossy magazine ... it can at least court smokers from the retailer's shelf, or from wherever it is placed by those already wed to it. (101)

Packaging designers remained optimistic about opportunities to increase the appeal of cigarette packs despite intrusive health warnings:

> With the uptake of printed inner frame cards, what we will increasingly see is the pack being viewed as a total opportunity for communications – from printed outer film and tear tape through to the inner frame and inner bundle. Each pack component will provide an integrated function as part of a carefully planned brand or information communications campaign. (122)

One packaging firm urged tobacco companies to skirt 'draconian legislation' by using pack over-wrapping to create an in-store advertisement.

> Where cigarette advertising is banned by law ... the retailer can 'quite coincidentally' stack up a kind of billboard using the products

at the point of sale if, for example, the cigarette cartons of a particular brand bear different parts of an overall design, which complete a puzzle or a caption when stacked up. (98)

Advances in printing technology have enabled printing of on-pack imagery on the inner frame card, (122) outer film and tear tape, (98) and the incorporation of holograms, collectable art, metallic finishes, (123) multi-fold stickers, (99) photographs and images in pack design. (124–126) In the early 1900s, collectable cigarette cards were a major form of in-pack promotion. (127) A contemporary return to the package as the primary source of advertising is apparent in numerous international examples.

Trends in tobacco industry pack design

Australia is a quintessential 'dark market' where all tobacco advertising is banned.[56] Subtle changes to cigarette packs and trademarks were observed on both *Benson & Hedges* and *Winfield* cigarette packs during 2000–2002. (42) When researchers called the company to inquire about the changes, an employee said they were 'playing with the logo because we can't do any advertising anymore.' (42)

British American Tobacco Australia (BATA) introduced split *Dunhill* packs in October 2006 (see Figure 3.5). (128) The pack could be split along a perforated line to create two mini packs, easily shared between two smokers perhaps unable to afford a full pack. Children, with limited pocket money, might be attracted to such an opportunity. Once split, one of the two packs did not bear the mandatory graphic health warning. BATA was forced to remove the packets from the market when they were found to be in breach of tobacco product health warning labelling laws. (129)

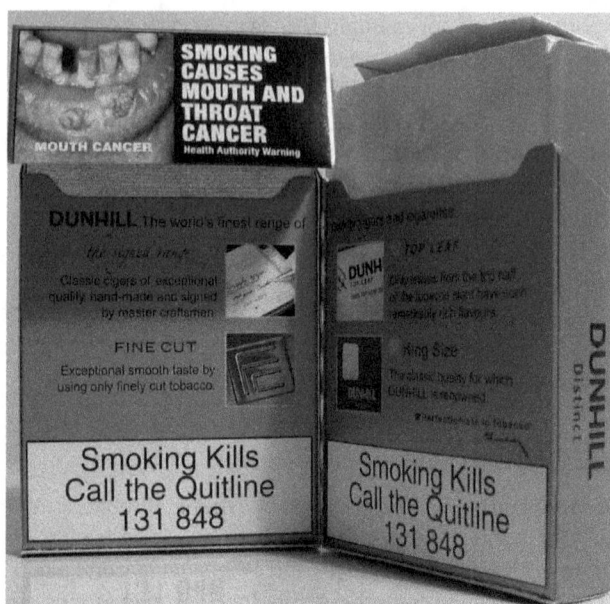

Figure 3.5 Split package of Dunhill cigarettes. Source: Quit Victoria.

In June 2005, Imperial Tobacco Canada introduced octagonal packs for the *du Maurier* brand, presenting an eye-catching package but also obscuring the health warning by wrapping it around the angled pack sides (see Figure 3.6). (130) Imperial's vice president of marketing received an international industry award for theinnovative design, 'considered an outstanding example of the capacity of product packaging to influence the end user.' (131)

Figure 3.6 Octagonal packs for the du Maurier brand. Source:
http://tobaccocontrol.bmj.com/cgi/content/full/15/3/150-a

In August 2006, BAT New Zealand packaged its *Benson & Hedges* brand in collectable tins, priced identically to those sold in cardboard packs; the required government issued health warning was affixed to the tin with an easily removed sticker. (132)

In December 2006, KT&G, Korea's largest tobacco manufacturer, released new packaging for the *Raison D'etre* brand. The pack featured a 'variety of colourful designs, including graffiti, Indie band, B-boy and X-sports' (see Figure 3.7). (133) The one month limited pack release sought to create a sense of product scarcity, a common marketing tactic to enhance product desirability. (134)

Figure 3.7 KT&G packaging for the Raison D'etre brand. Source: http://www.djtimes.co.kr/news/articleView.html?idxno=28832

Launched in December 2004 by the Thailand Tobacco Monopoly, *Chopper* (as in Harley Davidson motorcycles) was described as 'one of the most complex and in-depth package design undertakings.' (135) The name and motorcycle imagery reflects the popularity of motorcycles in Thailand.

In February 2007, RJ Reynolds (RJR) launched a new *Camel* cigarette aimed at women. *Camel No 9* is packaged in black and pink or teal (menthol variety) and designed to conjure images of sophistication, referring to being 'dressed to the nines' (Figure 3.8). (136) Women's internet sites featured positive commentary about the new packaging:

> ... with me being female and all, I have to say that the box and the pink foil inside are appealing, as is the actual look of the cigarette itself. (137)
>
> ... yeah my husband bought them for me last night, because I was so turned on by the black and pink package. (137)
>
> I don't smoke at all, but I keep seeing this [sic] ads for *Camel No 9*. The packaging alone makes me want to try them. It just looks damn good and doesn't follow that style that seemingly every other carton out there does. (138)

It is not possible to determine if these comments were posted by real women, public relations people, or by RJR employees.

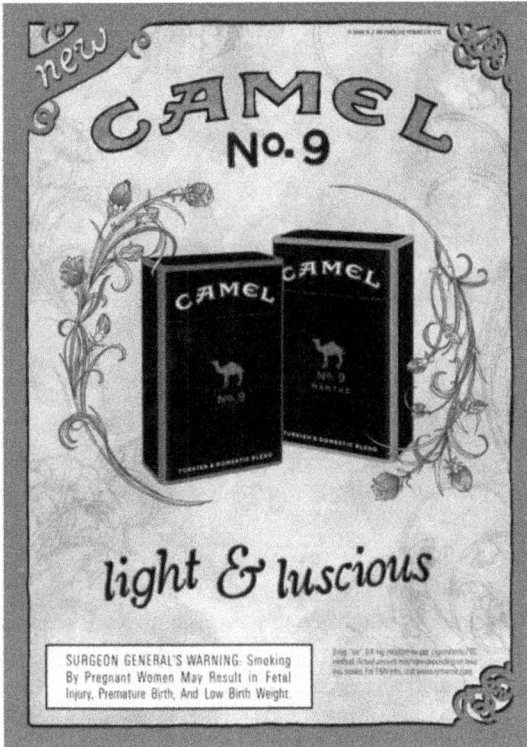

Figure 3.8 RJ Reynolds Camel No 9 cigarette aimed at women. Source: http://tiny.cc/e6iqox

RJR has proven to be particularlyinnovative in designing cigarette packaging. In 2007, smokers were recruited to rate and propose pack designs and logos. Consumers were directed to the *Camel* brand website and blog, where they could discuss package design and vote on what they wanted to see as a final concept. (139) The project, which was initially targeted to engage 6,000 people, netted 30,000 participants and resulted in four new flavours with eye-catching package designs being introduced onto the market (Figure 3.9). These four flavour and package variants were dubbed Frost, Mellow, Robust, and Infused. The cigarettes contain a small bead in the filter that delivers the unique flavours. The *Camel Signature Blends* packaging designs were subsequently modified for the retail market due to the cartoon-like imagery violating US advertising codes that tobacco packages not be appealing to children.

Figure 3.9 Open source package designs for the Camel Signature Blends – from left to right – Frost, Infused, Robust and Mellow.

Researchers from the Centre for Tobacco Control Research at the University of Stirling documented numerous changes in UK tobacco packaging following the introduction of comprehensive legislation banning tobacco advertising, promotion and sponsorship. (140–143) Packaging design strategies were categorised into key themes:

1. value-based packaging

   - selling products in smaller pack sizes
   - selling products in pack sizes larger than the traditional 20 cigarette and 12.5 grams of tobacco

2. revamping the packaging of brands traditionally seen as value
3. simplifying designs to communicate value-for-money
4. printing the price on the brand to imply a special low price
5. image-based packaging

   - designing packs to appeal to various segments of the market, in particular younger and female smokers

6. novel or innovative packaging

   - novel ways of opening the pack
   - novel shapes and sizes

- novel materials
7. themed packs to encourage collection of sets
8. environmentally sustainable packaging.

  - sustainably produced packaging
  - Rizla rolling papers certified by the Forest Stewardship Council.

Evidence supporting the likely effectiveness of plain packaging

The bulk of evidence about the possible impact of plain packs necessarily derives from experimental studies where subjects have typically been presented with both branded and mocked-up plain packs and asked about associations and preferences. A 2009 review of the evidence on the effects of plain packaging concluded: (144)

> The evidence indicates three primary benefits of plain packaging: increasing the effectiveness of health warnings, reducing false health beliefs about cigarettes, and reducing brand appeal especially among youth and young adults. Overall, the research to date suggests that 'plain' packaging regulations would be an effective tobacco control measure, particularly in jurisdictions with comprehensive restrictions on other forms of marketing.

International research on plain packaging

In 1995 an expert panel provided the Canadian health department with a comprehensive review of the likely effects of plain packaging entitled *When packages can't speak: possible impacts of plain and generic packaging of tobacco products.* (27) Until that time, only four sets of studies had been conducted on the plain packaging of cigarettes. (23, 26, 117, 145, 146) The expert panel found that all four studies produced some evidence to support the hypothesis that plain and generic packaging made cigarettes less attractive and less appealing.

The expert panel also conducted a series of studies to further assess the potential impact that plain packaging would have on smoking uptake, health warning recall and cessation, and evaluated the expected tobacco industry response to any packaging reforms. They found that teenagers were particularly vulnerable to linking specific tobacco brands to specific types of people and that tobacco brands served to help teenagers establish their own self-image. (147) On the basis of a detailed analysis of the findings of all the studies, the expert panel concluded:

> Plain and generic packaging of tobacco products (all other things being equal), through its impact on image formation and retention, recall and recognition, knowledge, and consumer attitudes and perceived utilities, would likely depress the incidence of smoking uptake by non-smoking teens, and increase the incidence of smoking cessation by teen and adult smokers. This impact would vary across the population. (27)

Since the Canadian expert review, further research has been conducted in Canada, (28, 112, 148–152) Australia, (153–156) the United Kingdom, (157) New Zealand (158) and the United States. (159) This research has focused on the effects of plain packaging on: awareness, recall and impact of health warnings, (23, 160) on perceptions of riskiness of tobacco products, (28, 150, 157, 159) and the appeal of brands and products. (26, 145, 148) (151–156, 158) Overall, this body of research confirms and strengthens the original findings of the Canadian expert panel.

Impact of plain packaging on effectiveness of health warnings

A multi-country tobacco survey examining the effectiveness of warnings showed that smokers in Canada, who were at the time of the study, exposed to large, picture-based warnings, were significantly more likely than others to report thinking about the health risks of smoking, to stop themselves from having a cigarette, and to think about quitting because of the health warnings. (161) The same study also showed that the larger and more prominent a health warning, the more likely it was to be recalled. Plain packaging enables the warning size to be increased and allows for additional information, elaborating on warnings and about smoking cessation, to be printed on packs.

An Australian study specifically explored the question of whether removing the colour and design features of packaging was more effective in reducing theappeal of brands than simply increasing the size of health warnings. (156) The study found that once packs were plain, increasing the size of the front-of-pack health warnings from 30% to more than 70% did not further reduce brand appeal. While other research indicates that larger health warnings are likely to be noticeable and memorable to consumers, in this study plain packaging was more effective than further increasing the size ofhealth warnings in reducing the brand appeal.

A New Zealand study (158) examined the combined effects of health warnings and plain packaging on the likelihood of young adults aged 18 to 30 years engaging in behaviours known to be linked to cessation. Smokers in this study were asked which pack they would be most and least likely to choose when presented with four cigarette packets featuring different branding and warning size combinations. Packs with the greatest number of branding elements were still preferred even when the warnings were increased from 30% to 50%. However they were less likely to be chosen with a 75% warning. Plain packets with 75% health warnings were significantly more likely to elicit stronger cessation-linked intentions, such as reducing the amount smoked, increasing quit attempts and seeking help to quit, than branded packs with a 30% front-of-pack warning.

Impact of plain packaging on perceptions of harmfulness

Unregulated package colouring and imagery contributes to consumer misperceptions that certain brands are safer than others. (43, 104, 150, 162) The colour of packs is also associated with perceptions of risk and brand appeal. *Marlboro* packs with a gold logo were rated as lower health risk by 53% and easier to quit by 31% than *Marlboro* packs with a red logo in a study of UK adult smokers. (157) A study of 8243 smokers from the US, the UK, Canada and Australia in 2006 similarly found that smokers of 'gold, silver, blue or purple brands were more likely to believe that their own brand might be a little less harmful' than smokers of red or black brands. (159) Researchers in both studies concluded that removing colours from packs, as well as misleading terms such as smooth, gold, and silver, would significantly reduce false beliefs about harmfulness.

Impact of plain packaging on reducing the appeal of products

An Australian study involving more than 800 adult smokers examined the effects on the appeal of tobacco products as the amount of pack branding was progressively reduced. As illustrated in Figure 3.10, the plainest packs were seen as less attractive (brand/pack characteristic), smokers of the packs were seen as significantly less stylish and sociable (smoker characteristic), and the cigarettes in the packs were thought to be less satisfying and of lower quality (sensory perception). (154)

A similarly designed study involving adolescents found that progressively removing brand elements such as colour, branded fonts and imagery from cigarette packs resulted in adolescent smokers seeing packs as less appealing, having more negative expectations of cigarette taste and rating attributes of a typical smoker of the pack less positively. (155)

Canadian studies (151, 152) examined the effects of removal of brand imagery on young female smokers aged 18 to 25 years. The researchers found that removing both descriptors and colours from packs substantially reduced the appeal of female-oriented brands for female smokers. For example, the appeal of the most desirable brand in the study, *Capri Cherry*, fell from 67% to 17% among women who viewed plain packs without the descriptor 'Cherry' on the pack. Plain packs were also associated with significantly fewer positive characteristics than fully branded packs, including glamour, being slim, popular, attractive and sophisticated. Among smokers who requested a pack at the end of the study, branded packs were three times more likely to be selected than plain packs. The researchers concluded that 'plain packaging and removing descriptors such as 'slims' from cigarette packs may reduce smoking susceptibility among young women.' (152)

Research has continued into many aspects of pack and cigarette design and the likely effects of standardisation. This has been summarised in a review for the UK government (76) and most recently by Hammond for the Irish government (163).

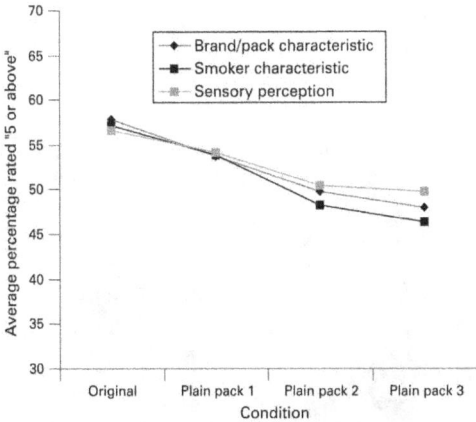

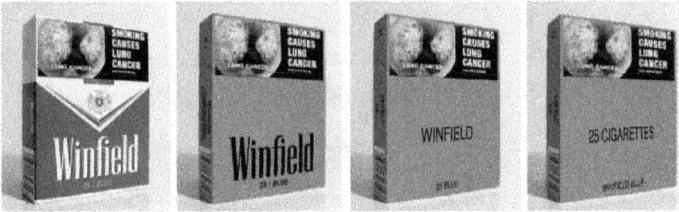

Figure 3.10 Level of attractiveness of increasingly plainer tobacco packaging. Source: Wakefield MA, Germain D and Durkin SJ. How does increasingly plainer cigarette packaging influence adult smokers' perceptions about brand image? An experimental study. Tobacco Control 2008;17:416–21. (154)

4
Tobacco industry arguments, strategies and tactics

In this chapter, we will review the main arguments, strategies and tactics used by the tobacco industry, its acolytes and messengers to attack plain packaging. At the end of the chapter, we will also describe some of the initiatives taken by advocates of plain packaging to counteract industry propaganda. We will start with the most prominent and common arguments and then move through to those used less often. Most of these were also used in the blogosphere by citizens and anonymous trolls, some of whom may well have been tobacco industry staff. (164)

It won't work, so don't do it!

Let us start with the most bizarre argument of all those used to oppose plain packs. This was the 'poacher turned gamekeeper' spectacle of those in the tobacco industry telling the Australian and later the Irish, British and New Zealand governments that they knew that plain packs would do nothing to decrease tobacco sales in children or adults, and that therefore the government should abandon the policy.

This was always going to be a highly fraught strategy for the industry. It is axiomatic that the tobacco industry wants as many people to smoke as much as possible. That is what all its employees understand as their collective key performance indicator as they arrive at work each day and what shareholders expect from their company. Their targets include those who smoke now, those who used to smoke and who might be tempted back into it (165), and those who have not yet started but who might be persuaded to start. This last group is overwhelmingly young people, including those under 18 years of age who are legally unable to buy tobacco products, but who of course often do.

It is equally axiomatic that the future of the tobacco industry depends on new generations starting to use its products. So for all the public statements from the industry that children should not smoke, and its denials that it ever tries to attract children via its marketing and promotions, its own internal documents contain many examples going back many decades about exactly the opposite. (91, 93) The tobacco industry is *intensely* interested in maximising the probabilities that young people will experiment with cigarettes, become dependent on nicotine and become daily, hopefully heavy smokers for many years.

Over the years, tobacco retailers have stood side-by-side with the manufacturers in opposing any measure proposed by governments or public health advocates that threatened to reduce their sales. Tobacco retailers similarly do not open up their shops each day hoping that sales will fall. Like any retailer for any product, they routinely offer price discounts knowing that this will increase sales. And like purveyors of any and all consumer goods, they appreciate that elegant, striking, eye-catching, desirable market-researched packaging helps promote the attractions of their products more than dull packaging incorporating hideous graphic warnings. On the eve of the release of the Chantler report on plain packaging, commissioned by the British government, Simon Clark from the tobacco industry-funded FOREST and 'Hands off our packs' campaign obligingly put the power of branded tobacco packaging this way: 'It's like showing them a picture of a Lamborghini and a beaten-up Ford Escort and saying "Which one do you prefer?"' (166)

Plain packaging poses two massive threats to the tobacco industry. First, it pulls the heart out of branding, the very core of tobacco marketing. As we saw in Chapter 3, branding invests tobacco products with rich signification and personal badging that is bound up in consumers being attracted to smoking and selecting brands, displaying them many times a day and remaining loyal to those brands. Plain packaging eviscerates the ability of tobacco companies to present packaging intended to make these products more desirable – and making smoking less appealing is a major goal of tobacco control.

Second, both tobacco manufacturers and retailers earn more from sales of some brands than others. Plain packaging poses a major threat to the profitability of premium, more profitable brands. Appearing identical to all other brands, apart from the permitted brand and variation names on the packs, many smokers reason: 'Why pay a lot more for a premium brand that looks exactly the same as a budget brand?'. These expensive brands are likely to taste little different to less expensive brands anyway (95). Plain packaging threatens to gut a major component of profitability of the tobacco industry as it dawns on smokers that they were paying more for a fancy packet that now looks identical to all others, except for the brand name.

In itself, this second effect is not of any primary interest to tobacco control because expensive cigarettes are no less deadly than cheaper cigarettes. It is just collateral damage to the tobacco industry caused by the policy objective of making *all* tobacco products less appealing. This is entirely the industry's problem, but one that is irrelevant to the prevention of diseases caused by smoking, and therefore to the public health goals of plain packaging.

On this, the Chantler report (76) makes this critical observation.

> The intent of standardised packaging is indeed to remove appealing brand differentiation. Standardised packaging is aimed at encouraging smokers to see all cigarettes as equally harmful and unappealing, rather than to identify with particular brands and associate them with positive qualities such as glamour, slimness or sophistication.

So when we hear anyone from the tobacco industry intoning earnestly that they believe that plain packaging 'won't work', and explaining that it would be sensible for government to abandon it, it is always sensible to decode such statements through a commercial reality checker. What possible motivation would anyone profiting from selling tobacco have to urge governments to *not* pursue strategies that supposedly would *not* impact on sales? The idea that anyone in the tobacco industry might seriously think that their advice on best practice in tobacco control would be given even a nanosecond's credibility is more than comical. But let's be generous for a moment and reflect that on hearing such advice, some people might think that those in the tobacco industry actually might know pretty well what might impact on smokers. 'They research smokers. Retailers talk to them every day. They might actually know.'

Yes, they certainly do know. It is instructive to watch delivery trucks dropping off tobacco supplies to retailers. These supplies have often been electronically ordered by retailers and the drivers electronically record every carton delivered. In this way, the tobacco manufacturers have instant access to data on every brand sold to every retailer in every suburb on every day. They can then map this data against any variable they choose: season, month, day of the week, macro-economic indicators, suburban demographic indicators, proximity of shops to schools or factories, the introduction of new brands and variants, of changes in pack design, price changes, tax rises, presence or absence of anti-smoking campaigns, and the introduction of new laws or regulations on smoking. They also know how long such changes to demand last.

Armed with such information, their statements about a policy not going to 'work' or having no serious impact, take on a different perspective. If a policy like plain packaging was *not* going to negatively impact on sales, why would they waste any breath, let alone many millions of dollars, in opposing it? As Hamlet's mother Gertrude might have put it: 'The [tobacco industry] doth protest too much, methinks.' The industry's frequent, insistent attempts to convince us that plain packaging is a silly idea ironically helps convince us that the exact opposite must be true.

It's never been done before

Equally bizarrely, the industry thought it was onto a winning argument by repeatedly emphasising that no nation had ever introduced plain packaging. They doubtless reasoned that this argument rested on several subtexts that would convey to the public that such a proposal was therefore reckless, adventurous, foolhardy and naïve. This argument implied that it was obvious that no other nation had introduced plain packs because all other nations – unlike the cavalier Australian government – had thought it through properly. If something has never been done before, it's always because it's been considered and rejected for good reason.

And because no country had ever introduced such legislation, another taunt therefore became available: there was of course no evidence to be found anywhere that plain packaging would achieve what it was meant to achieve. This evidence-free zone in turn allowed the industry to hitch a ride on the evidence-based policy mantra that has swept through governments over the last 15 or so years. How could the government possibly promote a policy for which there was no evidence? They were onto a winner, surely?

But in all the excitement, the industry had painted itself into the corner of championing opposition to innovation. It sought to make a virtue out of Australia only ever marching behind other countries. In a political science satire *Microcosmographia Academica* written in 1908, FM Cornford advised aspiring politicians that 'every public action which is not customary either is wrong, or if it is right it is a dangerous precedent. It follows that nothing should ever be done for the first time.' (167) This was the tobacco industry's mentality in a nutshell.

In public health and medicine, as in every facet of life, there are many examples of things having being done for the first time. Important examples from public health history include vaccination, countless new drugs, the introduction of seat belts in cars (which was first legislated in Victoria, Australia in 1970) and a huge range of product innovations. The *British Medical Journal* once published a tongue-in-cheek systematic review that pointed out that there were no randomised controlled trials that parachutes would save the lives of someone jumping from a plane before (or after) the first time someone jumped using a parachute. (168)

In tobacco control, there have also been many 'firsts' – policies adopted in one country before any other jurisdiction had done so. These included the first introduction of advertising bans; smokefree workplaces, restaurants and bars; strong public education (mass media) campaigns; health-based tax increases; the first pack warnings; and the first graphic pack warnings. Each of these vanguard innovations has now been adopted in many nations as tobacco control proliferates globally through the stimulus of the WHO's FCTC (75) and the strong support of international and national medical and health groups.

Senior *Sydney Morning Herald* journalist Ross Gittins was one who lampooned this argument:

> Plain packaging of cigarettes . . . has never been adopted anywhere in the world. Great argument: it has not been done before, therefore you shouldn't do it. This is the poor little stupid Australia argument. We should always merely follow the lead of other countries because we're not smart enough to dream up anything good ourselves. Its logic is foolproof: if it has never been done before there's no evidence it works, and if we never try it there never will be. But if the idea's so unlikely to work, why are the global giants fighting so hard to stop it being tried? (169)

There's no evidence it will work

The fraternal twin of the 'it's never been done before' argument is the even hairier-chested 'there's *no* evidence'. BATA ran advertising showing an empty filing cabinet to emphasise this point (Figure 4.1)

In fact, there was a good deal of published evidence. This was gathered together under the one cover in a review by Quit Victoria and the Cancer Council Victoria in August 2011 (170). Angela Pratt emphasised the importance of the assembling of this research:

> the amassing of the evidence base. I mean, the number of times that was in all of our talking points. That was incredibly, incredibly important because it enabled Nicola to make the case publicly that this was something that had an evidence base.

As we saw in Chapter 3, before Australia introduced plain packaging, there was considerable experimental evidence that consistently demonstrated that young smokers and potential smokers rate fully branded packaging as being far more appealing across many dimensions of appeal compared with plain packaging. In these studies, subjects are typically presented with fully branded and mocked-up plain packaging and asked to rate them on a variety of attributes and characteristics.

Five reviews summarising this extensive body of evidence showing how packaging influences consumer attitudes, beliefs and behaviour are

Figure 4.1 BATA advertisement 'Where's the proof?'

the *Tobacco labelling and packaging toolkit* (Canada, 2009) (171), *Plain packaging of tobacco products: a review of the evidence* (Australia, 2011) (170), *Plain tobacco packaging: a systematic review* (UK, 2012) (172), the Chantler review (England, 2014) (76) and Hammond's review for the Irish government (2014) (163). The main conclusions of this body of research are that:

- packaging is an important element of advertising and promotion, and its value has increased as traditional forms of advertising and promotion have become restricted
- packaging promotes brand appeal – it is difficult, if not impossible, to separate this from the promotion of tobacco use or to exclude children and young adults from its effect
- the inclusion of brand names and other design embellishments are strongly associated with the level of appeal and perceived traits associated with branding such as sophistication
- plain packaging is less appealing for young people who may be thinking of trying smoking
- on-pack brand imagery distracts from the prominence of health warnings and reduces their impact
- package colours and imagery contribute to consumer misperceptions that certain brands are safer than others
- plain packs reduce the appeal of cigarettes by lessening both the attractiveness of the product and the social desirability of the users of the product
- innovative packaging shape, size, and opening create strong associations with level of appeal and perceived traits associated with branding
- tobacco in plain packs is perceived to be less satisfying, of lower quality, and potentially more harmful.

Exploiting public misunderstanding of 'plain' packs

In the years since plain packaging was announced by the Australian government, we have often had to pause in our explanations of the concept when people interrupt and say, 'so, do you mean they are just . . . all plain? All white? Is there no health warning, for example?' Opponents of plain packaging sought to exploit this understandable lack of public understanding of the words 'plain packaging' and tried to give the impression that plain packs would be plain white boxes with no markings at all. For example, BATA ran the advertisement in Figure 4.2 in Australian newspapers. It proposed that if plain packaging were to apply to cans of cola drinks, then the cans would be all the one colour and only have the word 'cola' on the front, thereby not allowing purchasers to know if they had been sold the particular brand of cola drink they wanted. In Britain, plain packaging has been often depicted in the press as in Figure 4.3 following.

Depicting plain packaging in these ways is highly misleading for two reasons. First, unlike the BATA advertisement which shows a drink can with the word 'Cola', Australian tobacco plain packaging carries the brand and variant names of each different brand. Packs do not just say 'cigarettes' as the BATA advertisement implies, and as BATA knew full well would not be the case. Second, as Figure 2.1 shows, Australian plain packs do not look anything like the BATA comparisons with hypothetical 'plain' cola cans: they have massive coloured health warnings on them.

In March 2014, Linda McAvan, Britain's member of the European parliament for Yorkshire and The Humber, told the 6th European Conference on Tobacco or Health in Istanbul that tobacco industry lobbyists had been distributing plain white boxes like those in Figure 4.3 to members and staff of the European parliament. The mendacity of this exercise shows the tobacco industry today is little different to its decades of dishonest conduct we have witnessed repeatedly since the 1950s.

'Plain packaging' was the term initially used and that is now well understood in Australia.Plain packaging does *not* mean packaging without graphic health warnings. Other countries may wish to avoid potential confusion and could consider using terms such as 'generic' or 'standardised' packaging, which is the term used in the April 2014 Chantler review for the British government. (76)

It will be easier to make fake copies

This exploitation of the lack of understanding of 'plain' also played for the tobacco industry in proposing that plain packaging would create a paradise for counterfeiters. What could make life easier for counterfeit-

**WHAT COMPANY
WOULD STAND FOR THIS?**

Cola

The Tobacco Plain Packaging Bill could
destroy brands that are worth millions,
if not billions, of dollars.

No company would stand for having
its brands taken away and we're no
different. And it may infringe international
trademark and intellectual property law.

The Government could also end up
spending millions in legal fees defending
an idea unproven anywhere in the world.

Don't let the taxpayer
foot the bill for a bad Bill

Plain Pack.com

British American Tobacco
Australia Limited

Figure 4.2 BATA's attempt to depict the equivalent of 'plain packaging' for other products

ers than to reduce the challenges of counterfeiting sometimes complex packages by just requiring plain white boxes?

BAT's website featured a video sent to many MPs in the UK and Australia. The high production video dramatised the line that retail display bans (now adopted by a growing number of nations), plain packs,

Figure 4.3 How plain tobacco packs have been frequently shown in British news media.Source: http://www.examiner.co.uk/news/ west-yorkshire-news/kirklees-council-backs-call-plain-4928229

tax increases and banning additives would all contribute to increased crime, terrorism and prostitution. The video had everything from a cheesy script, to a swarthy eastern European drug dealer stereotype, an innocent and clueless European Union bureaucrat and a shifty English bad guy (see https://www.youtube.com/watch?v=lpFx7pLy2L0).

The entire premise of the message was that these control measures would be manna from heaven for organised crime: 'Plain packs – easy for us to copy . . . no logos to match . . . easier to counterfeit . . . lots more profit,' said a fingernail-removing Budapest crime boss from the back of a limo.

The truth, however, is that copying branded packs has never been a serious barrier to tobacco counterfeiters. On the streets of many low and middle-income nations, fake leading brands are openly sold through street vendors because of chaotic law enforcement and corruption. I once edited a research paper from Tehran showing that 21% of cigarettes are smuggled there. (173)

But that is not remotely the situation in Australia, nor in most OECD nations. Forecasts of massive black markets assume that smokers will be able to access these products with the ease that they today are able to buy cigarettes from every second shop.

As anyone who has travelled to nations where counterfeited consumer goods like watches, perfumes, clothing, books, DVDs, CDs, luggage and luxury pens are openly on sale, it is obvious that copying a cigarette pack is child's play. It has long been the case that counterfeiters have been able to easily make extremely good, near-to-perfect copies of fully branded tobacco packs. Australia's plain packaging would be no more or less easy for professional counterfeiters to copy than the fully branded packaging it replaced. It is a major misunderstanding to assume that challenges in copying packaging present a substantial barrier to professional counterfeiters. The tobacco companies know this, so for them it is nothing but the wilful attempt to promote a lie.

Former Scotland Yard chief inspector Will O'Reilly, now a regular 'spokesman' for Philip Morris, (174) emphasised another angle here, saying: 'If . . . we cut criminals' costs by giving them just one pack design to copy rather than 101, then it's criminals that win.' (175) This catchy sound bite rests on the falsehood that counterfeiters see their task as making faithful copies of every brand and brand variant that is available for sale in a licit market. Sometimes there are hundreds of legal brands and variants on sale, however counterfeiters have no interest in going to the trouble of copying brands with tiny market share. Few smokers want these brands when they are sold openly, so why would they suddenly want them, when popular brands are also cheaper when sold illicitly? In Australia a small number of brands are responsible for a large majority of market share.

Nonetheless, as shown in Figures 4.2 and 4.3, the tobacco industry decided that it should exploit the public misunderstanding that plain packaging meant all plain white boxes which any small business with rudimentary packaging equipment could make in a suburban factory. For many months it relentlessly promoted the idea that plain packaging would see the market flooded with such all white packs.

In 2011 the Australian prime time television news magazine program *A Current Affair* sent a reporter to Hong Kong where he interviewed a person said to be a tobacco smuggler. The reporter showed the smuggler a branded pack of a leading Australian brand, *Winfield Blue*, and asked: 'How close to that can you get?' In an instant the smuggler replied: '100 per cent'. *Winfield Blue* has a basic, minimalist pack design with just three colours: blue, white with black text. By contrast, Australia's plain packs have 14 different fully coloured rotated graphic warnings. They too, would be readily reproducible by anyone with the right equipment. But if anything, they would present far more of challenge to counterfeit than fully branded packs like *Winfield*.

The British government's 2014 Chantler report contained a bombshell admission from a BATA staffer who had spoken with the Chantler review team in March. Chantler summarised:

> There is no evidence of increased counterfeiting following the introduction of plain packaging in Australia and this is now accepted by tobacco manufacturers locally. [as] Mark Connell of BAT told the review team.
>
> [Mr Connell:] One of the things that we did say . . . is that there would be an increase in counterfeit of the standardised packaging. In other words, the legislation was virtually a blueprint that was given to counterfeiters . . . That hasn't happened, well, it may have happened in small quantities . . . Our biggest brand which was counterfeited all the time, very professionally I have to say, at least contained a health warning and a graphic health warning [unlike these illicit white brands now prevalent].
>
> Review team: Have you actually seen a reduction in counterfeit?
> Mr Connell: *Absolutely. Absolutely.* [our emphasis]

Illicit trade in Australia has nothing to do with plain packs. Such levels that exist are unquestionably a reflection of the high price of tobacco products in Australia, and a small section of the market's willingness to buy far cheaper illegal substitutes. As Connell says, there has 'absolutely, absolutely' been a reduction in such fake copies since the introduction of plain packs. Connell's now public emphatic statement should effectively put an end to tobacco industry claims that plain packaging encourages counterfeiters – but it won't. The industry will just keep on repeating the lie.

Illicit trade: pick a big number

This 'boon to illicit trade' argument was quite easily the most prominent of those run by the tobacco industry and its supporters in Australia. The same can be said about industry opposition in Britain, Ireland and New Zealand. For many months, the Twitter accounts of BAT's offices in London, Australian and New Zealand have tweeted on little else than the illicit trade, including claims that plain packaging would increase it.

Since 2005, there have been 10 tobacco industry-commissioned reports on illicit trade in Australia prepared by three consultancy firms – PricewaterhouseCoopers (PWC) in 2005, (176) 2007 (177) and 2010 (178); Deloitte between 2011 and early 2013 (179–183) and KPMG in 2013 (184) and 2014. (185) The PWC and Deloitte reports used interview data collected by a market research company for the tobacco industry in five Australian cities to then calculate estimates of the size of illicit tobacco consumption throughout the country.

The 2011 report from Deloitte contained a stop-in-your-tracks caveat:

> We have not audited or otherwise verified the accuracy or completeness of the information, and, to that extent, the information contained in this report may not be accurate or reliable. (179)

David Crow, CEO of BATA, gave evidence to the House of Representatives Standing Committee on Health and Ageing's hearings into the *Tobacco Plain Packaging Bill 2011*. Crow pushed the illicit trade argument and referred to the tobacco industry-commissioned Deloitte report, (179) saying:

> It is robust research. It is based on thousands of interviews of consumers done in a very thorough way by Roy Morgan Research, who work with Deloitte. The aim was to estimate – and you will never get a real answer?–?the size. That size has been consistent over the past 18 months. The last report found that about 15.6% of the industry is illicit. We say one in five; one in 5½ cigarettes smoked in this country is illicit. (186)

There were a couple of rather large problems with what Crow told the parliamentary committee. He presumably had read the Deloitte report, which states on page 20 that: 'This initial sample comprised of 9206 identified people. However after allowing for natural sample attrition, 949 respondents completed the survey.'

So 949 smokers in five capital cities, not 'thousands', answered questions about whether they believed they had used illegal tobacco (loose chop chop, counterfeit or contraband/duty not paid).

Then there was the problem with Crow's arithmetical (or was it his rhetorical) ability. 15.6% is not one in five (that's what 20% would be) or one in 5½ cigarettes. It is one in 6.41, which is less than one in six. So what's the difference between 'one in five' and 'less than one in six'? Not much you might think? But when you're talking about the number of cigarettes that would be involved, this means a difference of 741.69 tonnes of tobacco, using the Deloitte data. Depending on what assumptions are made about the average weight of a cigarette (0.75–1g), this translates to between 750 million and 900 million cigarettes and roll-your-own cigarette equivalents.

Crow would have been aware that in the week before he gave evidence, the Australian Institute of Health and Welfare (AIHW) published its then latest estimate of how many smokers regularly used illicit tobacco in Australia. Surveying 26,648 people across Australia, of whom 15.1% were daily smokers (and with 17% smoking at all?—?4530 smokers), the AIHW found just 1.5% of Australian smokers regularly smoked unbranded tobacco in 2010 – see Table 3.11 p39. (187) Crow did not refer to this substantially lower estimate.

The tobacco industry-sponsored reports rapidly became objects of ridicule as the manifold problems with them became apparent. The Cancer Council Victoria produced detailed critiques of the reports. (188, 189)

One commenced with:

The Deloitte report on illicit trade released 3 May 2012 once again beggars belief first because (like the previous years' reports) it features an implausibly large estimate of the size of the illicit market – does anyone seriously believe that one in every eight cigarettes they see people smoking in Australia are fake or come out of plastic bags? (188)

Ultimately, the idea that one in eight cigarettes being smoked (or as high as one in five, if you listened to BATA's chief executive) were obtained from illicit tobacco suppliers requires that there be an extremely widespread network of illicit tobacco retailers. These suppliers risk massive fines for tax evasion and so cannot trade openly. If one in eight ordinary Australians, predominantly from low socioeconomic backgrounds (190) and therefore often with minimal levels of education, could so easily find such a network of illegal suppliers, why could the Australian Federal Police, with all its resources, not find the same suppliers? While police corruption is not unknown in Australia, Transparency International ranks Australia 'very clean' in its 2013 Corruption Perceptions Index, (191) so the idea that police throughout the country may have been corrupt and turning a blind eye, was also not credible.

In April 2014 the three Australian tobacco companies released a report produced by KPMG LLP Strategy Group, London entitled *Illicit tobacco in Australia: 2013 full year report.* (185) This was an update of the half year report produced in October 2013. (184)

Again, Quit Victoria and the Cancer Council Victoria rapidly published a lengthy critical review of this report. (189) A key component of the KPMG report was a study of discarded packs found in streets. Quit Victoria's critique concluded that discarded packs were highly unlikely to be representative of total consumption of tobacco in Australia and that KPMG's 'estimate of the size of the illicit tobacco market is likely to be substantially higher than is warranted.'

The litter survey largely comprised packs either dropped by smokers or blown out of street rubbish bins but did not include domestic rubbish. Quit Victoria noted:

> The survey is therefore not a representative sample of all packs used in Australia and is likely to over-represent packs used by people who work or otherwise spend a lot of time outdoors, and packs used by people who litter. A review conducted by the International Agency for Research on Cancer has suggested that people who use illicit tobacco may also be more inclined to litter. . . .
>
> It is highly likely that the empty pack survey over-represents the packs used by tourists and other overseas visitors and students, all of whom are more likely than the average Australian smoker to be eat-

ing out and socialising at outdoor venues, and much more likely to be in possession of packs purchased overseas.

Areas frequented by high numbers of overseas students would also be places where there would be a high volume of discarded packs. Many overseas students live close to the institutions in which they study, in budget-style accommodation . . . Students also tend to eat out a lot in cheap eating places close by, including many serving cuisine from their countries of origin—for instance those in Swanston and Lonsdale Streets in Melbourne. It is interesting that each of the cities surveyed in the report – all of the capital cities plus Geelong, Newcastle, Wollongong, Cairns, Townsville, the Gold Coast, the Sunshine Coast and Toowoomba – is home to at least one university with high numbers of students from overseas.

Sir Cyril Chantler in his report (76) concluded about the KPMG report:

I note that Australian government departments, both Health and Customs, appear to be strongly of the view that KPMG's methodology is flawed. These departments point to official Customs data, which shows no significant effect on illicit tobacco following the introduction of plain packaging, backed by analysis undertaken by the Cancer Council Victoria (based on data from the National Drug Strategy Household Survey) that suggests that illicit tobacco in Australia is only 10–20% of the level proposed by KPMG. In a situation where estimates differ by such magnitudes, I do not have confidence in KPMG's assessment of the size of – or changes in – the illicit market in Australia.

The most bizarre claim about illicit sales was an online national interactive map promoted by BATA (interestingly since removed from http://www.illegaltobacco.com.au/) which allowed searching for the amount of illicit tobacco being sold in any Australian electorate. Browsers could look up the usage estimates in an outer suburban area of a large city like Sydney or Melbourne, as well as look up how much was being sold in the remotest central desert electorate (see a screenshot taken at the time in Figure 4.4). The amount per capita was exactly the same, regardless of location. Illicit sales rates per head of population were claimed to be the same throughout the country. The designers of the website had simply taken the highly questionable estimates of use obtained from the five-city (Sydney, Melbourne, Brisbane, Perth or Adelaide) survey of just 949 smokers and applied them across the country. Apparently, illicit tobacco is as easy to buy in the remote South Australian outback town of Oodnadatta as it is in the outer western suburbs of Sydney or Melbourne and in the most affluent suburbs of cities around the country.

Paul Grogan from the Cancer Council Australia picked up a lot of cynicism about the reports from politicians he often spoke with:

> Nobody I spoke to ever took them all that seriously. I'm happy to say most people saw them for what they were worth. Most people in government are pretty aware of reports that are produced to meet the goals of the commissioning agency. People get a report done by [a commercial agency] and it's got this disclaimer and everyone knows it's nonsense. It's good for a headline. It gets stuff stirred up in the media, but I never met anyone who was seriously worried about whatever it was . . . one in in five . . . cigarettes being illicit.

Price falls will drive up consumption

Tobacco companies make most profit from their so-called 'premium' expensive brands. I once received a BATA staff training video dating from 2001 from an anonymous sender which included the following exchange:

> Senior executive 1: Another example is our guys in marketing and trade marketing, they need to sell five packs of [a budget brand] to get the same profit they would get from one pack of [a premium brand].
> Senior executive 2: I mean, five packs of [the budget brand] for every pack of [the premium brand], I mean it's just a clear statement of fact of what our intentions are. If we don't sell [premium brand A] and [premium brand B] and [premium brand C], the amount of sheer volume we have to do of [budget brand] to make up for that is just ridiculous. I mean, the factory couldn't produce it.

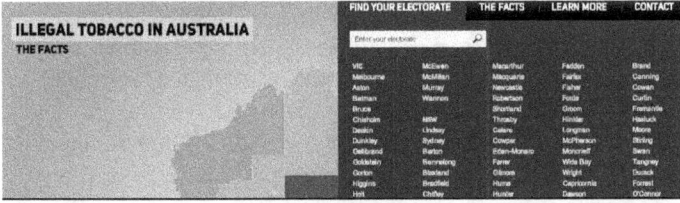

Figure 4.4 Screenshot from now removed BATA sponsored website showing illicit tobacco use in every Australian electorate

Tobacco companies promote and price expensive brands as being of
'superior' quality to less expensive brands. However, the industry has
known for decades that many smokers cannot tell the difference between similar brands (95) if they are not aware beforehand of which
brand they are about to smoke.

Smokers who buy more expensive premium brands to display their
supposedly more expensive taste in cigarettes have had this ability severely curtailed by plain packaging. Unless someone looks closely at
another's pack to see what brand is being smoked, all brands – budget
and premium – look exactly the same other than for the brand and
variant names. This may well cause smokers to 'trade down' to cheaper
brands, reasoning that they are getting no added value for paying more
for a brand that looks the same as all others. This scenario is known in
the trade by the dreadful expression 'commoditisation'. If this scenario
became widespread, it would be a major threat to company profitability,
forcing price to be a far greater factor in competition between companies. Here, there is some plausibility to the argument that plain packs
might cause a downward price war, which could make tobacco more affordable to young people and those on low incomes, which is why the
tobacco industry has emphasised this issue.

However, the 2014 Chantler report (76) found that post plain packaging, with the exception of some budget brands, the price of Australian
brands has been rising above those caused by tax rises because of the
industry increasing its prices. Chantler went on to say:

This objection also assumes that plain packaging is introduced in isolation, without any relationship with broader government tobacco

control policies. While tobacco companies may indeed seek to reduce price as a short-term countermeasure, this is a possible problem that is easily counteracted. When the Australian government announced its intention to introduce plain packs, it also introduced an immediate 25% increase in tobacco tax. In 2013, it announced a further four successive rises, each of 12.5%. Concerns or threats of price wars causing unintended greater affordability of tobacco can thus easily be countered by tax increases, which force prices up. Governments can monitor tobacco prices and if necessary increase tax to counteract such developments.

Importantly, with the exception of some ultra low-cost cigarettes, prices for leading brands in Australia have increased above tax rises. Rather than leading to complete commoditisation, it appears that the price differentials between premium and low-cost brands have widened, as the Australian pricing model moves closer to that of other high tax jurisdictions like the UK, with four distinct price segments. Some new ultra low-cost brands have been developed, *but this is likely to reflect tax changes more than plain packaging.* [our emphasis]

Therefore there is no evidence to date of a commoditisation of the market leading to immediate and widespread price reductions in Australia. It is too soon to make definitive conclusions, but the fact that leading brands are increasing prices above tax suggests that predictions of widespread price reductions are exaggerated, at least in the short run.

This was to prove something of an understatement. In July 2014, the *Australian Financial Review* ran a lengthy report (193) on what it headlined as a '$2.2 billion pay day for Australian tobacco companies'. While they had been vigorously prosecuting the case for plain packs and high taxes causing a race to the bottom of prices, the same companies had been quietly raising their own prices. And how. As Neil Chenoweth wrote, Cancer Council Victoria price monitoring showed that the local industry had regularly increased prices above tax increase rates, but this went into overdrive when the intent to introduce plain packaging was announced:

From August 2011 to February 2013, while excise duty rose 24¢ for a pack of 25, the tobacco companies' portion of the cigarette price (which excludes excise and GST), jumped $1.75 to $7.10. While excise had risen 2.8% over the period, the average net price had risen 27%. Philip Morris' budget brand *Choice 25s* rose $1.80 in this period, with only 41¢ of this being from excise and GST. (See Figure 4.5)

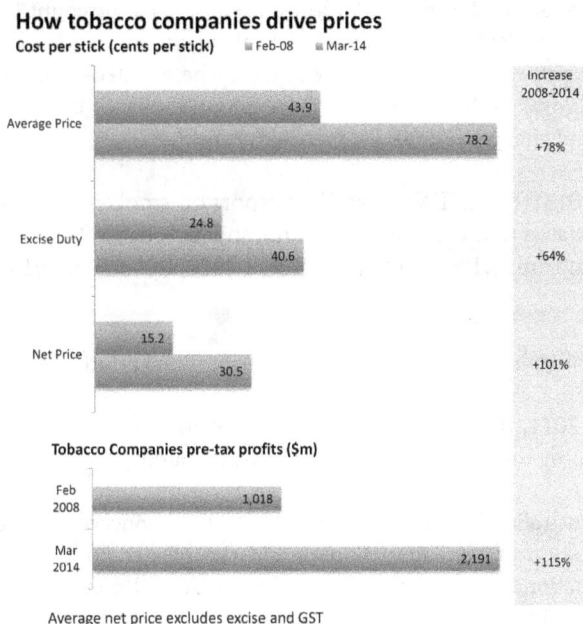

How tobacco companies drive prices

Cost per stick (cents per stick)   ▪ Feb-08   ▪ Mar-14

		Increase 2008-2014
Average Price	43.9 / 78.2	+78%
Excise Duty	24.8 / 40.6	+64%
Net Price	15.2 / 30.5	+101%

Tobacco Companies pre-tax profits ($m)

Feb 2008	1,018	
Mar 2014	2,191	+115%

Average net price excludes excise and GST

Figure 4.5 Contributions of tobacco tax to net sales price, Australia

An Imperial Tobacco Australia spokesman dismissed this by arguing that the data were recommended retail prices, not after-discount retail prices. But Chenoweth noted that:

tobacco industry sources say the level of the manufacturing rebates has remained relatively constant, which allows comparisons between time periods that show the sharp rises. Wholesale prices show similar gains, with *Winfields* up 13.2% from August 2012 to February 2013.

Chenoweth also wrote:

> The overall market moved to low-price and deep discount brands, which grew 5.6% to comprise 37.3% of the market in 2013. It's the higher prices for top and middle brands, where rusted-on customers stayed loyal to the brands, that have allowed tobacco companies to discount cheaper brands, yet increase profits.

In July 2014, the AIHW released its report on smoking in Australia in 2013. It stated that current use of 'unbranded' tobacco (ie: 'chop chop') had fallen from 6.1% in 2007, to 4.9% in 2010, to 3.6% in 2013. (194)

With retail display bans, plain packaging not needed

In April 2011, the trade magazine *Retail World* ran an item titled 'Retailers facing duplication of tobacco laws'. It stated:

> The Australian Retailers Association (ARA) is concerned about the duplication of regulatory burden and compliance costs associated with national plain packaging legislation. ARA Executive Director Russell Zimmerman said in a statement: 'Retailers have invested in new store fit-outs to ensure they are compliant with state tobacco display bans but they are now left wondering what exactly they are hiding behind cupboard doors if federal legislation will dictate standard packaging.'

Note here that the tobacco manufacturers pay for the new storage facilities, not the retailers. It continued:

> National Association of Retail Grocers of Australia Pty Ltd (NARGA) stated that tobacco products are already sold from closed

displays at one point of sale in a shop and are not generally visible to customers. 'The closed displays make the proposed plain packaging pointless,' NARGA said in a statement.

This argument was one that also featured in the TV ads run by the Alliance of Australian Retailers (AAR). Yet again, it was quite bizarre. Those using it appeared to acknowledge that keeping branded packs out of sight in shops might be appropriate in reducing tobacco's appeal ('out of sight, out of mind') and in further denormalising tobacco to be a non-ordinary consumer good. But of course as soon as tobacco products are sold and brought out from hidden display, they immediately become portable tobacco advertisements, being displayed every time a smoker takes them out to smoke, or places them on public display on a café table etc.

Plain packaging turns the cigarette pack from a glossy fashion accessory into an ugly product purposefully designed to be off-putting for both children and adults. Moreover, there is evidence suggesting that Australian smokers have reduced the 'display' of their cigarette packs after the introduction of plain packaging. In an observational study of smoking and pack display conducted before and after the introduction of plain packs, researchers found a 15% decline in pack display and a 23% decline in observed smoking in bars, cafes and restaurants with outdoor dining areas. Increases were observed in the proportions of smokers not displaying their packs face up, and covering them with wallets or other material, and a small increase in the (very small) proportion of smokers who had placed in their cigarettes in other containers. (195)

Plain packaging as an example of 'nanny state' legislation

In February 1985, *The Age* reported that at least three Australians had been disembowelled in the past two years after sitting on swimming pool skimmer box covers shaped like children's seats that have since been banned. Before the advent of mandatory shatterproof safety glass for showers, many people suffered major lacerations and occasionally died after bathroom accidents. Before 2008, it was legal for fast-buck retailers to sell children's nightwear that could easily catch fire: many children were hideously burnt and scarred for life. Random breath testing was first introduced in 1976, to the chagrin of the Australian Hotels Association. In New South Wales it was followed by 'an immediate 90% decline in road deaths, which soon stabilised at a rate approximately 22% lower than the average for the previous six years'.

These are just four of many examples of changes to laws, regulations, mandatory product standards and public awareness campaigns that were introduced following lobbying from health advocates. (196) With these, as with nearly every campaign to clip the wings of those with the primitive ethics of a cash register, there was protracted resistance. Bans and brakes on personal and commercial freedoms are routinely ridiculed as the interventionist screechings from that reviled harridan, the nanny state.

Similar attacks once rained down on Edwin Chadwick, the architect of the first Public Health Act in England in 1848. He proposed the first regulatory measures to control overcrowding, drinking water quality, sewage disposal and building standards. After he was sacked for his trouble, *The Times* gloated:

> We prefer to take our chance with cholera and the rest than be bullied into health. There is nothing a man hates so much as being cleansed against his will, or having his floors swept, his walls whitewashed, his pet dung heaps cleared away.

Yet on the 150th anniversary of the Public Health Act, a *British Medical Journal* poll saw his invention of civic hygiene, and all of its regulations, voted as the most significant advance in public health of all time.

Those opposed to state intervention in markets subscribe to often unarticulated social Darwinist values that imply that those with the misfortune to be killed, injured or made chronically ill by their participation in untrammelled marketplaces had it coming to them. The unregulated marketplace and community is a kind of noble jungle where the fittest survive thanks to their better education and judgement in their consumer choices, their better ability to pay for superior, less dodgy products, to keep up repairs on their cars and homes, and to get employment in work that is not dangerous or toxic. Children living in poorer housing near busy roads in the leaded petrol era had only their parents to blame for their lead-lowered IQs – they didn't have to live there! When a toddler drowned in a backyard pool before mandatory pool-fencing laws, it was the fault of the feckless parents for not being more vigilant, and nothing to with failure of government to mandate the cost of a fence as part of the cost of a pool. When kids ingested lead or other heavy metals from dodgy toys when these were legal, their parents should have just done their homework and not bought them.

So in the best traditions of nanny state invective, Imperial Tobacco ran a brief multimedia campaign in June 2011 seeking to conflate plain packaging and the government's greed for tobacco tax as the twin horsemen of a nanny state apocalypse. The centrepiece of the campaign was a severe, stout 'nanny', dressed like an archetypal state official-cum-Gestapo officer. In the TV ads (see http://www.youtube.com/watch?v=G-31ew2k95w) she bellowed and belittled an unseen but voiced young male smoker. Life-size cardboard figures of the nanny appeared in tobacconists.

Imperial's public statements accompanying the campaign were vacuous bluster about unspecified sinister 'unintended consequences' and 'dangerous precedents'. Without blinking, Imperial advised us that all Australians should be concerned about being on a 'path to a nanny state'. This pantomime-like campaign ran only briefly on television, suggesting that it was not effective.

Chaos in shops

Tobacco retailers joined the chorus of manufacturers protesting against retail display bans because the manufacturers had been giving retailers financial incentives to display particular brands in positions which maximised customer attention. ('Plain packaging would have a negative impact on retailers, who currently benefit from manufacturer payments for shelf displays and visibility.') (192). Some retailing representatives stood ready to support the tobacco companies in their attacks on plain packs.

Since December 2012, all Australian packs have been clearly marked with the brand name and any registered variant name (eg: 'smooth'). Each brand is delivered to retailers in brand-specific bulk supply boxes. Retail staff then transfer the new stock into the retail dispensers typically located behind them, behind the shop counters. Here, they are placed in brand-specific columns, with either the bottom or the top face of the lowest pack in the column showing to the shop assistant. Both the top and bottom panel of all packs show the brand name and variant. This is exactly the way that fully branded packs were stored, prior to plain packaging. The shop assistant then selects a pack of the requested brand from these columns, when serving a customer.

The tobacco industry and its supporters decided that they could make a big play about the utter chaos that all this was going to cause anyone selling tobacco products. In February 2011, it got the astroturf group it had created, the Alliance of Australian Retailers, (see p95) to run this message to the public, armed with a report from Deloitte, the global consultancy firm.

Astonishingly, Deloitte's research (197) was based on discussions with just six retailers around Australia ('Deloitte conducted consultations with two retail operators in each of the following categories: service stations/convenience stores, tobacconists and newsagents.'). These six told Deloitte's wide-eyed investigators about all the ways in which they imagined plain packs would increase transaction times with customers and Deloitte summarised this in Table 4.1 below.

Table 4.1: Estimated increase in transaction times and associated costs (Deloitte report)

Operator	Estimated number of daily transactions	Indicative additional time (hours)	Indicative extra annual costs ($)
Service station / convenience store	200–400	455–1,692	9,000–34,000
Tobacconist	100–200	323–1,218	6,500–24,000
Newsagent	50–200	216–834	4,500–17,000

Source: Data extracted from Deloitte, Alliance of Australian Retailers, Potential impact on retailers from the introduction of plain tobacco packaging https://www.australianretailers.com.au/downloads/pdf/deloitte/2011_01_31_AAR_Plain_Packaging2.pdf

The range in transactions reflects the different sizes of the six outlets researched. Aside from the unbelievably inept approach to sampling in this report, there would appear to be something very seriously wrong with this table. Consider tobacconists, who serve only tobacco products and so might be expected to be most familiar with tobacco transactions. Table 4.1 shows a range of 100 to 200 daily customer transactions, taking between 323–1218 *additional hours* (ie. between 193.8 minutes for the shops with 100 customers per day, to 365.4 minutes for those with 200 customers a day!) Later in the report, another table states a further additional 10–45 minutes per day would be needed for 'stock management' of the new plain packaging.

Somewhere out of this chaotic report the AAR extracted the sound bite of each transaction taking an additional 'up to 45 seconds', as it put in a submission to the government. (198) All based on the guessing of six retailers in a report published 17 months before plain packaging was actually introduced. As you read this, pause from your reading and say to yourself 'a packet of *Marlboro Red*, please' as if you were standing at the counter of a petrol station or convenience store. Then look at your watch and time out 45 seconds. Ask yourself if you can ever recall any interaction with a store employee needing to reach any item within a step or two from the cash register which has taken 45 seconds to find. And then remember that the claim was being made that 45 seconds was the length of the *increase* in time being claimed, not the actual time. Perhaps they were saying it would take well over a minute for a shop keeper to find an item that they would be asked for many, many times every day.

The really interesting question was what was a company with Deloitte's reputation doing putting its name to nonsense like this? The Deloitte report was prefaced with an interesting caveat: 'No one else, apart from the AAR, is entitled to rely on this report for any purpose. We do not accept or assume any responsibility to anyone other than the AAR in respect of our work or this report.' Fine: there was no reason to rely on the report for any purpose, unless you were the AAR.

In June, the AAR released another Deloitte report (199) with lots of shocking numbers and findings in it about an Armageddon that was going to descend on Australia's corner stores because of a policy that we'll recall wasn't going to work. Here was 'research' to prove it. So let's take a look at how this research was conducted.

First, Deloitte told us that: 'Roy Morgan Research was engaged by the AAR to conduct a consumer survey to verify the risk of channel shift following the introduction of plain packaging.' Channel shift is retail jargon for your customers switching to buying their tobacco from bigger outlets like supermarkets, which of course have been attracting small business customers for decades because of their cheaper prices on everything.

Note importantly, that the survey was not designed to examine whether there was a risk in channel shift arising from plain tobacco packaging, but to 'verify' it. It was a foregone conclusion, apparently. Great science!

We read that those surveyed 'were presented with an overview of the proposed regulation and asked whether they thought their shopping experience at a small retailer would be affected.' So they were presented with an overview that would assist in 'verifying' the risk of channel shift. Hard to imagine any chance of push polling effect operating there!

Catastrophically for corner stores, independent petrol stations and newsagents, more than one in three smokers (34%) and 18% of non-smoking consumers told the polling company after hearing the overview that they were 'either somewhat likely or very likely to change where they shopped as a result of plain packaging.' So why would they do this? Smokers thought they would be 'more likely to be given the wrong tobacco product'. So presumably they think that small shopkeepers are a cut below the staff in supermarkets and specialist tobacconists, and won't be able to read the name on the pack or the column on the pack shelving behind the counter. Why else would there be more mistakes in handing over the brand requested in small businesses than in larger outlets? They would be packaged the same wherever they are sold.

Another reason given was that small store staff 'would have a harder time finding what I want and so 'queues would be longer'. Again, how could this be different in small stores compared with large stores, given that the packs will be the same in all outlets? Particularly when we discover below that small shopkeepers think supermarkets will stock far more brands, which presumably might make the search more difficult in the larger outlets.

The report also presents results from focus groups with small retailers who believed that channel shift may occur because of:

- the increase in time required to complete a tobacco-related transaction would lead to customers becoming increasingly frustrated due to delays and longer queuing time
- the knowledge that a larger retailer, e.g. a major supermarket with a broader range of products, would always have what they require.

Let's repeat that. Small shopkeepers think that the introduction of plain packs will cause them to cut back on the range of products they offer, but that supermarkets won't do this? How could that be?

These unacceptable delays would have seriously consequences for small businesses, Deloitte argued, saying:

> The increase in time required to complete a tobacco-related transaction would lead to customers becoming increasingly frustrated due to the delays and longer queuing time. As a result, many small retailers believed such customers would leave their store without making a purchase and would opt to visit a larger retailer with more staff.

However, reading deeper into the report produces not a little amusement. At the end of Table 3 (see top of page 24) (199) we read reasons why customers shop at small retailers. 'Convenience' and 'location' rank highest. And what is the least important reason that tobacco customers choose to shop at small retailers? That's right. It was 'quick service', at just 2%. Plain packaging might only improve matters!

The industry then promoted this 'big enough' number, hoping that no one would question it. It also had a small chorus line of dedicated supporters who were willing to repeat this nonsense. One was Alex Hawke, one of the federal Opposition's rusted-on opponents of 'excessive regulation'. In July 2011 he intoned in parliament:

> I also rise tonight to put on record my opposition to proposals such as plain paper packaging legislation – ill thought out proposals put forward by government committees and the bureaucracy which will not achieve their ends and which will artificially burden small businesses around our country. I was visited by the Alliance of Australian Retailers on behalf of those small businesses which will be most im-

pacted by this bad legislation – an ill-considered idea put forward by a government addicted to legislative response. An independent report by Deloitte, funded by the Australian Alliance of Retailers, identifies key areas in which small businesses will suffer from such a piece of legislation. One area is stock management – the legislation could double the time spent managing cigarette stocks. Increases in sales transaction times could cost independent retailers up to $30,000 a year. Other problem areas identified were product selection errors and increases in shrinkage. The list goes on. We must remember that these are products which are already required by law to be behind a counter.

We now have a situation in our country where we pay a government bureaucracy to determine – by government decree – that the ugliest colour in this country is olive green. What if you happen to like olive green? What if you happen to be a government-mandated freak? That is what the government has paid a bureaucratic committee to determine – that olive green is the ugliest colour in our country. That is what we are paying people in government to determine today. I want to record my sympathy for all of those small retailers and those people making a stand against this ridiculous form of nanny state legislative response to ordinary, everyday problems. (200)

The Australian Retailers Association ran a similar line:

> Like retail display bans, plain packaging is likely to significantly increase the time taken to complete a transaction including the sale of tobacco products. Regulations that increase transaction times have been estimated to cost businesses up to half a billion dollars [$461 million], equivalent to 15,000 jobs. Increased transaction times also often lead to 'retail rage' at the checkouts which is a health and safety concern for retail employees, particularly young workers. (201)

Five months after the December 2012 implementation, this 'store chaos' theme continued unabated. Jeff Rogut, a store owner and chief executive of the Australasian Association of Convenience Stores, flew to London to speak at a Philip Morris sponsored meeting about plain packs in April 2013. In an article published in *Asian Trader* he wrote that staff:

> ... have to put the stock away, which has again caused enormous angst in terms of layouts in the stores. Remember they are behind closed doors already, they then have to open the doors and where do they put the packs? Previously you used to have the best sellers in the middle, easy to reach and easy to identify. Now we've had to think through – do we do it by brand, alphabetically, by company? How do we make it easier for our people to serve? And that decision has really not been made – every store is working through finding the most efficient way to get their staff to recognise the product.

Every time *any* new product or newly packaged existing product is sold in any store, staff obviously have to make decisions about where to store these products. Cigarettes in new packages are no different.

Rogut then painted a fascinating story of plain packs being responsible for the collapse of security in Australian shops:

> Generally you have one person behind the counter and they have to physically turn their back to the customer to look for the product. In that time, a car could have filled up and driven off, somebody could have pulled out a knife, a gun or a baseball bat. It really is a security issue for our industry.

The problem with this ludicrous account is that those serving in Australian tobacco retailers have *always* had to 'physically turn their back to the customer' when selecting a pack of cigarettes from the storage shelves – plain-packaged or not.

And finally, Rogut painted a picture of utter chaos with not 55%, not 60%, but 59% of cigarette transactions resulting in the wrong brand being passed to the customer.

> About 59% of the products being given to customers are actually incorrect because staff are confused. Fortunately when they scan it, it recognises it's not a *Windfield [sic] Blue* but happens to be a *Windfield [sic] Red* – the feedback is that there has been a high incidence of that. Recording of the stock was easy before – you could see it was a

Red, Blue or *Green*. Now they physically have to read it using a hand scanner to make sure that they have the right stock in store.

But this gripping apocalyptic vista was still not yet finished. Rogut continued about stores having to bring in additional staff to train shop assistants where to look for the different brands and 'how to serve customers better.' Imagine such a training session:

Trainer: Now, behind you – as they have always been – is your tobacco stock. Open the doors to reveal the storage columns. Now, try and find a pack of brand X.
Trainee: Well, here it is, where it's always been . . . in the column for that brand.

So what does independent research show actually happened in shops after plain packaging was introduced? It shows that plain packaging had no lasting impact on serving times. A study examining cigarette retrieval times before and after the introduction of plain packaging has been published (202). In June and September 2012 (before plain packing was implemented), and in the first two weeks of December 2012 (the first two weeks after plain packaging became law in Australia), and again in February 2013, 303 stores were visited in four Australian cities by trained fieldworkers. They asked for a cigarette pack of a pre-determined brand, variant and pack size, unobtrusively recording the time from the end of the request to when the pack was scanned or placed on the counter.

The study found that the average

. . . December retrieval time (12.43s) did not differ from June (10.91s; p=0.410) or February (10.37s; p=0.382), but was slower than September (9.84s; p=0.024). In December, retrieval time declined as days after plain packaging implementation increased (β=-0.21, p=0.011), returning to the baseline range by the second week of implementation. This pattern was not observed in baseline months or in February.

The study authors concluded that:

Retailers quickly gained experience with the new plain packaging legislation, evidenced by retrieval time having returned to the baseline range by the second week of implementation and remaining so several months later. The long retrieval times predicted by tobacco industry-funded retailer groups and the consequent costs they predicted would fall upon small retailers from plain packaging are unlikely to eventuate.

Here is a link to a video of a person buying cigarettes in a Sydney shop in early 2013. The time taken for the shop assistant to find the requested brand is negligible. The time taken to transact the credit card payment takes far longer. (203) http://tiny.cc/yttrox

Plain packaging will cause great financial hardship to small retailers

This was a highly misleading argument that sought to conflate the sales reduction threats posed by plain packaging with the competitive price disadvantage that small retail tobacco outlets experience when competing with large retail chains like supermarkets. Large retailers can offer cheaper prices for cigarettes (and all products) because of economies of scale that allow them to trade off smaller profit margins per pack against the much larger volume of trade they attract. Small retailers have long been aware that smokers can buy their supplies at cheaper prices from supermarkets or 'cigarette barn' chains. The threat of plain packaging to all retailers is of reduced sales caused by more smokers quitting and fewer new smokers starting. Any such effects will impact *all* retailers across the board – not just small retailers – because all packs, regardless of where they are sold, come in plain packaging. There is no plain packaging impact for small business and another one for larger tobacco retailers.

Further counters to these arguments follow:

- Efforts to engender sympathy for small retailers should not blind us to the reality that they are knowingly selling a lethal product. Nobody now selling cigarettes has taken up this role without being aware that they are lethal. Many small retailers also sell cigarettes to children. The interests of consumers and public health should override sympathy for those who may not make so much profit from sales of a product that kills one in two of its regular users.

- Changes to smoking patterns occur over time. Retailers can and do develop other sales lines. When smokers quit, they do not place all the money they would have spent on cigarettes in a box under the bed. Like people who have never smoked, they spend their money on other goods and services instead. These purchases benefit many small retailers.
- There is an obvious contradiction between the industry argument that plain packaging 'won't work' and their frequent claims that it will harm retailers through loss of sales.

The slippery slope

No other consumer good kills half of its long-term users (13) when used as intended by the manufacturer. No government or recognised health authority in any nation has ever called for the plain packaging of any other consumer product. While governments and health authorities are rightly concerned to reduce harms from alcohol or junk food, tobacco is unique as a consumer product where the clear and intended aim of government policy is to end use.

Tobacco advertising began to be banned in Australia from September 1976, when the government implemented legislation to end direct advertising of cigarettes on radio and television. Over the next 16 years further legislation incrementally stopped tobacco advertising and promotion through other media, with state bans starting in 1987 in Victoria, culminating in 1992 with the national Tobacco Advertising Prohibition Act. In 2014, 38 years after tobacco advertising began being banned, and 64 years after the lethal nature of cigarettes was incontrovertibly demonstrated, other categories of harmful products (eg. alcohol, energy dense foods) have not been subject to similar forms of legislative restrictions on their advertising. If there is a slope leading from tobacco advertising bans to those in other areas, then that slope appears to be decidedly non-slippery.

You're on your own with this, Big Tobacco

The desperate tobacco industry sought to pull in likely allies from other industries into its slippery slope campaign. But this was likely to prove difficult: even the corporate world has now started to turn on its own rotten apple, with an editorial in *Packaging World* stating: 'The tobacco industry should steer clear of complaining of being singled out, which, in large measure, stems from its products being like no other consumer packaged good.' (118)

The slippery slope 'what product will be next to fall to plain packing?' argument was implied in a BATA advertisement, but this drew immediate criticism from a section of the alcohol industry. Stephen Strachan, chief executive of the Winemakers Federation of Australia said his industry rejected any suggestion of an equivalence between alcohol and tobacco implied in the ad. 'Our industry does not like any association between tobacco and alcohol' (204) he said. Tobacco was on its own in this one.

Illicit drugs aren't sold in glossy packaging but many still use them

The obvious retort to this claim is to point out that, if illicit drugs were beautifully packaged, displayed in shops and advertised, even more people would be likely to use them than do now. Of the few nations and states that have decriminalised the personal possession of cannabis, only Colorado, USA, allows it to be sold openly in shops, as if it was another ordinary item of commerce. None allow it to be commercially packaged or advertised.

The repackaging turnaround time was too short

The industry argued that companies needed many months to set up the new printing processes to completely repackage all of their brands at once. However, the requirement to change all packaging to 'plain' poses exactly the same challenges to a nation's tobacco industry as a requirement to introduce new pack warnings when all packs are required to be reprinted by a specified date. With almost every nation requiring health warnings, and as of November 2012, 63 nations required graphic warnings (205), there are many nations which have experience in setting deadlines for the tobacco industry to comply with legislation to change the printing for all packs.

In Australia, Imperial Tobacco issued a press release in November 2011 arguing that it would need 17 months after the plain packaging legislation was declared law to change its printing for all its brands. Asking colleagues in other nations, the typical time given to companies to change all packaging for new generations of pack warnings has been 6–12 months.

There is ample evidence from other consumer products that companies can move speedily to introduce new forms of packaging either following legislation or for commercial reasons. While the tobacco industry needs to be given a reasonable period to comply with repackaging of all its products, government officials should be very circumspect about any claims for lengthy transition periods, and share information with other nations about the times that were required for repackaging in the past for packaging changeovers.

Won't plain packaging prevent the industry and governments from providing information about less harmful tobacco products?

The tobacco industry often cites freedom of speech protection, arguing that they have a right to inform consumers about their products, especially those that may be potentially less harmful (although the tobacco industry has a long history of misleading consumers about such claims (206)). This erroneously implies that cigarette advertisements contain important consumer information and that smokers base their decision to smoke by weighing up such information and making an informed choice.

The tobacco industry has used this argument for decades to try to retain the right to advertise. In fact, as discussed in Chapter 3 tobacco advertising is one of the least informative forms of all advertising. And aside from a number indicating the number of cigarettes in a pack, packs rarely if ever contain any 'information' beyond the brand name and number of cigarettes in the pack. The last time Australian tobacco companies tried to be 'informative' on their packs was when they used descriptors like 'light' and 'mild'. In 2005, the Australian Competition and Consumer Commission (ACCC) accepted court-enforceable undertakings from the three major Australian tobacco manufacturers, Philip Morris (Australia) Limited, British American Tobacco Limited and Imperial Tobacco Australia Limited, under which the companies agreed to stop using terms such as 'light' and 'mild' and to provide a total of $9 million for corrective advertising to be run by the ACCC.

Tobacco companies are the last bodies who should be involved in making decisions about health information. If the government wishes to provide such information, on the basis of expert advice rather than tobacco company lobbying, it has many different options.

Covering up the packs

With the exception of the first very small pack warning introduced on packs in 1973, with all three subsequent warnings, Australia saw a succession of knowing predictions from talk-back radio callers that smokers would be one giant step ahead of out-of-touch governments by simply transferring their cigarettes to elegant cases, or buying natty covers to hide their eyes from the warnings. But it never happened to a less than trivial and rapidly vanishing degree with any of the three generations of pack warnings, including the graphic warnings required from 2006. With plain packs, we didn't have to wait long before it started again.

First out of the blocks was a cartoonist for Rupert Murdoch's *The Australian* newspaper, Bill Leak, who was incensed about the nanny state implications of the imminent plain packs. He sought legal advice on whether he could produce covers with fake brand names like Honeymoon, Post-Coital Cigarettes, Tree Huggers, Vegetarian Cigarettes, Man Up: Smokes for Blokes, Ripped: Fitness Cigarettes and Fatales: Diet Cigarettes 99 per cent fat free ('with a sexy sheila on the pack'). His legal advice was apparently that he would likely end up in court. Health Minister Nicola Roxon responded to this superbly, saying: 'Everyone likes a laugh, but when so many people die from smoking, it doesn't seem so funny anymore.' (207) We never heard from Bill again.

But with the 1 December 2012 full implementation date, an opportunistic small businessman from Queensland was not to be denied his

15 minutes of fame, announcing that smokers could now buy stickers to cover the front and back of the new packs (see http://boxwrap.com.au/). Just $8.75 would buy enough for six packs, with choices ranging from a map of Australia to a rear view of a young woman with her legs apart.

A month after the launch, I noted that since launching his box wrap stickers in early December, he had been deluged with a whole 386 Facebook 'likes', and 1319 views of his YouTube promotion. A whole 24 people had followed him on Twitter, 21 of whom lived outside Australia. These were mainly pro-smoking groups who saw plain packs as a strike at the heart of their inalienable freedom to buy a product in beautiful packs, all market tested to their last square-centimetre, that will kill half its long-term users. English libertarian Chris Snowdon got characteristically very excited when he came across publicity for the wraps, blogging triumphantly: 'You'd have to be simple not to have predicted this (Simon Chapman said it would never happen, natch). Plain packaging was always going to create commercial opportunities for those who make covers, stickers and cigarette cases.' (208)

The threat of covers and wraps being taken up extensively never eventuated. In an observational study of people displaying cigarettes packs before and after the plain packaging legislation, use of 'covers' rose from only 1.5% to just 3.5%. In 1000 smokers, only 35 were observed to have gone to the bother of using covers. (195)

Like all the opportunists who lost their money with previous cover gimmicks for the older health warnings, our Queensland entrepreneur looked like an early candidate for a 2013 Darwin award for heroically failed business acumen (see http://www.darwinawards.com/). On 2 February 2014, his Twitter following had fallen to just four (https://twitter.com/boxwrap) and his Facebook page (http://www.facebook.com/boxwrap) had grown to just 687 likes – less than many 14 year olds have – with the last post made in July 2013.

Anyone who takes the trouble and expense of hiding their eyes from the pack warnings is engaging in obvious denial. Evidence shows that smokers who actively try to avoid exposure to pack warnings by covering them up, have higher subsequent rates of quit attempts than those who don't. (209)

The news media were interested in this for about two days in early December 2012, and then the story died. Advocates prepared the following communication points in the improbable event that it might have spread.

- Every generation of new pack warnings over last 30 years has seen minor entrepreneurs trying to cash in like this. We are now seeing it with covers.
- A tiny minority of smokers buy them maybe once, but then can't be bothered.
- Many suburban markets have forlorn vendors with tables covered with pack covers, but nobody is buying. They have lost their money.

When you think about it, the very act of going out of your way to cover up a warning shows that such people are actively avoiding being reminded of what smoking is doing: a bit like a child covering up their eyes for the scary scenes in movies – but unlike movies, the scare here is real and won't going away by not looking at it.

We now turn to a consideration of the strategies and tactics used by the tobacco industry across the four years of their campaign.

Astroturfing: the Alliance of Australian Retailers

As discussed, the tobacco industry had long sought to avoid coverage in the Australian news media because of the endless potential embarrassment provided by its now very public internal documents, made public in the 1990s through whistleblowers (210) and the millions released under the Master Settlement Agreement. (211) It also knew it had very poor public credibility and was held in low public trust. So it invested further in the time-honoured strategy of 'astroturfing': the finding and/or founding and funding of seemingly independent third party organisations and spokespeople. It hoped that many would not understand that these groups were connected to the tobacco industry. Tobacco companies have used astroturfed organisations for many years globally, including in Australia.

Knowing the welcome mat laid out for it was like that offered to the Grim Reaper,[1] the Australian tobacco industry was an early pioneer in

---

1   Indeed, in this segment from The Chaser, the Grim Reaper seeks employment at BATA https://www.youtube.com/watch?v=wu8TqMRBNk4

the development of apparently independent lobby groups set up to attack everything from pack health warnings to attacks on sponsorship. For example, it helped establish the Confederation of Australian Sport in 1976 where 'the salary and office expenses of the confederation's president, Wayne Reid, are paid by the Australian tobacco manufacturers under a separate consultancy agreement with each of the three companies.' (212)

Less than three weeks out from the federal election polling day of 21 August 2010, we learned of the existence theAlliance of Australian Retailers. No one had ever heard of it before it took to the media, opened a website (https://www.australianretailers.com.au/) and began running advertising in newspapers and on television. Initially, it was publicly fronted by Sheryle Moon, the executive director of the Association of Convenience Stores.

The board of the Association of Convenience Stores was chaired by the supermarket conglomerate Coles, owned by the Wesfarmers group. On learning that it had been misled about the funding for what was ostensibly an anti-Labor party campaign, Coles ordered the association to withdraw from the campaign. (213) Moon was no longer the public face of the alliance. Two days later, the other main supermarket chain, Woolworths, revoked its membership of the association over the campaign and demanded that its $15,000 in annual fees be returned. (214) Any tiny ray of respectable big retailer support the alliance might have hoped for was now gone. But as we'll see below, it had major funding from the three tobacco companies and advertisements continued to be published and broadcast.

Those in tobacco control were incredulous when Moon made her debut. Angela Pratt from Nicola Roxon's office told us: 'When Sheryle Moon first appeared, we kind of thought, well, is this the best that they can do? Surely not?'

When she first appeared, I searched for Moon on Facebook, to learn more. I found this https://www.facebook.com/pages/Sheryle-Moon/119524304805507?ref=ts and noticed that Moon had no Facebook friends. Feeling sorry for her as she struggled through questions about smoking and disease on the *Lateline* program, I became her first and only Facebook friend, telling the *Sydney Morning Herald* that 'the loneliness of a tobacco industry shill is something special.' (215)

It transpired that the Facebook account was almost certainly a fake. Moon never posted to it. No one in tobacco control ever owned up to setting it up. Moon later made occasional statements against plain packaging wearing her association hat. (216)

Advertising blitz

The AAR's television (http://tiny.cc/a0trox, http://tiny.cc/81trox) and print media pre-federal election ads featured shopkeepers – apparently real, although possibly played by fully scripted actors – who ran the following arguments around the themes of 'It won't work. So why do it?' and 'Good policy requires more than good intentions.' It used the following messages:

- plain packing was rejected in the UK and Canada
- there's no real evidence it works
- governments can rush into policies without good evidence
- this is just another poorly conceived government campaign that won't work
- because all states already ban retail displays of tobacco, how will plain packs make any difference?

Big Tobacco funding

From the very start of the campaign, the AAR was open about being supported by the tobacco industry. But it was not for some weeks that the extent and purpose of the support became understood when a dossier of emails and documents between Philip Morris Australia and staff at the Civic Group, a public relations agency, found its way to ABC television's *Lateline* reporter Peter Lloyd, who was one of the first to cover the entrance of the AAR. (217)

The dossier opened with a helpful guide to the various organisations and individuals who would feature in the pages to come. It then gave a breakdown of the amount of funding contributed to date by the three tobacco companies, Philip Morris, BATA and Imperial ($5.44 million together) and noted that a further $3.74 million had been promised for the next phase of the campaign, talking the total to $9.18m.

One of the emails from Philip Morris in the dossier stated plainly that the launch and planned activities of the AAR was targeted directly at attacking the Labor government in the forthcoming election (August 21), stating: 'We envision the election being a major decision point'. It asked the public relations (PR) agency to provide a budget for a three-phased campaign. Emails in the dossier commented on Moon's media performances – they thought she was 'not spooked', but then noted that she had been accepting media interviews without first checking with the PR agency ('They called her and she agreed without telling us. Could be long couple of weeks!').

An email from a media buyer to the Civic Group dated 1 September 2010 post-campaign showed that the group's commission on the advertising expenditure was $145,788. The jubilant sender asked: 'Would you like me to transfer it to your bank, or hold it for drinks in Barbados? Let's know either bank details or flight number. Regards, and thanks!'

An invoice from the Civic Group to Philip Morris, dated 31 August 2010, requested that $788,444.10 be paid within 14 days.

A particularly interesting email between staff of the Civic Group dated 1 September 2010, after Moon's exit, showed the gossamer-thin status of the alliance:

> They still have not registered the business name.
>
> Why, you ask? Because instead of asking Bob Stanton to just sign the form and get one of the three legal departments or three external law firms to do it, the Alliance asked him to take care of the entire process. But because the Alliance has no bank account and it costs $83, Bob does not think it should come out of his own pocket.
>
> Therefore a month later nobody has done it.
>
> So, if this campaign is successfully stopped over a legal challenge, it will be over $83. (218)

A Craig Clasby would emerge as the new spokesperson in early 2011 (219) by which time the alliance's website listed only the Service Station Association Pty Ltd, the Australian Newsagents' Federation Ltd and the National Independent Retailers Association Inc. as its member bodies.

With the exception of newsagent's federation, these bodies do not represent the majority of retailers trading in retailing or petrol stations.

Mike Daube tells the story of the dossier:

> We didn't know who they [the AAR] were, and some of that advertising was getting a bit of traction and it was clearly continuing. It was a bit frustrating and I remember one night I woke up at around midnight and checked my emails, as you do. There was an email from somebody I had never heard of, I still don't know who he or she was or is, and it said 'Dear Professor Daube, I have seen you on television. Would you like some real time confidential tobacco industry documents about plain packaging?'
>
> So I of course emailed back saying, 'yes please'. They came absolutely piling in, more than 40 pages, all showing that this was astroturfing on a grand scale. Everything was being run from London and New York. Direct instructions in detail. Why is such-and-such appearing on this program and so on? Telling them what they should do.

ABC TV's *Lateline* also obtained the documents. (217) Daube says: 'It did a huge amount to undermine the industry because (a) that campaign, if it was getting any traction, lost it and (b) it just showed how the industry hadn't changed its spots.'

The leak bore all the signs of being an inside job. It was unlikely to be a hacker, as it would have been unclear where a hacker might begin to look once inside a tobacco company, or which of many advertising, PR and lobbying agencies might have been involved. The industry probably reached this conclusion as well. Knowing its internal security was breached, this would have put a major brake on how those involved communicated freely about what their next steps were.

Sunlight on the cockroaches

In the 1970s and 80s, the companies and their (now defunct) jointly-funded propaganda arm, the Tobacco Institute of Australia, (220) were regularly seen and heard across all Australian news media. Their agenda included reassuring smokers about smoking and health, (221) denying that nicotine was addictive and attacking policies like health warnings and smoking restrictions. This clip from the early 1980s shows John Dollisson, then head of the Tobacco Institute, and Bill Webb from Philip Morris issuing point-blank denials under questioning from the ABC's Huw Evans (see video here (222)). But during the 1990s the tobacco industry began withdrawing from making public comment when whistleblowers and a succession of US court cases saw a flood of some 14 million, previously internal, documents running to over 80 million pages, become publicly available.

California's Professor Stan Glantz is fond of saying that tobacco companies are like cockroaches: they spread disease and dislike sunlight. These millions of documents put white hot, withering sunlight on the industry and caused them to retreat from all public debate.

All the industry's standard policy platforms (health harms from smoking unproven; nicotine not addictive, only a 'habit'; secondhand smoke harmless; we don't want children to smoke) were contradicted by hundreds and sometimes thousands of their own documents which showed that they knew, and thought, quite the opposite. All these positions could therefore no longer be sustained against the revelations in the documents, which henceforth acted like a public truth serum against industry lies. Continuing to make public comment, and appearing in interviews and debates suddenly became highly risky.

In a 2008 interview BATA's Bede Fennell, then head of public affairs, told the interviewer that she was the first journalist for at least a decade to be admitted to the company's national headquarters in Sydney. For years, the policy was to keep as low a profile as possible. 'When I got here, we never talked to the media,' he says. 'We didn't even return the calls.' (223)

But plain packaging panicked the industry so much that this long-standing policy was shelved as it stared down the barrel of the biggest threat it had arguably ever faced.

British American Tobacco Australia

Of the three transnational companies operating in Australia, BATA was by far the most prominent in its public attacks on plain packaging. May 2011 was an historic month for the company. It held its first press conference in many years, commenced an aggressive advertising campaign against the policy, started several web sites, and opened Twitter accounts. A company account (@BATA_Media) and at least three staff (chief executive David Crow (@DavidCrow_BATA), 'company spokesperson' Scott McIntyre (@Scott_BATA) and Louise Warburton (@Louise_BATA – now deleted) began tweeting regularly on plain packs.

Both Crow and McIntyre seem to have had advice from the corporate lawyers when they tweeted early that '[this] Twitter account has not been set up to sell or promote BATA products in any way.' In just over six months in 2011 McIntyre tweeted 420 times, with a modest 370 followers, but in 2012–2014 tweeted only 31 times. McIntyre's boss Crow seemed to tire of it more quickly, sending only 66 tweets. The decision seemed to be to mainly use the @BATA_Media account (937 followers and 688 tweets by 18 April 2014).

BAT plainly has a global Twitter policy. In three nations (Australia, New Zealand and the UK) BAT's Twitter accounts have been almost totally preoccupied with tweeting about the folly of plain packaging, particularly the extent of illicit trade and how plain packaging will allegedly make this worse.

On 17 May 2011, BATA's years of near total absence from public statements was broken by Crow, who held a press conference in Sydney. It caused a frisson of anticipation among journalists. Several called me earlier in the day saying pretty much the same thing: 'You'll be amused to know that BATA is holding a press conference. They must be pretty worried. They generally won't comment on anything.'

A press release (224) and Crow's presentation covered the usual industry lines about there being no evidence, the fearsome legal costs the government was risking, and the inevitability of the market being flooded with black market tobacco. But the big news to emerge was that BATA would be running a multi-million dollar advertising campaign produced by the advertising agency G2, and a threat by BATA that it would significantly drop its retail prices (and so its profit margins) in order to compete with the certainty of downtrading the industry was promoting. Crow told journalists: 'If we have to lower our prices, we will to compete with illegal product flooding in from abroad.' (see https://www.youtube.com/watch?v=FTldddUlrls) He thought this would be tragic as it would make cigarettes more affordable to children. Crow was a parent too, and didn't want to see this happening: 'I've got a 13-year-old, an 11-year-old and a seven-year-old and if they smoke I tell them absolutely, categorically, "Do not smoke"' (225). But with his duty to his company, this concern that more children might smoke would unfortunately just have to take a back seat. It was all the government's problem.

Crow has a reputation as an ebullient, 'blokey', swaggering CEO. A 2008 portrait of BATA's senior staff in a weekend newspaper by Jane Cadzow described him thus:

> Crow, 45, is a strapping figure – 195 centimetres tall, with broad shoulders and such an exuberant personality that he seems to take up more space than he actually does. The son of an oil company executive, he went to Cranbrook, one of Sydney's most expensive private schools, then studied economics and commerce at university. He is a keen sailor and a former rugby player.

He described his company, whose most dedicated customers have at least a 50% mortality experience because of their smoking, (13) as a 'fun and funky place'. (223) A bemused Roxon staffer remarked that Crow signed some of his letters to the government with just 'Crowie'.

The *Sydney Morning Herald*'s Mike Carlton was the most acerbic about the re-emergence into public view of industry spokespeople:

> So the chief drug dealer at British American Tobacco Australia, one David Crow, is threatening to flood the country with cut-price fags if the federal government brings in plain packaging for cigarettes. That would mean 'more people will smoke, more kids will smoke,' he said on Tuesday, oozing regret from every pore, as if he were helpless to prevent such wickedness . . . As a corporate bully-boy attempt to browbeat a government, it doesn't come more crude than that. The insolence is staggering. Mr Crow will not like being called a drug dealer, I suspect. But that's what he is, the bumptious twerp. (226)

Cadzow reported that photographs of staff in the BATA building are captioned with quotes explaining why the person likes working there.

> Says one: 'All my heart and mind needs are met.' Says a second: 'It makes me happy and alive.' Says a third: 'The people I work with are

like a family to me and the goals of the company are close to my heart.' (223)

Other tobacco companies

Philip Morris and Imperial took far lower profile roles than BATA. Imperial ran a brief 'nanny state' campaign (see p 82). Philip Morris set up a website www.plain-packaging.com, which was later taken down, and started another in April 2011 called *I deserve to be heard* https://www.ideservetobeheard.com.au/ to attract smokers opposed to the legislation and other forms of tobacco control. The site invited smokers to share their stories, to invite friends to join in and to write to their MP. None of our colleagues nor any politicians we spoke with could recall anything that seemed to flow from this name-gathering exercise. This was very predictable: most smokers wish they didn't smoke and many support tobacco control measures that might help them stop or reduce the amount they smoke.

Here is an example of the sort of robot-generated messages that those who registered with *I deserve to heard* received.

Dear [name],

Did you know that your local MP [name] supports plain packaging legislation for cigarettes? Click [here] to find out more.

You have every right to be disappointed that your local representative is not listening to your concerns about plain packaging.

It's time to send a clear message that you oppose plain packaging and that you deserve to be heard.

Many people like you have told [politician's name] that they oppose plain packaging and other policies that unfairly target smokers.

Despite this, [politician's name] has chosen to push a policy that just does not make sense.

With cigarettes already hidden behind doors in most shops across the country, plain packaging will just make it harder for you to identify and purchase your cigarettes, causing long queues and all for a policy that has not been proven to prevent or stop people from smoking.

The government will put legislation for plain packaging into Parliament within the next couple of months, so the time to let [politician's name] know that you oppose plain packaging is now!

Write to [politician's name] and have your say to today!

How did the industry perform?

I asked a senior lobbyist from a non-government organisation (NGO) and Mike Daube about their perceptions on how the tobacco industry had handled their campaign against the legislation.

Daube was unimpressed:

I think they performed very poorly. The reason for that, and I know it's a point we slightly flippantly mention from time to time, but I think it's real – it's hard for the industry to get really good people. They pay a lot of money, but it's very hard for them to get good people. Second, it's hard for them to get good groups to work with them. Third, their public credibility is zilch, so they're always battling against that. When people and politicians hear that it's thingamajig from BAT, initially just a blanket distrust descends over them. So that's an issue.

The next issue, which I think is a pretty fundamental one, is that it's not an indigenous industry. It's all controlled from London and New York. So my guess would be that for years the industry here had stayed below the parapet because they'd learned from experience that once their heads appear, then we will kick them with glee and nobody believes them and so on. My guess would be that the industry people here would probably have preferred a similar approach to plain packaging. They would probably have liked to have worked more in the dark, but there were people screaming down the phones from London and New York saying: 'Do something!' You must do this, you must do that. You must run advertising campaigns. You must do some astroturfing. You must this, you must that.' And that just backfired monumentally.

The campaign, the whole approach was being directed from London and New York, [which] meant that they just didn't read Australia. They didn't understand how much the industry was on the nose. Those awful nanny state ads, they were enough to repel anybody.

The astroturfing approach: setting up phony organisations, guaranteed to come out in the end and to hit them slap bang in the face. Same with the lobbying of politicians. Some of what I heard was pretty crass stuff. The commentary in the media, do you remember one of them, I have forgotten what her name was, saying on radio: 'Yes I do understand that smoking kills people and that's very sad, but . . .?' Do you remember that?

I think they just totally mishandled the lobbying. They could all have done a whole lot better. Also even the people they used, so demonstrably second rate. They just sounded like junior PR interns and very little credibility. They put a cartload of money in and I don't think we should fool ourselves, you can spend a lot of money on advertising and you can do a bit of turning around, but it didn't get them very far.

A senior health NGO employee reflected on BATA's main spokesperson:

The guy who always popped up, I mean every time he'd just put his foot in it so badly that I think people would also ask the question, I mean, people who work in public affairs would think 'Is this the best they can do?' Every time this guy opened his mouth it would be a free kick.

Angela Pratt was equally blunt:

I was surprised, and I think we were all surprised, at how unsophisticated their public spokespeople were, both during the election campaign at the very beginning and subsequently. None of their people seemed to have any credibility. Their arguments were unsophisticated, over the top, extremist and ultimately that, for my money, characterised their campaign broadly and that's why it was unsuccessful, because they went so extreme, but also kind of not in a very sophisticated way.

For example, in August 2013 BATA's Scott McIntyre was asked on radio: 'How many people do you believe that tobacco kills in Australia?' He replied: 'We're not in the business of running health departments. We're in the business of selling cigarettes.' Pressed, he continued: 'I don't have any figures off the top of my head.' (http://www.abc.net.au/newsradio/content/s3815878.htm at 4m01s) This was a stunning statement. Here, the main spokesperson from Australia's largest tobacco company was claiming to not be able to recall what was probably the most repeated statistic in Australian tobacco control: that some 15,000 people die annually from tobacco-caused disease.

I asked Daube if anything the industry did got them any traction.

> Yes, some traction. They planted various stories, particularly in the Murdoch media. I think some of their advertising, just the constant weight of advertising, probably did have some impact, and that clearly comes through from some of the tracking work they did, but overall, it took them from a D minus to a D, rather than even a D plus, rather than getting a significant change. I don't think it had good traction.

Submissions to government and international lobbying

In April 2011, the Australian government began a 60-day public consultation period to allow the Australian public and international community to comment on the proposed Tobacco Plain Packaging Bill (2011). By the close of the public consultation period in June 2011, 265 submissions had been received by the Australian government, not including 1566 'form letters' received (see below). Ninety-nine submissions supported the bill (many from substantial health or related organisations, themselves with many member groups and individual members), and 158 opposed it. Another eight submissions commented on matters relating to the bill, but in a way that was not clear whether they supported it or were against it. Most submissions were from Australian-based individuals or groups, (221) with only some from overseas (44).

Form letters

Three different form letters were submitted, all opposed to the policy. One sent by 1100 people came from smokers; a second (n=447) came from small retailers; and a third was sent in by 19 respondents.

With the exception of a few individuals (and even here it is difficult to identify which were indeed linked indirectly with or generated by tobacco interests), the only opposition is likely to have come from tobacco interests and their associates, and possibly organisations with philosophical or commercial objections to curbs on industry.

Overseas-based organisations making submissions against plain packs in Australia included: tobacco companies, intellectual property associations, civil liberties associations and chambers of commerce. Australian retailer and business groups opposing plain packaging included those involved in packaging, and retailing (supermarkets, liquor, newsagents, motor vehicle service stations). A summary of the submissions can be found here (227).

The American Legislative Exchange Council (ALEC) had already sent the Australian Cabinet a copy of a unanimous resolution (228) originally sent to the Obama administration. It detailed a diatribe of specious arguments about the importance of free trade. To anyone with any familiarity with the global tobacco industry, this was as predictable as Father Christmas appearing in stores in December. PR Watch has a large entry on ALEC, noting that it 'is an influential, under-the-radar organisation that facilitates collaboration between many of the most powerful corporations in America and state-level legislative representatives. Elected officials then introduce legislation approved by corporations in state houses across the US, without disclosing that the bills were pre-approved by corporations on ALEC task forces.' It has a long relationship with the tobacco industry, dating from 1979, and it has essentially worked in total lock-step with that industry's interests. (229)

Freedom of information deluge

In October 2011, the *Sydney Morning Herald* (230) reported that Big Tobacco was 'abusing' the freedom of information (FOI) process over plain packaging. The Department of Health and Ageing had been swamped with 64 FOI requests relating to plain packaging, with 53 of these lodged by the tobacco industry. The department's secretary Jane Halton detailed to a Senate estimates committee in February 2012 how the industry was inundating the government with FOI requests in a move she said was designed to 'tie up resources'.

In July and August 2010, BATA lodged 17 FOI requests concerning plain packaging and related issues. Halton told the committee:

> Our initial estimate of processing these requests was over $1.47 million, based on the need to examine 5265 files and make decisions on an estimated 81,791 documents. The department negotiated with BATA to reduce the scope of these requests and the associated charges over a five-month period. As part of this negotiation, BATA withdrew seven of the requests and reduced the scope of the remaining 10. This left 242 files and an estimated 13,137 documents to be processed.
>
> We issued a revised charges estimate of just over $367,000 in July 2011. BATA agreed to the charges estimate and paid the deposit – it sounds like buying a house – of $91,776. . . . Because of the large amount of duplication on the files and a smaller number of documents on which decisions had to be made and due to efficiencies in decision making as officers became more familiar with the documents, the final charge arrived at for the BATA 10 was $135,734.60. The department estimates the actual cost of processing the requests at over $643,000. The charges therefore represent only 21 per cent of the final costs. I should say that the net cost to the department is worth four staff who should have otherwise been working on population health issues.

'In a separate case, BATA took legal action in June 2011 against the Australian government after the Department of Health and Ageing refused to reveal confidential legal advice written for it 16 years ago. BATA applied for the advice under FOI laws but was rebuffed. Lawyers for BATA told a federal court that the legal advice, written in 1995, was needed in the current public debate about plain packaging in Australia.' (231) BATA's case was unsuccessful. (232)

In June 2010, Philip Morris lodged FOI requests with six government agencies concerning 19 questions on tobacco plain packaging and related matters. Halton told the committee:

> Again there was a lengthy negotiation over scope and costs, and a decision was made to release a number of documents in February 2011. PML (Philip Morris Limited) requested an internal review of this re-

quest, which was completed in April 2011. They then appealed to the Administrative Appeals Tribunal. A hearing was scheduled for 4 November and significant work was done in the department to prepare for the appeal, including the release of some additional documents. They withdrew the case a week before the hearing, on 26 October. That is just to give you an indication of the costs and the tactics, which are basically designed to tie up departmental resources which we cannot cost recover.' (231)

Pro-plain packaging tactics

The Australian government did not run any advertising campaigns to inform the public about why it was planning to introduce plain packaging. It ran a national information campaign for tobacco retailers informing them of their obligations at the time of implementation. (233) Australian health NGOs rarely run mass reach advertising campaigns on any issue because of the costs involved. Instead they rely on 'earned media' (news coverage and commentary) on internet-based information and awareness raising, and very occasionally on 'packaged' advocacy campaigns targeted at politicians.

The Cancer Council Victoria produced two video ads, but could not afford to run them on television. Sometimes TV news will cover such campaigns, sending lots of traffic to websites for viewing. One of the Victorian ads released just after the December 2012 implementation was titled 'No more hiding', and showed smokers trying to hide and cover up large graphic health warnings on the new plain packs. It ended with the words 'You can't hide the effects of smoking' (see http://www.youtube.com/watch?v=GgcYn2YQ0t4#t=16). As of 5 October 2014 it had received 66,773 views.

Another featured a well-known political satirist, John Clarke, impersonating a tobacco industry chief talking earnestly about a total product recall and then laughing like a drain as he said: 'Because we care about your health' (see https://www.youtube.com/watch?v=3jKDW9MTF48). As of 5 October 2014 it had attracted 16,361 views.

A coalition of NGOs ran one print media advertisement (see Figure 4.6) in 2010 to underscore that the AAR campaign was merely a front for Big Tobacco.

Quit Victoria was contacted by a marketing executive with 27 years experience, including four years with the former tobacco company, Rothmans. Craig Seitam spoke at a seminar (https://www.youtube.com/watch?v=cEqt0n40aX0) and wrote an opinion piece in the *Sydney Morning Herald* and *Age* newspapers where he supported the case for regarding packaging as advertising by emphasising the importance of packaging to branding, and particularly to young smokers. (234)

I've seldom been persuaded that petitions and open letters were an advocacy strategy worth the effort involved. On many occasions, I've heard staff from political offices remark that they are over-used, seldom read and of little impact. But our experience with a plain packs multi-signature open letter caused me to revise this negativity. The Australian Council on Smoking and Health (chaired by Mike Daube), Cancer Council Australia, the National Heart Foundation, the Public Health Association of Australia and I organised the collection, within two weeks, of a list of over 200 health and medical professors from around the country, and all seven medical former Australians of the Year to sign an open letter addressed to parliament. When I sent an email to all professors within my own medical faculty at the University of Sydney, replies began pouring in immediately. Feedback from politicians was that the letter, which was cited in federal parliament, played a valuable role. This approach has since been used by other groups in the health arena.

Australian smokers' reactions: not with a bang, but a whimper

Australian smokers were made conspicuous by their absence from opposition to plain packaging. The voices that were heard against the introduction of the packaging were almost all connected with the tobacco industry and industries associated with it, particularly retailing. Other than the industry, the industry-funded Institute of Public Affairs, a few fringe libertarian internet forums like Menzies House, (235) and the usual presence of mostly anonymous trolls on blog comment sections,

Figure 4.6 Guess who's pulling the strings? Source: http://tiny.cc/59trox

(164) there was no apparent organised local opposition to plain packaging nor evidence of any widespread anger among smokers. Enquiries to politicians revealed negligible complaints from their constituents.

The tobacco industry is well aware that most smokers wish they had never started smoking – 90% regret ever having started to smoke (236) and around 40% make a serious quit attempt each year. They would also be aware of national and international polls that show that many smokers support tobacco control measures, particularly if the measures are explained as being principally targeted at preventing children from starting to smoke.

For example, a paper published in 2013 found that 25% of New York smokers surveyed favoured increasing taxes on cigarettes, climbing to 60% if taxes were used to fund healthcare programs. Thirty per cent smokers favoured limiting the number of tobacco retail licences, and 60% supported raising the minimum age to purchase cigarettes from 18 to 21 Almost half of smokers favoured keeping tobacco products out of customers' view and prohibiting price promotions. (237)

A telling indication of the extent to which smokers will put their 'rights' about other considerations ahead of those about their smoking came in the 2013 national election where a Smokers' Rights party fielded Senate candidates in all six states. (238) Its candidates attracted just 25,123 first preference votes out of 13,464,123 votes cast in these states (or one vote for every 536 votes cast). In Victoria, only 78 people voted for two individual Smokers' Rights candidates out of 3,499,438 who voted – one in every 44,865 voters.

5

Plain packaging – why now?
And why Australia?

Any history of tobacco control in Australia, and indeed in nearly all nations, would report with incredulity the lack of urgency in the pace with which governments went about trying to reduce smoking. In Australia, in 1957 the NHMRC noted the research being published from 1950 in the USA and Britain on the association between lung cancer and smoking, and recommended to the minister for health that publicity campaigns should be considered to warn the public about the risks (see Figure 5.1).

It took another 16 years before Australians saw the first health warnings peeping in small font from the bottom of cigarette packs. And it was not until 1982 – 25 years later – that any significant (multimedia) statewide anti-smoking campaigns commenced in Australia at a level going beyond simple posters and pamphlets.

Smoking was first banned in cinemas, in public halls and on buses and trains from the mid-1970s. The Australian Capital Territory began to stop indoor smoking in pubs and bars under health ministers Wayne Berry (1994) and Michael Moore (1998), but other states and territories delayed until 2005 and later.[1]

Advocacy for banning smoking in cars carrying children commenced in Australia in 1995. It took until December 2007 – another 12

---

1   See details of Australian smoke free environments legislation here http://tiny.cc/ydurox

years – before Tasmania became the first state to introduce legislation on smoking in cars in Australia. (239)

Direct forms of tobacco advertising ended on Australian radio and television in September 1976, but it was another 16 years until all remaining forms under the control of Australian governments ended with the 1992 Tobacco Advertising Prohibition Act.[2]

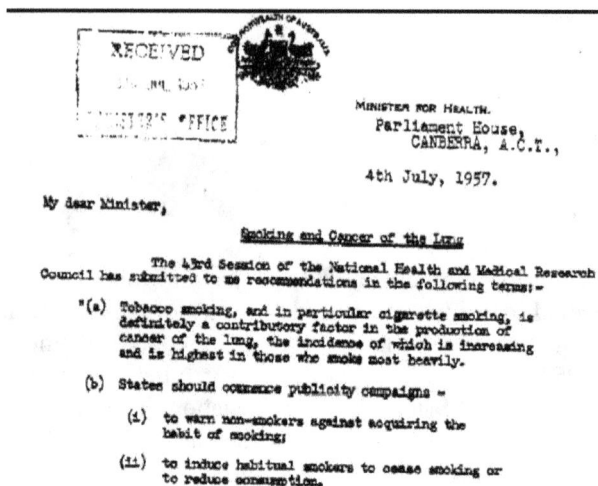

Figure 5.1 Extract of letter from NHMRC to minister for health, 4 July 1957

Those working in tobacco control in Australia were therefore used to long gaps, perhaps of decades, between early advocacy for a proposal and its eventual complete political adoption. All major advances in tobacco control policy have been subject to heavy attack and sustained lobbying by the tobacco industry. As outlined in Chapter 1, there had been advocacy for plain packaging since the late 1980s, with the evidence base steadily growing. It is always interesting to consider what makes proposals once considered radical, like tobacco advertising bans

2   See http://tiny.cc/4eurox

and smokefree public places, morph into sensible ideas whose times have now come.

Table 5.1: Major milestones in the introduction of plain packaging in Australia

Year	Milestone
2008	9 April: Nicola Roxon announces establishment of the National Preventative Health Taskforce
	10 October: Release for consultation of the draft report of the National Preventative Health Task Force recommending plain packaging (240)
	17–22 November: Parties to the Framework Convention on Tobacco Control adopt guidelines on advertising and package labelling that recommend the use of plain packaging (241)
	October 2008 to February 2009: Public submissions and consultation sessions by the National Preventative Health Taskforce (242)
2009	30 June: National Preventative Health Task Force provides final report to government (243)
	1 September: Minister releases final report of the National Preventative Health Task Force, which includes recommendation on plain packaging
2010	29 April: Kevin Rudd and Nicola Roxon announce plain packaging will be introduced (244) and an immediate 25% increase in tobacco tax
	24 June: Prime minister Kevin Rudd deposed by deputy prime minister Julia Gillard
	4 August: Public launch of tobacco industry astroturf group, Alliance of Australian Retailers
	21 August: Federal election. Gillard government returned to power, but relies on support from three crossbench members in House of Representatives to pass legislation
	12 September: Coles and Woolworths withdraw from Alliance of Australian Retailers
2011	1 March: Release of Deloitte report on illicit trade

Year	Milestone
	7 April: Australia notifies the WTO of its intention to implement plain packaging (245)
	17 May: BATA launches major advertising campaign against plain packaging
	31 May 31: Nicola Roxon honoured by WHO; Coalition decides it will not oppose plain packaging legislation
	June: 260 submissions received by government on bill (246)
	7 June: First discussion at WTO of Australia's move (247)
	21 November: Final passage of amended bill through House of Representatives (248)
	21 November: Philip Morris Asia Limited, Hong Kong, owner of Australian affiliate, Philip Morris Limited, announces that it has begun legal proceedings (249) against the Australian government by serving a notice of arbitration under Australia's bilateral investment treaty with Hong Kong
2012	17 April: High Court case commences
	15 August: High Court decision
	1 October: Henceforth illegal to manufacture or import fully branded packs
	1 December: Plain packaging fully implemented – henceforth illegal to sell any non-complaint packs

Table 5.2: Milestones in passage of Plain Packaging Bill through Australian Parliament, 2011

Date	Action
6 July[3]	Bill introduced into House of Representatives, read and second reading moved (250)
7 July	House of Representatives refers bill to Standing Committee on Health and Ageing (251)
22 July	Submissions close for House of Representatives Standing Committee on Health and Ageing – Inquiry into Tobacco Plain Packaging Bill 2011: 63 submissions received (252)
4 August	Hearings of the House of Representatives Standing Committee on Health and Ageing (253)
18 August	Senate refers bill to Legal and Constitutional Affairs Committee which calls for submissions by 2 September (254)
22 August	House of Representatives Standing Committee on Health and Aged Care tables the report on its inquiry into plain packaging (255)
24 August	Second reading debate, third reading agreed to passage of legislation through House of Representatives (250)
25 August	Bill introduced and read a first time in Senate, then second reading moved (250)
2 September	Submissions received by Senate's Legal and Constitutional Affairs Committee (256)
13 September	Hearings of the Senate's Legal and Constitutional Affairs Committee (257)

3   It is common for politicians to acknowledge the presence in the public parliamentary gallery of people who are affected by new legislation or who have played a major role in its development. In speaking to the bill, Nicola Roxon noted 'Can I particularly say that it gives me great pleasure that the parliament has been able to accommodate Mike Daube on his 63rd birthday. I hope that this is a good birthday present for him.'

Date	Action
11 October	Second reading debate in Senate commences (250)
2 November	Nicola Roxon, announces that the implementation of plain packaging will be delayed until 1 December 2012 as a result of delays in the Senate review of the bill (258) which followed industry lobbying
9–10 November	Second reading debate continues and second reading agreed to. Third reading agreed to (with amendments) (250)
21 November	Final passage of amended bill through House of Representatives. Vote on Tobacco Plain Packaging Bill and Trademarks Amendment Bill as amended by the Senate. (250) Official Hansard No 18, Monday 21st November, Forty-third Parliament, First session – Fourth period 2011:12913. (248)
28 November	Signing into law by Governor General of *Tobacco Plain Packaging Act 2011* (72)

I asked Nicola Roxon a question asked of me many times: 'What made the government you belonged to take such an important step?' She emphasised several factors, including the evidence base, the reputation and coherence of the tobacco control community, and expertise in the public service, legal profession and in the public health sphere.

The evidence base

Roxon repeatedly highlighted the critical role that evidence played in the government's decision to adopt plain packaging. The public health effort to reduce smoking in Australia from as far back as the 1970s has been an evidence-based enterprise. Australian researchers have been major contributors to the international research literature in all areas of tobacco control.

The most important group researching tobacco packaging in Australia has been Professor Melanie Wakefield and her team at the Cancer Council Victoria. The Centre for Behavioural Research in Cancer at Cancer Council Victoria was established in 1986 as a scientific research centre specialising in the understanding and monitoring of behaviours that contribute to cancer, and in the evaluation of programs and policies aiming to change such behaviours. It is funded largely through competitive research grants which depend on the high levels of academic rigour and strong track records of publication in the peer-reviewed scientific literature. As noted in the government's response to the recommendations of the National Preventative Health Taskforce, the results of studies by Wakefield et al of the effects of reducing design features on smokers' perceptions of attractiveness and social desirability of smoking provided important evidence of the potential impact of plain packaging. Wakefield also advised the government on research it conducted to guide the design of standardised packaging and size and placement of health warnings.

An associate of the centre, Dr Michelle Scollo also deserves particular mention. Her meticulous and encyclopaedic data banks on nearly every aspect of tobacco control in Australia that form the backbone of the massive online resource, *Tobacco in Australia: facts and issues* (http://www.tobaccoinaustralia.org.au/), and her peerless grasp of issues concerning tax and apparent consumption, brought invaluable expertise to the development and evaluation of plain packaging.

Reputation and coherence of Australian tobacco control community

As well as the research evidence on the appeal of tobacco packaging, another crucial factor in the government's decision to proceed was the national and international reputation of Australian tobacco control in all its achievements over the previous decades. Roxon said:

> It was an attractive next step after all the Australia had done successfully over decades. It would be fair to say that there wasn't any groundswell from the public service at that time [about plain packs]. The taskforce pulling together the evidence and presenting options helped move that significantly – and they [the public servants] were very enthusiastic converts once we, as government ministers, said we were interested in it. My interest was definitely sparked by the cohesive arguments the whole public health community in Australia put

to us. Without their track record, the strong impression made when groups put those ideas to us would have been much weaker.'

The tobacco control research and policy advocacy communities in Australia have long been a relatively small, tightly knit, personally close and extremely communicative network. Most of the leading individuals in these communities today have been working in it for well over 10 years, with several approaching or exceeding 30 years. (259) Their strategic research contributions and advocacy have often been followed by sweeping policy change successes, such as ending all forms of tobacco advertising and promotion and the roll-out of smokefree areas. Unlike some other areas of public health where policy goals are more complex and nuanced, tobacco control's goals have long been clear and consistent.

Roxon was very aware of this coherence, talking about:

> ... well respected people, coordinated. So not 10 different people all asking for 20 different things. That [cohesiveness] happens much more rarely than you would imagine in politics. I think the value of the cut-through of a message like that, and how easy it then is for governments to pick it up, shouldn't be underestimated.

She also emphasised the attraction of plain packaging as being a strategy that would not be expensive for government to implement, with all packaging costs being borne by the companies. 'What were the options for interventions that could have an impact and not necessarily be expensive?' she asked. 'Plain packaging ticked that box.'

Besides the researchers who were publishing the evidence for the policy, there were several other groups of highly skilled and experienced individuals working in different areas to whom Roxon would have been referring as 'well respected' people.

Legal white knights

Lawyers have played important roles in several stanzas of Australian tobacco control over the last 35 years. They have assisted in drafting laws and regulations, advising governments on potential legal risks and, especially in the case of Peter Gordon from Victoria, have run cases for individuals who were seeking redress for harms. But plain packaging acted like a clarion call to a phalanx of academic legal experts who produced a small tsunami of legal scholarship on the many domestic and international issues arising from the legislation. These included Greg Craven, Mark Davison, Tom Faunce, Jonathan Liberman, Benn McGrady, Andrew Mitchell, Mathew Rimmer, Don Rothwell and Tania Voon. Most of these lawyers contributed to a large volume of both scholarly and journalistic writing, and several were often heard in radio commentary. An edited book of legal papers was published. (36) Several of them worked closely with the government at different stages of the saga.

It is also critical to acknowledge the vital role of the Australian government's lawyers who provided legal oversight at all stages of the legislation and its regulations, and of the successful defence of the bill in the High Court (see Chapter 6). Their work is continuing in international forums.

Commonwealth public servants

Everyone with even the slightest engagement in the passage of the bill through to law appreciated the extent and sheer quality of the expertise available in the health department and in the solicitor general's office in Canberra. These were beyond consummate public servants who rose magnificently to meet the extraordinary range of challenges that were their responsibilities in the passage of the bill. They provided detailed input to the development of the regulations preparing the government's defence for the High Court case, they weathered the carpet-bombing freedom of information requests from the industry (see pp107), and they collated and summarised public submissions. They also handled numerous public enquiries and much correspondence, and provided close collaboration with other government agencies on a range of issues pertinent to the legislation, and on the conduct and handling of targeted and public consultation on the legislation and the regulations.

Angela Pratt from Roxon's office was effusive about the role played by staff in the Department of Health and Ageing:

The health department, Jane [Halton], Simon Cotterell, there are a couple of different deputy secretaries that oversaw it at different stages of the process, were all magnificent. Really seriously magnificent. The detailed work involved in the legislative drafting was really difficult, complex work. If we had had a lesser team of people on that job, the kind of risk for problems in the legislation would have been very high. But the health department team were absolutely magnificent.

Very fittingly, the department was awarded the American Cancer Society's Luther L Terry Award for outstanding leadership by a government ministry at the 2012 World Conference on Tobacco or Health, held in Singapore.

Public health experts and advocates

In addition to the lawyers mentioned above, Professor Mike Daube (Curtin University and chair of the Australian Council on Smoking and Health in Western Australia), Anne Jones and Stafford Sanders from ASH (Action on Smoking and Health), Cancer Council Australia and Victoria staff Professor Ian Olver, Paul Grogan and Fiona Sharkie and ourselves were the most frequent voices being interviewed, calling radio stations and writing opinion pieces and blogs over the four-year period since the April 2010 decision to proceed was announced.

Mike Daube played a pivotal quarterback role in plain packaging from the time of his chairing the National Preventative Health Task Force's tobacco committee. Vastly experienced in both senior levels of government (he spent time as director general of health in Western Australia) and in advocacy dating from his time as inaugural director of ASH UK in the 1970s, Mike was in on every important conference call. He and I would speak often several times a day, whether to share information, review an incident or plan a line of attack. Most important of all, Mike was the main go-to person for the minister's office.

Angela Pratt:

It was absolutely helpful to the government and the fact that all of you guys were incredibly well organised. You know, Mike Daube would ring me and say we've got a new opinion poll; when would be a good time to release it? I'd sort of say, well, don't do it on Tuesday because something else is happening on Tuesday and it will get lost. But if you could do it on Thursday week that would actually be great because on Friday we're planning to do X, Y or Z. So there was this very strong sense that we were working very closely together in support of a mutual goal.

I knew that if I talked to Mike the message would get out. It was just this great sense of there being a very well organised group of NGOs and academics in support. No single thing is decisive, but it all kind of builds into a campaign.

Mike travelled from Perth to Australia's east coast so much that we all joked that he must have had not a platinum frequent flyer card, but a black diamond one. We referred to him as 'Midnight Mike' for his indefatigable willingness to give live interviews seemingly around the clock nationally and internationally. He is a consummate media performer whose instincts on how to best respond to the latest tactic from the industry are remarkable.

Non-government agencies

Australia's network of health and medical NGOs all sang from the same song sheet on plain packaging. The Cancer Council Australia and the Heart Foundation both employed in-house lobbyists (Paul Grogan and Rohan Greenland) who both gave high priority to supporting the bill throughout its course. Both of these organisations had for years jointly funded ASH, and tobacco control for them was core business.

ASH in turn provided a large amount of media commentary on the issue and orchestrated a coalition of smaller NGOs to contact MPs at strategically important times to show their support. Stafford Sanders, who worked at ASH for 10 years, told me: 'What most MPs would have experienced was a flood of letters and calls from small NGOs, parent groups, local health professionals and other influential local figures supporting plain packs.'

The Australian Medical Association is widely regarded as having a more natural affinity with politically conservative parties. They were at loggerheads with Roxon and the Labor government on a range of proposed reforms (including nurse practitioner and midwife reforms, Medicare Locals, hospital funding and various Medicare rebate changes) but, to their great credit, were resolute supporters of plain packaging. They issued many press releases, were often heard providing commentary, and were known to have urged the Opposition to support the bill.

Other health organisations, in particular the Public Health Association of Australia and its CEO Michael Moore, also made substantial contributions as part of the lobbying team.

News media

With a few exceptions (particularly News Corp newspapers), Australia's news media reported the saga of plain packaging in overwhelmingly positive ways. I had no hostile interviews across the entire period, but recall a good many openly negative, and often scathing, comments about the tobacco industry's response from journalists, producers and camera and sound operators before, during and after interviews. Tobacco control has almost attained the status of a no-brainer issue for most in the news media. Like immunisation, it has long evolved into a story that does not need 'two sides' in its telling. (260)

Angela Pratt shared this view:

I think by and large the media were supportive, and I think that just goes to show how discredited the industry has become, that basically anything the industry said, they kind of scoffed at. Ridiculed is too strong a word, though in some cases they did because some of the things that the industry said were ridiculous. I don't remember it being something that we felt like the media were part of the enemy, whereas other issues we absolutely felt like we were in the trenches against the media.

Columnists

A large number of opinion pieces on plain packaging were published in Australian-based newspapers and online news outlet and blogs.

Table 5.3: Opinion page and blog authors on plain packaging, 2008–14

Supportive	Opposed
David Campbell (261)	Leo Bajzert (advertising worker) (314)
Mike Carlton (226)	Chris Berg (IPA) (315)
Simon Chapman (262–279)	Julie Novak (IPA) (316)
Simon Chapman and Becky Freeman (280, 281)	Tim Wilson (IPA) (317)
Mike Daube (282, 283)	
Mark Davison (284–287)	
Matthew Day (288)	
Simon Evans (289)	
Thomas Faunce (290)	
Becky Freeman (291)	
Mia Friedman (292)	
Ross Gittins (169, 293)	
Steven Greenland (294)	
Nathan Grills (295)	
Paul Grogan (296)	
Paul Harrison (297)	
David Hill (298)	
Jessica Irvine (299)	
Stephen Leeder (300)	
Ross MacKenzie (301)	
Colin McLeod (302)	
Rob Moodie (303)	
Ben O'Shea (304)	
Reema Rattan (305)	
Matthew Rimmer (306–309)	
Don Rothwell (310)	
Craig Seitam (234)	
Kyla Tienhaara (311)	
Julian Vieceli (312)	
Tania Voon (313)	

These were overwhelmingly positive to plain packaging, and often scathing of the tobacco industry and congratulatory of the government. Table 5.3 lists authors of all those that we have been able to locate, written by both professional journalists and guest authors.

Cartoonists and satirists

Australian cartoonists, satirists and current affairs panel programs feasted on plain packaging, rarely with anything but biting support. This site features 18 such cartoons, nearly all of which rained down vicious blows on Big Tobacco's arguments: http://atodblog.com/2012/11/20/editorial-cartoonists-did-their-duty-in-australias-tobacco-war/

'Everyone hates them'

For many years, tobacco companies in Australia have suffered from public perceptions that they are not to be trusted, that they are corporate pied pipers with intense interests in children, rapacious corporate leviathans who put profit before all else, and are indifferent to the suffering that their products cause (260). Two surveys of Australians' attitudes to the tobacco industry put it very plainly (318, 319). One of these found that:

> 80% of respondents and 74% of smokers thought tobacco companies mostly did not or never told the truth about smoking and health, children and smoking and addictiveness of tobacco. With regard to perceived standards of honesty and ethics, tobacco company executives were rated the lowest of all professional groups, with 74% of respondents judging them to have low or very low standards. (319)

Philip Morris' own commissioned market research from 1993 had told them the same thing:

> Philip Morris is almost universally known among the public and opinion leaders . . . The company's overall favourability ratings average in the low 30s on a 100-point scale places it in the company of two other tobacco companies – W.D. & H.O. Wills and Rothmans –

well below the normal mid-50s to mid-60s typically found for most companies. These ratings for the company are very similar to those found among comparable audiences in the United States. (320)

Eighteen years later, things had, if anything, sunk even lower for Big Tobacco. In 2011, the Reputation Institute published results of a global survey of 85,000 respondents (including an Australian sample of 5,611) conducted by the Reputation Institute and AMR Australia in January and February 2011. It rated all major industries in 25 categories for reputation. The top categories were consumer products (73.8), electrical and electronics (73.2) and computers (70.3). By far the worst performing category was tobacco, which scored only 50.1, well behind the next lowest category (utilities with 59).

A Google search with the string 'just like the tobacco industry' returns many thousands of examples of how the tobacco industry has become an index case or benchmark in everyday talk for all manner of malfeasance in corporate conduct. It has set the bottom feeder standard on trust, ethics and grubby conduct. No other industry is subject to widespread policies of academic institutions refusing to allow their staff or students to accept tobacco industry research grants or scholarships. Our own university (Sydney) has long refused to allow tobacco companies onto the campus to run job opportunity stalls at its annual student employment fair. It is the only industry thus refused.

Politicians are highly sensitive about who they are seen to be associating with. Political scandals involving associations with sex workers, criminals and corrupt land developers are common around the world, but in an increasing number of countries, being seen to be cosy with tobacco companies has become a hallmark of political poor judgement. As the CEO of the American Cancer Society, John Seffrin, has put it: 'Politicians don't like to stand next to a pariah in the next photo opportunity.'

Roxon was similarly emphatic that the industry's appalling reputation as corporate pariahs (260) was important to the decision to run with plain packaging:

When the taskforce report came, marshalling all the evidence for various measures including plain packaging, this was when I really started to give it serious thought. I can remember one of my advisors, my personal staff, not the bureaucrats, saying to me well, this is just a 'no-brainer'. Meaning, it might be new and bold, but it hit a political sweet spot too – you have good evidence, you have doctors and researchers on side, you're trying to protect kids and the only one lining up against you is the tobacco industry. With a sceptical media and pretty well informed public, fighting such a discredited industry was not as dangerous as people thought.

Angela Pratt told us:

Basically my view about it at the time and since has been it was a good old-fashioned political fight between good and evil. When you're fighting with the AMA [Australian Medical Association] about something, it's never that clear cut. It's not really ever that great to be in a big fight with the doctors. Even if it's worthy and justified and they're being bastards, as a political strategy it's never really that great. I would almost say that the prospect of a fight with Big Tobacco was something that people relished the thought of, rather than shied away from it. That's not the reason that we did it, but a fight with the tobacco industry was not something that scared people off.

Pratt said that Rudd shared this view:

I think it's probably fair to say that he didn't mind the idea of a big fight with the tobacco industry. You know, in politics it's not bad to have a fight. I mean, we didn't do it *because* we wanted a fight. We did it because we thought it was important and would make a difference. But the prospect of the fight with the tobacco industry wasn't something that put people off, particularly.

Like millions of Australians, Rudd had lived through several decades where tobacco control was rarely absent from the news media (321, 322) for more than a week. In this time there had been years-long advocacy campaigns to get rid of all tobacco advertising and sporting and cultural sponsorship, to upgrade pack warnings, to introduce smoke-free indoor air on public transport, and in workplaces, restaurants and bars. (323) There had been the train wreck of revelations about the tobacco industry's duplicity on health and addiction and designs on children when millions of their internal documents were made public in the late 1990s. There had been large-scale public awareness campaigns on the risks of smoking. And through all this, we saw virtually continual declines in smoking, growing antipathy toward the tobacco industry and support for governments to do more to reduce smoking, particularly among young people.

Nicola Roxon

No analysis of why Australia acted on plain packs could fail to place Nicola Roxon at centre stage. Across 35 years I have encountered many federal and state ministers responsible for aspects of health, and worked with several closely. Barry Hodge (Western Australia 1983–86), John Cornwall (South Australia 1982–88), David White (Victoria 1985–89), Michael Wooldridge (Federal 1996–2001), Frank Sartor (New South Wales 2003–07 and 2009–11) and Verity Firth (New South Wales 2007–08) were all ministers who implemented major tobacco control reforms while in power. Each of these people painted their reforms on a state or national canvas, as did Roxon. But Roxon's contribution to tobacco control history looms as one of the most important initiatives with global ramifications ever taken. If, as expected, dominoes fall around the world over the next decade, her contribution will have been monumental.

Roxon was a spectacularly good media performer. Those of us who had several decades of experience in advocating and debating for policy reform in the news media have had many hundreds, if not thousands of opportunities to rehearse particular framings, sound bites and lines of arguments. On a big news day in tobacco control, it is not uncommon to do 10 or more interviews for different media outlets, all about the same issue. You quickly get a sense of how journalists see an issue, and about which questions they see as central to a debate. You often get these questions early and develop a sense about how you have handled a question: which parts if an interview were strongest and which needed work. Subsequent interviews then allow you to push forward responses that you have used earlier to good effect. In this way, interviews throughout the day tend to get more polished. It's a common experience to feel as thought you have nailed an interview with a turn of phrase, an analogy, a killer fact or statistic.

Nicola Roxon gave many interviews on plain packs over 2010–12. Seasoned advocates for tobacco control were in awe of her abilities to calmly and firmly explain the policy, to defend every aspect of it from attack and to go to the heart of the case for strong tobacco control. For example, on releasing the report that recommended plain packs, Roxon put the importance of firm action on tobacco by simply saying: 'We are killing people by not acting'. (65) This stunningly direct, simple, clear-sighted and courageous statement of moral principle was one of several powerful sound bites she was to use in the months ahead. Another was her compelling observation that she had 'never met a smoker who hoped their children would grow up to become a smoker.' There was just no comeback on that point.

Angela Pratt told me that working with Roxon was an experience she never expected to better.

> Nicola was an outstanding minister. She was outstanding in everything that she did. She was always across her brief. Whenever she did an interview, she was extremely well prepared. She knew the ins and outs of the arguments, and she wouldn't agree to do the interview until she knew that she could be. I guess with this issue, she had an amplified sense of the importance of getting it right because she knew that every word uttered on television could be something that the industry would use in their legal case against us if she said slightly the wrong thing.
>
> She really believed in plain packs. She's a formidable person. She's incredibly smart. She's incredibly articulate. She has an incredible ability to go right to the point of an issue. She was very clear from the beginning about the strategy for defending this, that it needed to be placed in the context of a long history of tobacco control policy so that we could argue that it was the next logical step.
>
> She was very clear about the limits of what you could say about the evidence base: while there was no *proof* that it would work – there never is when you do something for the first time – but there was *evidence* that it most likely would work. She was very clear about the fact that we didn't expect that it would have a major impact on long-term smokers. Rather, it was all about preventing young people from

starting up smoking. So it was for all those reasons that she was a formidable advocate for the policy, and why it was such a delight to work for her during that period.

The Coalition, the Greens and the crossbenchers

After the August 2011 election, the Labor Party was returned to power in a hung parliament requiring the support of at least three of the five crossbench members of the House of Representatives to pass its legislation, such as the plain packaging bill. In the Senate, it was assured of safe passage because the Greens Party was rock solid in its support for the bill, and in voting with the government, guaranteed that it would pass. Cross-party support was important, not only for the safe passage of the legislation, but to ensure continuity of support in the event of a change of government. It was also considered important to show the world that plain packaging was unanimously supported in Australia, historically a two-party nation, particularly at a time of minority government.

Health groups such as the Cancer Council and the Heart Foundation enjoy excellent relations with all political parties, and it soon became apparent that the three needed crossbench votes were assured with the support of the sole Greens representative, Adam Bandt, and two NSW independents Tony Windsor and Rob Oakeshott. Tasmanian independent Andrew Wilkie was also emphatically supportive of the legislation. None of these three, who had often voted in a bloc on other legislative issues, needed any convincing. Maverick Queensland independent MP Bob Katter described the policy as 'rampant wowserism' (324) and would have never voted for it.

But the tobacco control community knew how important it was to make sure that the bill gained the support of the Opposition. This would better ensure its preservation and consolidation down the track, should they come to power.

As explained earlier (pp97), the conservative Liberal/National Coalition Opposition was by no means pro-smoking. It had introduced and sustained important platforms of tobacco control when previously in government. But in Opposition, the task of trying to find fault with most government activity is standard. The Abbott-led Opposition took this duty very seriously and developed a reputation for being extremely negative about almost everything the Labor government supported. Many expected that the Opposition would not be any different when it came to plain packaging.

The Coalition had a good number of members – including Abbott himself – who were almost genetically opposed to 'unnecessary' regulation of business and human behaviour. After the government had announced its intentions on plain packaging, several equivocated and publicly expressed reservations or declined to comment. Shadow health minister Peter Dutton said in June 2009: 'In my books, in the current debate, providing a ban to packaging and to branding on packaging is a bridge too far.' Pushed in May 2010 by prime minister Julia Gillard to say yes or no to plain packaging, Abbott eventually said: 'If it shuts you up for a second, yes Julia.' (see https://www.youtube.com/watch?v=pjR9JbThk1I) In May 2011, on the day BATA launched its campaign with a press conference, Abbott said: 'My anxiety with this is that it might end up being counterproductive in practice.'

Fragments of intelligence from Opposition members and occasionally tobacco industry staff were gathered about the likelihood of support for the legislation. These painted a mixed picture. For example, a tobacco control colleague had been on holiday in Fiji resort in 2010 and got talking to some Australian businessmen. They turned out to be staff from an Australian tobacco company and some retailers who were being rewarded for achieving high tobacco sales levels. Without disclosing her interest, the colleague asked whether they were worried about the impact of plain packs. They brushed it aside and said that their management had assured them that Tony Abbott would drop the policy on gaining power.

But this may have been mere company bravado, because a leaked fax from Philip Morris's head of corporate affairs to a PR agency in May 2010 (see pp15) noted: 'Please note that contrary to the proposal, the Coalition's "resolve" is not "strong". It is at best neutral.' This resolve referred to the industry's hopes that the Opposition would oppose the legislation.

However, there were at least four Coalition members (Liberals Dr Mal Washer, Ken Wyatt and Alex Somlyay, and West Australian National Tony Crook) who expressed support for the policy. (324) Rumours spread that some of these may have been willing to cross the floor and vote with the government if a division had been necessary. Of these, Mal Washer was the most forthcoming about his intentions. A highly respected Perth general practitioner, Washer was a popular and trusted figure across all sides of politics, often acting as a doctor to politicians while in Canberra for parliamentary sittings. He was not someone easily ignored.

When interviewed by *The Age* on 22 May 2011, just nine days before his party would decide that it would not oppose the bill, Washer was asked about industry claims about increases in smuggled products. His words were blunt:

> All this talk of chop chop [loose, illegal tobacco] and crime gangs sounds like bullshit to me. The tobacco industry is jumping up and down because they're worried about their businesses. I support these reforms unequivocally and whatever my party decides to do, I don't give a shit. (325)

On 26 May 2011, the Cancer Council held its annual Australia's Biggest Morning Tea fundraiser event in parliament house. Opposition leader Tony Abbott attended and told those present: 'We all should do what we can to fight cancer.' (326). Lung cancer is Australia's leading cause of cancer death, with 8410 victims in 2012, more than double the cancer causing the next most deaths (colorectal with 3950), prostate (3294) and breast (2940).

The next day Michelle Grattan, perhaps the most senior member of the Canberra press gallery who had attended the event, wrote an opinion piece about the Opposition's lack of leadership on plain packs. She wrote:

> There are issues that should be elevated above politics, and trying to find ways to reduce the killer habit of smoking is one of them. So it is particularly disappointing that Tony Abbott, a former health minister, is dithering on the Opposition's attitude to government legislation for the plain packaging of cigarettes. The case for this measure is overwhelming . . .
>
> Abbott has to contend with serious divisions within his ranks on the packaging issue . . . But Abbott will have to deal with the differences within the Opposition eventually, and he might as well do it

sooner rather than later. The packaging legislation appears set to get through the House of Representative even if the Coalition opposes it – thanks to the crossbench and the Liberal dissidents' will to cross the floor. Politically it would look bad for Abbott to appear doubly impotent; unable to stop the legislation and unable to keep his own troops in line.

2011 World No Tobacco Day

On 31 May 2011 (World No Tobacco Day), Mike Daube and I, together with the Public Health Association of Australia, arranged a special event in Canberra to thank Nicola Roxon and the Labor government for what it was doing in tobacco control, particularly with plain packaging. This was the biggest policy advance any of us had ever experienced, and we wanted to bring together all who had played big roles in both the years leading up to it, and in all the defence of the bill described in this book.

We had earlier nominated Roxon to the World Health Organization to receive a WHO World No Tobacco Day medal. We had also arranged for her to receive the Nigel Gray Award, named in honour of the long-time head of the Cancer Council Victoria (1968–1995), widely regarded as a global 'godfather' of tobacco control.

She was presented with both awards that day at parliament house, where the WHO's regional director for the Western Pacific, Dr Shin Young-soo, flew down from Manila to make the presentation. Nigel Gray was there to present the award under his name. (She was later also awarded the Public Health Association's Sidney Sax Medal).

Mike and I had drawn up a list of those around Australia who had made outstanding contributions to tobacco control since the 1970s. About 50 were able to attend, including politicians from all sides, senior health department bureaucrats, long-time researchers, heads of leading NGOs, John Bevins (the advertising writer who had created the 'Sponge' ad (see https://www.youtube.com/watch?v=UbwsET7_6kQ)) and many others, and Dr Arthur Chesterfield-Evans, a leading figure in the BUGA UP anti-tobacco billboard graffiti movement from the late 1970s and early 1980s. (327)

The award ceremony took place at 11am. Unbeknown to most of those attending, the Opposition was also meeting at the same time in the parliament building, and one of its agenda items was plain packaging. At noon, Rohan Greenland and Lyn Roberts from the Heart Foundation met with Andrew Robb as part of their ongoing engagement with the Coalition on the issue. Robb came straight from the party room and told the two that the Liberals had decided not to oppose the plain packs legislation, and that they were the first to know. Greenland told me: 'He was very happy to break the news to us.'

Angela Pratt saw the timing of announcement as no mere serendipity:

> We, in combination with you and all your colleagues, had sort of set out to create a real sense of building pressure on the Opposition in the lead-up to and on that day. So I remember all of those things coming together and culminating on that day successfully, because that was the day the Liberal Party announced that they wouldn't oppose the legislation.

I asked Nicola Roxon and Angela Pratt to comment on the Opposition's behaviour over the bill. Both took the stance that the Coalition were never comfortable with the issue, but were clearly able to read the very negative political realities of being seen to effectively side with Big Tobacco and having principled party members being seen to cross the floor of parliament.

Roxon said:

> My personal view is they got embarrassed into it. Ultimately Opposition support came because the tobacco industry had no credit in Australia, because of their past behaviour. Once the Liberals could see that we were sticking to our guns – I think they were waiting to see if we buckled or changed direction – but because we weren't, they saw that they were going to be very much on the wrong side of public opinion.

Pratt's view was similar. She said:

> [Mal Washer] was prepared to cross the floor, if necessary. So really I think Abbott and the political leadership of the Liberal Party made a judgement that the risk of disunity – with Washer crossing the floor –

was worse than any political downside of their supporting the legislation. So they made a judgement that supporting the legislation was the lesser of two evils. It was a pragmatic political judgement to avoid an ugly show of disunity in the floor of the House of Representatives.

Angela Pratt's view was that Washer's position was made all the easier because of the antics of the tobacco industry:

What gave strength to Mal Washer's hand was this sense that the tobacco industry's campaign was actually just really quite abhorrent. It was over the top. They were being seen to be bullying the government. And it's the tobacco industry!

So I have always had the view that it was the extremity of the industry's campaign – the fact that they went so hard, so extreme, so over the top – that hurt them. I think it became clear to the Liberals that it was politically completely unpalatable for them to be on the same side as all of that.

I absolutely think that it was not Abbott's or Dutton's instinct to support it, but it became a political liability for them not to be supporting it. Because by not supporting, they were on the same team as the tobacco industry, which was a kind of pretty unpalatable prospect.

Pratt also acknowledged that:

Graphic health warnings were introduced under Abbott, so there is sort of shared sense of pride in Australia's tobacco control history. It's a shared sense because both parties have some ownership of different parts of it. I still think that the Liberals would have preferred not to support the plain packaging legislation. I have never seen any evidence of them having become enthusiastic supporters of the policy. So while broadly I would say tobacco control is a bipartisan issue, I'm not sure that I would say plain packaging is a bipartisan issue.

The Adelaide *Advertiser's* headline the next day was: 'Libs *yield* on smokes packaging' (our emphasis). The article stated:

There were also fears that Mr Abbott's 'brand' could be damaged, given the Government's initiative had been unanimously supported by health groups and normally conservative lobbies, including the Australian Medical Association. (328)

On the evening of the day the awards were presented and the Coalition made its decision to not oppose the bill, the Public Health Association hosted a dinner in parliament house for Nicola Roxon, Nigel Gray and the 50 or so tobacco control stalwarts who had been there for the ceremony. Roxon's very proud mother came along, as did Mal Washer and the Greens Senator Rachel Siewert.

I sing in a Sydney rock covers band. Our lead guitarist is Paul Grogan, the Cancer Council Australia's lobbyist. We had put an impromptu version of a new take on the 1960s Shangri-Las' hit *Leader of the Pack* on YouTube (see http://tiny.cc/8qurox), recorded after dinner one night at Paul's house. Paul and I sang the song that night in tribute to Roxon. Everyone in the room roared the chorus lines.

On the morning that the High Court case began in Canberra (17 April 2012), Tony Abbott went out of his way to make his support even clearer. He said: 'I think this is an important health measure. It's important to get smoking rates down further. We didn't oppose the legislation in the Parliament and I hope it withstands the High Court's scrutiny.' (329) It is noteworthy that after the 2013 election, the new Coalition government maintained strong bipartisan support for tobacco control, including plain packaging, regular excise increases and mass media campaigns.

6
Legal challenges, massive costs

The legislation has already faced one legal challenge (the one in the High Court of Australia) and is set to face two more:

- World Trade Organization (WTO) disputes
- the challenge under Australia–Hong Kong Bilateral Investment Treaty.

The High Court of Australia

When the passage of the government's bill on plain packaging became assured with the support of the Opposition, the Greens and key independents, an ever-desperate tobacco industry began to concentrate on threatening the legal apocalypse that they promised would descend on Australia first through the High Court and if necessary, through international trade bodies like the WTO. Indeed, within hours of the April 2010 political announcement of plain packaging, two tobacco companies (BAT and Imperial) declared they would challenge the decision in court using seizure of intellectual property arguments, and seek billions in compensation. (eg: https://www.youtube.com/watch?v=wEXH7mqEEWE) and Figure 6.1.

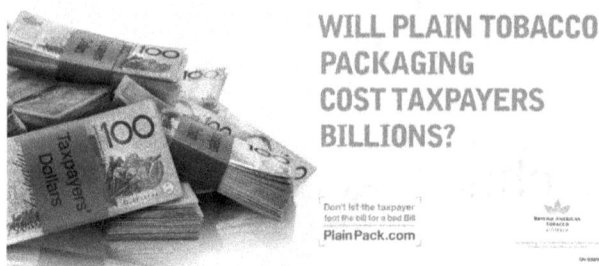

WILL PLAIN TOBACCO
PACKAGING
COST TAXPAYERS
BILLIONS?

Don't let the taxpayer
foot the bill for a bad Bill
PlainPack.com

Figure 6.1 BATA advertisement about the 'billions' government might have to pay in compensation.

BATA ran several ads promoting the idea that plain packaging would see the government, and therefore ultimately the taxpayer, having to incur stratospheric legal bills and pay out compensation to tobacco companies. Figure 6.2 shows an advertisement arguing that the government has had poor legal advice before, and plain packaging was likely to be another example.

These arguments were a house of cards, starting with the central problem that plain packaging would not extinguish the industry's valued brand identities. All packages would still carry brand and variant names, allowing smokers to clearly exercise their freedom to select between the much-vaunted but often non-existent differences in brands. In the highly unlikely event of a ruling by the High Court in favour of the industry, any calculation of compensation would need to take account that branding differences had only been diminished, not extinguished. The companies would have needed to demonstrate with precision that sales losses arose from losing colours, logos and different pack shapes, but not brand names and variants.

Few of those megaphoning this legal Armageddon appeared to have even read the draft bill itself. Section 11 of the bill made it clear that plain packaging would not proceed if it were to be determined (by a court) that its operation would result in an acquisition of property other than 'on just terms'. So in the unlikely event that the High Court determined there was an acquisition of property (more on this below), Section 11 created a fallback provision under which 'the trade mark may be used on the packaging of tobacco products, or on a tobacco

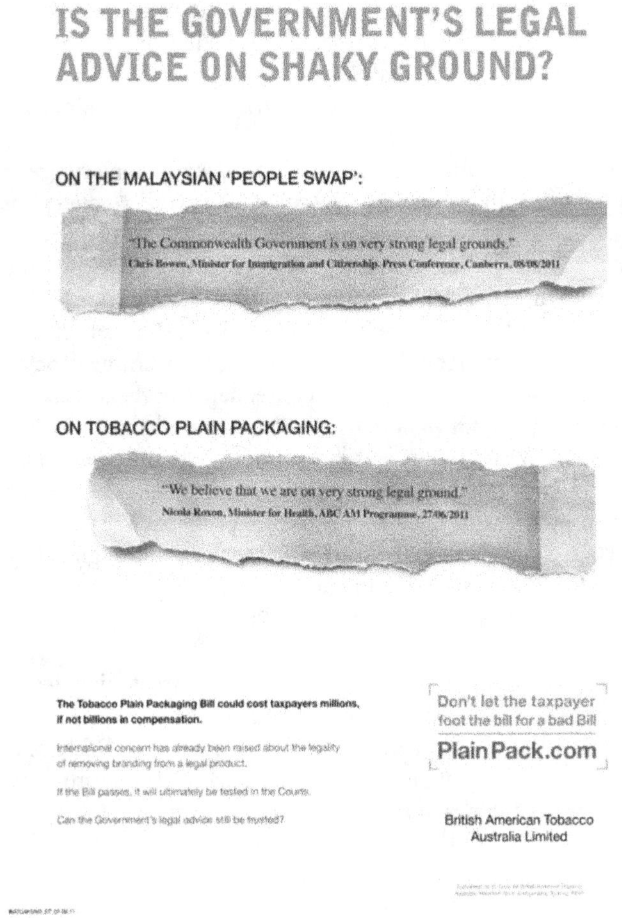

IS THE GOVERNMENT'S LEGAL ADVICE ON SHAKY GROUND?

ON THE MALAYSIAN 'PEOPLE SWAP':

"The Commonwealth Government is on very strong legal grounds."
Chris Bowen, Minister for Immigration and Citizenship. Press Conference, Canberra, 08/08/2011

ON TOBACCO PLAIN PACKAGING:

"We believe that we are on very strong legal ground."
Nicola Roxon, Minister for Health, ABC AM Programme, 27/06/2011

The Tobacco Plain Packaging Bill could cost taxpayers millions, if not billions in compensation.

International concern has already been raised about the legality of removing branding from a legal product.

If the Bill passes, it will ultimately be tested in the Courts.

Can the Government's legal advice still be trusted?

Don't let the taxpayer foot the bill for a bad Bill

PlainPack.com

British American Tobacco Australia Limited

Figure 6.2 BATA newspaper advertisement about poor advice received by government.

product' in accordance with requirements to be prescribed in subsequent regulations.

In other words, the bill had been drafted with a get out of jail free card under which plain packaging would not proceed if the High Court ruled that it involved an unjust acquisition. As a result, there could have been no compensable damage or loss incurred by any tobacco company mounting a legal challenge before implementation of the Act, even if such a challenge was successful.

Moreover, Monash University's Mark Davison explained:

> As for the constitutional argument that the legislation acquires property on other than just terms, Professor Craven, a noted constitutional expert, has since observed on Radio National's *Background Briefing* that the tobacco industry's prospects of success are about the same as a three-legged horse has of winning the Melbourne Cup. The reason for his view is simply explained. The extinction of rights or the reduction of rights is not relevant. The government or a third party must acquire property as a consequence of the legislation. The government did not want to use the tobacco trademarks. Nor does it want third parties to do so. It does not desire to or intend to acquire any property. The proposition that prohibitions on the use of property do not constitute an acquisition of property was confirmed by the High Court as recently as 2009. In that case, the High Court held that the government was entitled to extinguish property rights in licences of farmers to take bore water. (287)

Immediately the tobacco companies began threatening legal action, Australian legal experts in constitutional and intellectual property law began publicly ridiculing their prospects of success. Professor George Williams (University of New South Wales) said: 'The Commonwealth is able to regulate the use of IP [intellectual property] and that is quite different to it acquiring that property.' Professor Greg Craven (Australian Catholic University) said: 'I'm sure it would fascinate the High Court all the way to deciding "No"' and Professor Mark Davison (Monash University) described the industry's argument as:

> ... so weak, it's non-existent. There is no right to use a trademark given by the World Trade Organization agreement. There is a right to prevent others using your trademark but that does not translate into a right to use your own trademark. (330)

In May 2010, Tim Wilson of the Institute of Public Affairs (IPA) participated in a seminar on plain packaging at Melbourne University.

Wilson's videoed contribution can be seen here (http://vimeo.com/ 12106765), where 'as a staunch constitutionalist' he summarised his take on the various laws and international treaties said to be possibly relevant to a case against plain packaging. The next speaker, Professor Mark Davison, critiqued Wilson's presentation in a demolition job that went near to being academic bloodsport for many of those present. (266)

Of Wilson's constitutional argument that plain packaging would be an acquisition of property by the Australian government, Davison had this to say:

> I thought for example, you might have . . . I don't know . . . picked up a textbook. Look[ed] at a case. See, there is no acquisition of property being proposed here. The mere extinguishment or deprivation of rights in relation to property does not involve acquisition. The government does not want the pretty pictures [the branding colours and logos]. It wants them not used. [pointing to his slide] There are six cases. Six. And there are a lot more, that say precisely that . . . (see http://vimeo.com/12108576)

No tobacco company ever compensated for pack health warnings

Governments all over the world have been 'seizing' parts of the intellectual property of tobacco companies since 1966 when the United States became the first nation to require packs to carry a health warning. Over the next 45 years, these warnings have become slowly more detailed and explicit, embracing language like 'addiction', 'cause' and 'kill' that saw protracted national and global lobbying against every new step that was taken. After Canada became the first nation in 2000 to introduce graphic, pictorial warnings in full colour, 63 nations followed suit over the next 12 years, with Uruguay leading the way with 80% front and back, until Australia's new requirements saw it temporarily become the new leader with 75% of the front and 90% of the rear given over to health warnings. Thailand took the lead in June 2014 when it required 85% of the front of the pack to be a graphic heath warning.

But in all these years, no tobacco company has ever received a cent in compensation from any government for these sometimes massive appropriations. There were no financial barriers to any tobacco transnational taking legal action against governments for this heinous alleged theft of a part of their intellectual property. Such actions would have posed negligible financial barriers to any tobacco transnational. The big stick of legal action and compensation the industry keeps warning governments that they hold behind their backs is the threat of legal action and massive compensation for trademark violation. But as we shall see, in the case of Australia – at least within the domestic legal system – this was a big case of crying wolf.

The $3 billion compensation factoid

There's nothing quite like the threat of a massive legal penalty to get headlines and frighten the political horses about proposed legislation. A big number is required for such threats and the number that was selected for plain packaging that the government was said to be facing was $3 billion ... per year! So where did this satisfyingly very large number come from? It began circulating in May 2010 and was repeated many times in the months ahead by frothing radio shock-jocks, and by some who should have known better.

Step forward Tim Wilson, the then 'director of intellectual property' at the tobacco industry-funded IPA. Wilson is a prominent ideological spear-carrier for deregulation and a sworn enemy of the odious nanny state. In 2014 he was appointed by the new Abbott-led conservative government as a Commissioner for Human Rights, with a focus on 'free speech'. In late April 2010, just a month after the government had announced its intentions with plain packs, while not holding a law degree, Wilson was all over the Australian news media promoting the likelihood that the Australian government would be hit with a compensation bill of up to $3 billion a year for having 'confiscated' the tobacco companies' intellectual property in the form of their packaging. (331)

So where did Wilson get his $3 billion number from? What were his 'rough calculations' (332) as he described them in *The Australian* newspaper? Wilson sent a submission to the Senate Community Affairs Committee enquiry into the Family First-proposed Plain Tobacco Packaging (Removing Branding from Cigarette Packs) Bill 2009 which had been triggered by a bill proposed by the one-term Families First Party Senator, Steve Fielding. The submission was based on an IPA report also authored by Wilson. Here, (333) in all its embarrassing glory, we can examine Wilson's prowess with the numbers and the birth of one of the most ludicrous factoids in many years. His report's subtitle, presumably added with no trace of irony, was *Australian governments legislating, without understanding, intellectual property.*

In his executive summary, Wilson provided 'an indicative calculated range' of between \$378m and \$3027m per year that a High Court order under Section 51 (xxxi) of the Australian Constitution could award the tobacco industry over plain packs. From whence did Wilson pluck these estimates? Table 2 in his report shows two lines of numbers showing the total value of tobacco sales in Australia in 2006: one for the value including excise tax and one for the sales value ex-tax. Excise tax is paid by tobacco companies to the government, but is then repaid to tobacco companies by smokers when they purchase tobacco. This means that it is smokers, not the tobacco companies, who actually pay the tax. The sales value ex-tax represents the returns to manufacturers and retailers combined.

By taking the trouble to differentiate the two like this, Wilson must have known that no court would order the return of the tobacco tax component of retail sales to the companies, for the elementary reason that they never would have been entitled to that component of the retail price: it is the ex-tax value only that fuels the industry's pipedream of massive compensation should any government be silly enough to take the plain packs route. Wilson then calculated the tax-included and the ex-tax values on two assumptions: a 10% and a 30% fall in sales *each year* that might follow the introduction of plain packs. He calculated these two figures at \$378m and \$1.135b. So where does the \$3b factoid come from? Are you ready for this? The *tax-included* sales value of a 30% fall is \$3.027b – the biggest number on the page.

Even setting aside inclusion of tax in this \$3 billion figure, how reasonable were Wilson's assumptions that plain packs would cause a fall of a minimum 10% through to 30% *each year*? Between 1999 and 2003 the average annual fall in total dutied cigarettes was just 2.6%. The most sales have *ever* fallen in one year was just shy of 10% in 1999 after the combined impact of a change in the way cigarettes were taxed (from weight to per stick) and a big budget boost to the national quit campaign by the then Liberal health minister Michael Wooldridge.

Wilson's $3 billion number was thus based on a projected decline which was the stuff of fantasy land. Worse, it appeared to be a wilful selection of the tax-*included* biggest number he could sight in his own specious table. To the delight of the industry, it quickly became a virulent factoid. Google '$3 billion' and 'plain packs' and you will see what we mean.

ABC television's *Media Watch* program was tipped off about Wilson's antics and ran a segment about his claims in May 2010. (334) *Media Watch* is said to be a program that many people like to watch but no one wants to appear on. The segment highlighted the policy of the IPA, Wilson's employer, of never disclosing its funders. This is a paradoxical position to take for an organisation obsessed with freedom of speech. A tape of Wilson saying on radio that: 'any funding [they might have from the tobacco industry] has no impact on the policy positions we take whatsoever,' was included in the *Media Watch* segment, with the host noting that Wilson undoubtedly 'sincerely' held his views, regardless of whether the IPA was funded by Big Tobacco or not. However, another IPA employee Alan Moran, told a Productivity Commission enquiry in 2001 that '. . . the IPA doesn't represent anyone in particular . . . we don't represent the firms. . . there are occasions when we may take positions which are somewhat different from those of the funders. Obviously that doesn't happen too often, otherwise they'd stop funding us.' (335)

Undeterred by any suggestion that the tobacco industry may have had any influence over the IPA's views on plain packaging or on Wilson's economic flatulence, *The Australian's* Christian Kerr (who has also written for the IPA) kept the flame alive as late as mid-September 2010 for Wilson's 'rough' calculation, describing it as an 'independent estimate' (336).

In September 2011, when the plain packaging bill entered the Senate's Legal and Constitutional Affairs Legislation Committee, David Crow of BATA affirmed the 'billions' ballpark figure.

> Senator Cash: In relation to your submission at 7.2, you actually state whilst the amount of any compensation would ultimately be a question of the courts, commentators have put a compensation figure for the TPP [Trans-Pacific Partnership] bill and the proposed increase in graphic health warnings could be in the vicinity of $3 billion. Is that

a fair estimate? Is that an estimate that you have had a look at? Is that just a figure that has been plucked out of the air?

Mr Crow: No, we are currently doing work on trying to do the evaluations of this, getting ready for any potential challenge.

Senator Cash: Are we talking millions, hundreds of millions or billions?

Mr Crow: It would be in the billions.

Senator Cash: It is in the billions?

Mr Crow: I think when they reviewed it in 1995 . . .

Senator Brandis: In the billions, did you say?

Mr Crow: In the billions, yes. Our business is worth approximately probably $7 billion or $8 billion. The brands would be worth roughly probably half of that.

In June 2013, the matter of whether the IPA received funding from the tobacco industry was settled when BAT's Simon Millson confirmed in a letter to ASH (London) that it was a corporate member of the IPA. (337)

The judgement

The tobacco industry's challenge in the High Court of Australia commenced in Australia in April 2012 and judgement was handed down in August, with the reasons for judgement published in October of the same year. (338) The case against the Commonwealth of Australia was brought by five tobacco companies (British American Tobacco Australasia Ltd, Imperial Tobacco Australia Ltd, JT International SA, Nelle Tabak Nederland BV and Philip Morris Ltd). Of the full bench of seven judges hearing the case, six rejected the pleadings brought by the plaintiffs. The McCabe Centre for Law and Cancer provides a good summary of the case made by the applicants, the reasons for the judgement and many links to scholarly commentaries and media coverage of the case. (339) A paper by Jonathan Liberman, the centre's director, also provides an excellent review. (340) A slightly edited version of the McCabe Centre summary follows.

In challenging plain packaging, the tobacco industry made two principal arguments:

... that the restrictions on its property and related rights (including trademarks, copyright, goodwill, design, patents, packaging rights and licensing rights) effected by the Tobacco Plain Packaging Act and Regulations constitute an acquisition of its property (for which just terms had not been provided); and

that the Act and Regulations give the Commonwealth the use of, or control over, tobacco packaging, in a manner that effects an acquisition of the tobacco industry's property (for which just terms have not been provided).

In her judgement, Justice Crennan observed that what the tobacco industry 'most strenuously objected to was the taking or extinguishment of the advertising or promotional functions of their registered trademarks or product get-up'.

The essence of the 6:1 majority's reasons for dismissing the tobacco industry's challenge is set out in the summary provided by the court:

On 15 August 2012 the High Court made orders in two matters concerning the Tobacco Plain Packaging Act 2011 (Cth) ('the Act'). Today the High Court delivered its reasons in those matters. A majority of the High Court held that the Act was valid as it did not acquire property. It therefore did not engage s 51 (xxxi) of the Constitution, which requires any acquisition of property effected by a Commonwealth law to be on just terms.

The Act imposes restrictions on the colour, shape and finish of retail packaging for tobacco products and restricts the use of trademarks on such packaging. The plaintiffs brought proceedings in the High Court challenging the validity of the Act, arguing that the Commonwealth acquired their intellectual property rights and goodwill otherwise than on just terms.

A majority of the Court held that to engage s 51 (xxxi) an acquisition must involve the accrual to some person of a proprietary benefit or interest. Although the Act regulated the plaintiffs' intellectual property rights and imposed controls on the packaging and presentation of tobacco products, it did not confer a proprietary benefit or interest on the Commonwealth or any other person. As a result, neither the Commonwealth nor any other person acquired any property and s 51 (xxxi) was not engaged.

All six members of the majority affirmed that under the Australian Constitution, for there to be an 'acquisition of property' requiring just terms compensation, the Commonwealth or another must obtain a benefit or interest of a 'proprietary nature'. As Justices Hayne and Bell put it, this is a 'bedrock principle' which must not be eroded: 'There must be an acquisition of property' (emphasis in the original). The tobacco industry's arguments '[ran] aground' on this bedrock.

As (now Chief) Justice French expressed it:

> On no view can it be said that the Commonwealth as a polity or by any authority or instrumentality, has acquired any benefit of a proprietary character by reason of the operation of the TPP Act on the plaintiffs' property rights.

The achievement of the Commonwealth's legislative objects would not be such a benefit. As Justice Kiefel wrote, if the Act's central statutory object were to be effective, the tobacco companies' business 'may be harmed, but the Commonwealth does not thereby acquire something in the nature of property itself'.

In addressing the tobacco industry's argument about use of, or control over, packaging, Justices Hayne and Bell observed that the requirements of the Act:

> . . . are no different in kind from any legislation that requires labels that warn against the use or misuse of a product, or tell the reader who to call or what to do if there has been a dangerous use of a product. Legislation that requires warning labels to be placed on products, even warning labels as extensive as those required by the TPP Act, effects no acquisition of property.

Justice Crennan noted that: 'Legislative provisions requiring manufacturers or retailers to place on product packaging warnings to consumers of the dangers of incorrectly using or positively misusing a product are commonplace'. Similarly, Justice Kiefel wrote that: 'Many kinds of products have been subjected to regulation in order to prevent or reduce the likelihood of harm', including medicines, poisonous substances and foods.

Justice Crennan underlined the significance of the tobacco industry's ability to continue to use brand names on tobacco packaging, 'so as to distinguish their tobacco products, thereby continuing to generate custom and goodwill'. She noted that the 'visual, verbal, aural and allusive distinctiveness, and any inherent or acquired distinctiveness, of a brand name can continue to affect retail consumers despite the physical restrictions on the appearance of brand names imposed' by the Act; 'an exclusive right to generate a volume of sales of goods by reference to a distinctive brand name is a valuable right'.

The High Court's judgement reverberated around the world, confirming the analyses of many legal scholars and commentators who had anticipated the judgement almost to the letter. Those few who had confidently predicted that the court would order the Australian government to compensate the companies to the tune of 'billions' were oddly silent.

The IPA's Tim Wilson was one who kept quiet. What had he learned from all this? In February 2014, a reporter included the following exchange in a magazine portrait of Wilson (341):

> But would Wilson concede he was wrong on plain packaging?
> 'No.'
> 'Have you ever been wrong on anything?' I ask.
> 'I'm sure there have been things,' he says. 'But I can't think of them right now.'

World Trade Organization disputes

While plain packaging has been upheld domestically in Australia's highest court, challenges in international law are ongoing at the time of writing.

In the World Trade Organization, five governments – Ukraine, the Dominican Republic, Honduras, Cuba and Indonesia – have initiated complaints against the Australian government's plain packaging law.

In May 2014 the WTO composed the three person panel who will examine the dispute of the five complainants together. (342) The panel will next set a timetable for hearing the dispute. Typically, the WTO's dispute settlement system aims for panel reports to be provided to all parties approximately six months from the panel's appointment, and then to all WTO members three weeks later. However, due to the large number of complainants and the complexity and breadth of the issues argued, it is likely this panel will take much longer. If either party appeals, the matter will be considered by the WTO's appellate body, which is expected to provide its report within a few months.

With the exception of Indonesia, none of these nations have any significant trade of any sort with Australia, let alone in tobacco products. (343, 344) For all Big Tobacco's outraged global tub-thumping about plain packs and its success in whistling up sternly worded submissions from a variety of US-based trade associations, it is telling that with the exception of the geopolitically very important neighbouring country of Indonesia, these other puppets are the heaviest hitters it could influence to run its case with the WTO. Big Tobacco's best team are nearly all global minnows.

It has been reported that Philip Morris is providing support to the Dominican Republic, and that British American Tobacco is doing the same for Ukraine and Honduras. (345)

The WTO complaints are based on three WTO agreements: the General Agreement on Tariffs and Trade (GATT), the Agreement on Technical Barriers to Trade (TBT) and the Agreement on Trade-Related Aspects of Intellectual Property Rights (TRIPS), In essence they claim that what Australia has done is unnecessarily burdensome to trade, that the new law is somehow discriminatory, that it is more trade restrictive than necessary, and that it unjustifiably infringes upon trademark rights.

Australia argues that its laws are a sound, well-considered measure designed to achieve a legitimate objective – the protection of public health. It is vigorously defending the complaints.

Several legal scholars have published detailed examinations of the merits of Australia's stance that its laws comply with WTO obligations. (346, 347) In support of Australia's position, the McCabe Centre for Law and Cancer notes that the laws represent a sound exercise of Australia's sovereign power to regulate, are non-discriminatory, are based on evidence, are well-drafted and have behind them the legal and political force of the WHO FCTC, its article 11 and article 13, other decisions of its Conference of the Parties, and other international instruments including the Doha Declaration on TRIPS and Public Health. (348)

Many governments restrict trade for health and cultural reasons

In all this, it is also important to reflect that there are many examples of governments introducing strong restrictions, bans or penalties on the sale or promotion of different commercial products for cultural or health reasons. Many nations – including Australia (349) – severely restrict civilian access to firearms. Asbestos products are banned in several nations. Pharmaceutical products are subject to stringent formulation, dosage, access, packaging and sales controls, with direct-to-consumer advertising of prescribed products allowed in only two nations (the USA and New Zealand). Several Islamic nations totally prohibit the sale of alcohol. Food safety regulations have been accepted as the norm for many decades. Many nations impose strict quarantine regulations on the importation of exotic animals, insects and biological material. Every year, governments ban or restrict consumer goods deemed to be unsafe. Prohibitions on pornography are common in many nations, while not in others.

We have not seen, for example, firearms manufacturers seek to lobby nations to bring cases to the WTO or other global tribunals in an attempt to force such nations to relax their gun control laws. This is because of the principle of nations being able to have sovereignty over their own internal laws and regulations.

Restrictions and regulations on tobacco packaging need to be seen against this background and against the *exceptionally* deadly and addictive status of tobacco – a product which sees half of its long-term users die prematurely from using the product directly as intended by the manufacturers. In this, tobacco is unique among all consumer goods; one of the reasons why tobacco was also the subject of the world's first global health treaty, now ratified by 178 nations – the WHO's FCTC. (75)

What if Australia were to lose in WTO?

WTO rulings against a nation can result in the WTO sanctioning trade retaliation against the nation. So in the highly unlikely event that Australia were to receive an unfavourable decision in the WTO, the prospect of Australia being subject to trade retaliation from nations like Honduras and Ukraine with whom it has negligible trade would involve all the pain of being flogged with a damp lettuce leaf. Notwithstanding this, the Australian government would probably seek to 'bring itself into compliance' by bringing the legislation into compliance with any ruling given, in order to preserve its reputation as a country that follows international trade rules.

Challenge under Australia – Hong Kong Bilateral Investment Treaty

After losing the challenge in the Australian High Court in 2012 (along with five other companies), Philip Morris, through Philip Morris Asia (PMA), has brought proceedings against the Australian government under a bilateral trade agreement between Hong Kong and Australia signed in 1993. (285) The claim being made is that the Australian plain packaging law breaches the agreement between the government of Hong Kong and the government of Australia for the promotion and protection of investments. This bilateral investment treaty is known as the BIT, hence is known as the BIT claim. (350)

Unlike in the WTO system, this agreement contains a dispute settlement provision which permits investors, in this case a tobacco company, to bring their own claim against governments directly. PMA has made a number of arguments, including that plain packaging would expropriate its intellectual property, and that it has not been afforded fair and equitable treatment. PMA is seeking 'billions of dollars' in compensation for potential corporate losses arising from the new legislation. (351)

The timeline of facts/events in this instance are likely to be of critical relevance to the prospects of the case. On 29 April 2010, the Australian government announced its intention to introduce plain packaging. At that time Philip Morris tobacco products in Australia were manufactured by Philip Morris Australia. On 23 February 2011, Philip Morris Asia purchased Philip Morris Australia and on 27 June 2011 – a full 14 months after knowing the government intended to introduce plain packs – PMA served its notice of claim to the Australian government. (285)

Why is this sequence of events important? Imagine someone considering purchasing a property who had learned, 14 months earlier, that the property would be badly affected by a new freeway being built nearby. Then imagine them going ahead and purchasing the property. And then imagine them taking the government to court for compensation over damage to their investment. The PMA case would seem to have the same prospects, quite apart from all the arguments against the idea that a trade treaty should be able to override any government's sovereignty in public health matters in perpetuity.

The proceedings are governed by the United Nations Commission on International Trade Law Rules of Arbitration 2010 (UNCITRAL Rules), (352) and are being overseen by a three-member arbitral tribunal. (353) The process of arbitration differs from that in the WTO in several respects. Despite the Australian government's expressed commitment to transparency in investor-state arbitration and request for open hearings and published hearings, PMA has requested that the case be heard in secret and only limited documents published (with redactions), as it is entitled to do under the UNCITRAL rules. (354)

Mark Davison (285) was convinced that the case for compensation was worthless.

> Article 6 of the BIT specifically refers to how compensation should be calculated. It states that the compensation shall amount to 'the real value of the investment immediately before the deprivation or before the impending deprivation became public knowledge whichever is the earlier'.
>
> The investment is defined in Article 1 of the BIT as the investment of the Hong Kong investors, that is, PMA. So what was the value of the 'investment' that PMA had before the impending 'deprivation' became public knowledge? It seems that it did not have any investment at all at the time that the impending 'deprivation' became public knowledge.

No doubt PMA will have some argument on the point but, as a general rule, the value of nothing is nothing.

It appears that PMA's claim for 'billions of Australian dollars' has about as much life as the parrot in the famous Monty Python sketch. (see https://www.youtube.com/watch?v=aqz_4OgMi7M) It will be interesting to see whether PMA argues that its claim is just resting or, perhaps, just temporarily stunned by the Australian government taking it out of its cage and giving it a good hard whack with the facts.

In April 2014, Australia received a favourable order when the tribunal decided to divide the proceedings into two phases (the 'bifurcation question'), in line with a request by Australia. As a result, the tribunal will now first examine the jurisdictional objections raised by Australia and will only then turn to the argument on the merits, if necessary.

Australia is arguing that the tribunal does not have jurisdiction to hear the case for three reasons, summarised in an email circulated by the US-based *Tobacco Free Kids*:

1. The dispute falls outside of the scope of the Treaty because PMA did not have any relevant 'investment' in Australia at the time the introduction of plain packaging was announced on 29 April 2010. PMA only acquired its interest in Australia on 23 February 2011, 10 months after the government announced plain packaging.
2. Further or in the alternative, PMA's 'investment' needed to be 'admitted' by Australia subject to its foreign investment laws and policies. The burden of proof falls on PMA to prove that its investments were so admitted, a burden which it has not discharged.
3. Further or in the alternative, PMA's claim relies heavily on a series of treaties over which an arbitral tribunal could have no jurisdiction. The Treaty's article 2 (2) umbrella clause does not extend to obligations owed by Australia to other states under multilateral agreements. Even if it were correct (which it is not) that article 2 (2) could somehow be understood as extending the tribunal's jurisdiction to obligations Australia owes pursuant to other treaties, all of those treaties have their own dispute settlement mechanisms. It is not the function of the tribunal to establish a roving jurisdiction to make determinations that would potentially conflict with the determinations of the agreed dispute settlement bodies.

The court will deal with these jurisdictional arguments as a preliminary matter. If Australia prevails, the case brought by PMA will be dismissed. Bifurcation is beneficial to Australia because the case will be dealt with more expediently and the financial and other resources expended by the parties will be reduced if the case is decided in this first phase. The hearing of this first phase has been set down for three business days (and two additional days in reserve) from 16 February 2015 in Singapore.

7
Evaluating the impact of plain packaging

For different reasons, the Australian government, other governments around the world, and the Australian and international tobacco control communities, are intensely interested to know what impact plain packaging might have on the goals of the legislation, as are the tobacco industry and its supporters (see p53).

The Department of Health commissioned a team led by Professor Melanie Wakefield to conduct a suite of research projects evaluating the impact of the legislation on these goals. Wakefield is an international giant in tobacco control research. In 2012 she was voted by a panel of her international peers to receive the American Cancer Society's Luther L Terry Award for research in tobacco control. This is the field's peak global award for research excellence. Other winners have included the late Sir Richard Doll and Sir Richard Peto, both from Oxford University and authors of some of the most seminal 'big epidemiology' on smoking and health ever published. She has also served as a senior editor on a National Cancer Institute report on mass communication in tobacco control (355), and is an elected Fellow of the Australian Academy of Social Sciences.

The contract for research awarded to Wakefield's team is a confidential document. Other than the parties to the contract, the research questions and the ways that these are being approached are unknown to others. This confidentiality has no doubt been put in place because the tobacco industry has an intense interest in doing what it can to show the world that what Australia has done has 'not worked' and that other governments should therefore not go down the same track. If the industry knew full details of the nature, timing and study populations involved, there are almost certain to be actions that the companies could take to try to disrupt, confound and artificially influence the outcomes of some of these studies.

'Has it worked?'

The seemingly most obvious and basic question that is most frequently asked about what Australia has done with plain packaging is 'has it worked?' In the 20 months since the new packs began appearing in shops, we and our colleagues have both been asked this many question many times by Australian and international journalists, colleagues working in other fields, friends and students from all around the world doing assignments.

As will be discussed at length in this chapter, this apparently very obvious question invariably rests on a number of assumptions by the questioner about the objectives of plain packaging. These assumptions are about the timing, magnitude and causal attribution of changes in smoking (to uptake, cessation and total cigarettes smoked). What might seem like a very simple question rapidly emerges as being very complex as the often naïve assumptions beneath it are interrogated.

This complexity was fully appreciated by those responsible for drafting the plain packaging legislation and is reflected in the objectives contained in the legislation (see p53). The goal of Australia's comprehensive approach to tobacco control is to reduce tobacco use, exposure to tobacco smoke and diseases caused by it. When public health advocates and researchers think about a policy like plain packaging 'working', they do not think about a cartoon-like caricature of a smoker robotically responding in immediate Pavlovian hot-wired simplicity to a single policy. They think about how one ingredient like a price rise, a new health warning or campaign works over time in conjunction with all the others. Everyone working in tobacco control knows that the various elements of tobacco control policy and programs do not work in isolation from each other but in concert, with relationships that, to be best understood, need to be researched longitudinally over many years.

Proximal and distal factors influencing smoking

The decisions individuals make to not take up smoking or to stop smoking are sometimes made suddenly and sometimes unpredictably in response to specific stimuli named by those involved. These stimuli can include the onset of symptoms like coughing up blood or a coronary incident. Other common precipitating reasons for quitting include pregnancy, highly memorable and personally relevant pre-operative 'doctor's orders', a plea to quit from a loved one like a spouse or child, a sharp tax or price rise, perhaps taking the cost of a pack through a psychological barrier like $20 a pack, or the impact of a powerful new piece of information via an anti-smoking campaign. These sorts of immediate, sometimes quick-acting influences are called proximal factors, and have often been reported in research literature on smoking.

But the far more common natural history of someone not ever taking up smoking or finally deciding to quit reflects the confluence of many years of influences, both specific and general. Children and adolescents might grow up in nuclear and extended family environments where they never or rarely see a family member smoking. They may also have few friends who smoke. They may be exposed in classroom settings as well as via mass media to anti-smoking information. They may often see smokers huddling outside of buildings and think that being a smoker doesn't look much fun. If they are aged 22 or under in Australia today, they would have grown up never having seen tobacco advertising or a tobacco-sponsored sporting event, because these were all finally banned in 1992. They may have read that a pack a day smoker could spend more than $7000 a year on cigarettes, and count their blessings that they do not have to accommodate such an outlay. The chances are that they would be exposed to all or many of these influences.

Similarly, smokers who quit most commonly nominate a general 'concern about health' as the outstanding reason why they quit. This concern may have been nascent for many years, but became steadily amplified by emotions like regret, personal resentment at being addicted, concern about the expense of smoking and about not enjoying being a smoker in a society where smoking is exiled from every indoor public space, and from many private spaces like homes and cars. One day, often after a history of several failed attempts, many such smokers finally decide to quit. Every year, many thousands succeed in permanently stopping. Any attribution of this decision to just *one* of the preceding factors, or an account of why they quit which was blind to the complexity of the distal, life-course factors that have acted to finally get a smoker to a point where they decide to quit, would explain little.

Plain packaging might well function as a 'slow burn', distal negative factor against smoking, than as a precipitating proximal factor akin to those described above. Plain packaging removes a major positive influence on smoking: the ability of smokers to handle and display a richly semiotic connotative badge designed to reinforce a chosen sense of self or to be an accoutrement of personal style.

Accordingly, in setting the objectives of plain packaging, those who drafted the Australian legislation would have almost certainly reflected on the likely role that the removal of this final form of tobacco promotion would have in the overall mix of factors that together act negatively on smoking.

For this reason, the Australian government appropriately did not forecast any precise effect of plain packaging, but instead emphasised the longer-term focus (especially in relation to preventing uptake of smoking by children) and, through its National Tobacco Control Plan (356), its commitment to a comprehensive, long-term approach to reducing tobacco use.

The objectives in the legislation included 'discouraging' people from taking up smoking, 'encouraging' cessation, 'discouraging' relapse, reducing the appeal of tobacco and the ability of packaging to mislead, and increasing the effectiveness of health warnings. Each of these objectives embody what the Chantler report (76) calls 'intermediate' effects that lie in three broad areas: reductions in the appeal of smoking, increases in the salience of pack health warnings and increases in perceptions of harm from smoking.

Studies monitoring the possible role of plain packaging in achieving these intermediate goals could for example consider changes in:

- negative attitudes about smoking
- negative views about the desirability of smoking
- knowledge about harms of smoking
- intentions to not smoke
- increased effectiveness of health warnings.

For its part, the tobacco industry decided that acknowledging the sub-
tleties and complexities in all this would not be in its interests. Instead,
it opted to commission studies and frame data and expectations as
if plain packaging was a classic proximal variable. The test of the effectiveness of the policy was put succinctly by one of the industry's
leading acolytes, the English libertarian Chris Snowdon, who wrote that
nothing less than 'a sharp decline in smoking prevalence, particularly
underage smoking prevalence' (357) was the test of whether plain packs
worked. He did not define the magnitude of 'sharp', but the average annual fall in adult smoking prevalence over the past 30 years in Australia
has been just 0.5%. (358)

Critics of plain packaging played the game of demanding 'hard'
evidence that would unambiguously show the precise impact of the legislation, uncluttered by any other variable. The logical consequence of
this line of 'hard' argument was that nothing less than a randomised
controlled trial of the introduction of plain packaging which showed
that it reduced smoking prevalence in children would be satisfactory.

The Chantler report was brutally dismissive of such a demand:

I do not consider it to be possible or ethical to undertake such a
trial. To do so would require studies to be carried out within a suit-
ably large and isolated population free of known confounding factors
that influence smoking and prevalence. Such studies would expose
a randomised group of children to nicotine exposure and possible
addiction. Australia does not constitute that trial because a number
of things have happened together, including tax rises. Disentangling
and evaluating these will take years, not months.

I have been asked whether the evidence shows that it is likely
that there would be a public health impact. This is clearly not an issue
which is capable of scientific proof in the manner one might apply,
for example, to the efficacy of a new drug. There have been no double blind randomised controlled trials of standardised packaging and
none could conceivably be undertaken. The most direct experiment
to test the efficacy of standardised packaging might be to compare
the uptake of smoking in non-smoking children with cigarettes in
branded packaging and to see which group smoked more. But given
the highly addictive and harmful nature of smoking, such an experiment could, rightly, never receive ethical approval. In any case such

an experiment would need to be conducted over a long period and within a large population in which other variables were held constant. Indeed in Australia it will be difficult in due course to separate the effect of plain packaging from other factors such as changes in pack sizes introduced by the manufacturers, and price and tax increases.

Chantler concluded that the best evidence that could be in fact be obtained would be in the form of the 'intermediate outcomes'.

Having reviewed the findings of the Stirling Review and subsequent Research Update, and the detailed critiques made of them, I believe the evidence base for the proposed 'intermediate' outcomes is methodologically sound and, allowing for the fact that overall effect size cannot be calculated from it, is compelling about the likely direction of that effect. Taken together the studies and reviews based on them put forward evidence with a high degree of consistency across more than 50 studies of differing designs, undertaken in a range of countries. (76)

Industry claims about impact

Various tobacco industry statements and reports about the impact of the legislation began appearing from as little as five months after implementation and continue as we go to press. Almost uniformly, the spin put on these reports by the tobacco claimed that plain packaging had already been shown to be a failure.

Devastating to sales or zero impact?

In forecasting the impact of plain packs, the tobacco industry and its supporters seemed to be intent on imitating the mythical creature from Hugh Lofting's Dr Dolittle series, the pushmi-pullyu. This was the two-headed beast with two minds of its own. The beast would try to move in opposite directions at the same time. For example, the Alliance of Australian Retailers ran an industry-funded multimedia campaign asserting that plain packs 'would not work' (see pp97) – meaning they wouldn't reduce sales.

This was a refrain megaphoned at every opportunity. But it created a small problem for another central plank of the industry's case, where the other end of the pushmi-pullyu, the BAT-funded IPA, was warning that plain packaging would work like nothing in the entire history of tobacco control: it would reduce sales by up to an unprecedented 30% in the first year and by further 30% tranches in every year after that (see pp145). A back-of-an-envelope calculation shows that starting at annual consumption of 24,032 million cigarettes and cigarette equivalents[1] in 2010–11, and reducing this by 30% every year, by 2020, consumption would have fallen to just 969.4 million sticks – just 4% of the starting point. The IPA confidently predicted that the High Court would order the government to compensate the companies concerned for all of this massive loss.

But after being humiliated in the High Court, the industry quickly moved the pushmi-pullyu beast out of sight into a back paddock and put all its efforts into three main arguments: (1) the packs were not causing any reduction in sales; but (2) they were driving smokers downmarket to buy cheaper brands with lower profit margins for manufacturers and retailers, and (3) the illicit market was booming, all because of plain packaging.

Imperial Tobacco: market down by 2% to 3%

In April 2013, just five months after plain packaging implementation, Imperial Tobacco's global CEO, Alison Cooper, appeared on a video for the company's shareholders. (359) Cooper said: 'I should also mention Australia – we've had the first six months of the plain pack environment in Australia. We've seen the market decline roughly 2% to 3%, so maybe *not as bad as we might have anticipated.*' [our emphasis].

Coming from a tobacco company with access to its own sales data, and almost certainly high-level intelligence on that of its competitors, this was an important declaration about expected and actual changes to sales in the first months of the implementation. To get perspective on

---

1   See http://tiny.cc/huurox

this statement, we need to look at changes in consumption in Australia in the years before plain packs were introduced. In April 2010, on the same day that the government announced plain packaging would be introduced, it announced an immediate and unprecedented 25% increase in tobacco tax. A Treasury paper reported that while a fall in consumption of 6% had been predicted, the impact was nearly double that at 11%. (66) In the years between 2003 and 2009, the annual change in the number of cigarette equivalents dutied ranged from an increase of 2.3% to a fall of 2.5%. The average change was a decline of 1.1% per annum prior to the April 2010 tax increase. So a half year fall of 2–3% would appear to be at least double the rate of the average *annual* fall.

The Imperial CEO's carefully chosen rough '2–3%' fall, rather than precise estimate, might suggest that the fall was more toward the 3% end. If the fall had been more toward 2%, this would have been clearly worth stressing given the company's strenuous efforts to attack plain packs.

Another early example of the 'it's failing' performance came from Jeff Rogut, chief executive of the Australasian Association of Convenience Stores. Rogut spelled out the unfolding disaster to an English audience at a Philip Morris sponsored meeting in London in April 2012. He'd spoken to 'a number of retailers' to get 'some open and honest feedback on what's happened in the last five months'. Using this robust methodology, he told the audience that smokers were trading down:

> People are saying 'why should I pay $17 when I can pay $12 or $13? Nobody's going to judge me in terms of what brand I'm smoking – I might as well smoke the cheaper brand.

He explained that by paying cheaper prices *'actual unit sales are up. People are buying more cigarettes more frequently.'* But then a few sentences later he asked: 'Has it done anything to smoking rates or the tobacco sales? *Nothing at all. Our sales have been steady.* After five months there has been no noticeable reduction in people smoking or buying cigarettes. ' (360) [our emphasis]

So here we can presumably just take our pick: 'actual unit sales are up' or 'there has been no noticeable reduction in people smoking or buying cigarettes. . . nothing at all'. All with the benefit of the authoritative Mr Rogut having supplied no data on national smoking prevalence beyond his recollections of speaking to 'a number' of retailers and reporting this at a Philip Morris organised meeting in London.

London Economics report

In November 2013 a press release on 'one of the first comprehensive surveys of smoking prevalence since the introduction of plain packaging in Australia one year ago' was issued by a private UK consultancy, London Economics, sponsored by Philip Morris. It stated:

> Over the time frame of the analysis, the data does not demonstrate that there has been a change in smoking prevalence following the introduction of plain packaging despite an increase in the noticeability of the new health warnings.

The message was that the legislation was not working.

Within hours, Cancer Council Victoria produced a critique of the report, that would have seen any undergraduate researcher who had authored the nonsense it contained humiliated by the basic methodological flaw in the study and its serious lack of statistical power, to make the claims its authors made for it. The demolition is so complete, we publish it in full.

> This Philip Morris-funded survey has been conducted on the mistaken assumption that adult smoking prevalence ought to have markedly declined immediately following the introduction of plain packaging and refreshed larger graphic health warnings in Australia. No tobacco control intervention in history has ever achieved that. Unsurprisingly, this was therefore not the expectation of government or the public health community.
>
> Rather, the more proximal aims of the plain packaging legislation were to reduce appeal of packaging, especially for young people; increase the salience of health warnings; and reduce the ability of packaging to mislead consumers about the harmful effects of tobacco use. The legislation was introduced as one of a number of tobacco control strategies, including tobacco tax increases and mass media campaigns, to contribute to reducing overall smoking prevalence.

The most important methodological difference between this at- tempt to assess smoking prevalence and the approach used in the three-yearly government-funded survey called the National Drug Strategy Household Survey (NDSHS), is that the Philip Morris study failed to use a probability-based sampling approach. It is a basic tenet of population survey research that the most representative samples are those where every population member has an equal probability of being included in the survey.

Because the Philip Morris survey used an online panel to obtain responses from Australians and it used those responses to estimate prevalence, only Australians who are members of online market re- search panels could be included. While panel members comprise people of a wide range of demographic characteristics, these people opt-in to become members of an ongoing online panel for the pur- pose of taking part in many different surveys or studies and they earn rewards each time they participate. In this way, they are going to be different from a representative cross-section of the Australian population. The Philip Morris survey would likely have mixed to- gether several online panels to achieve these numbers. The survey used quota-sampling (that is, it required its sample to have a partic- ular mix of age, gender and regional characteristics), presumably to try to compensate for its non-probability-based sampling approach. However, quota-based sampling cannot ensure the survey is repre- sentative of the wider Australians population who are not members of online survey panels.

By comparison, the NDSHS uses a household sampling ap- proach, where all residential Australian private households are eli- gible for inclusion in the sample. The non-representative nature of internet panels in Australia is the most likely reason that the London Economics Philip Morris report estimates daily smoking prevalence (around 20% in each survey attempt) to be much higher than the far more representative NDSHS, when it recorded 17.4% daily smoking among 18+ year olds back in 2010.

The three attributes the report authors highlight to suggest it is a high quality survey (under 'quality assurance') are in fact or- dinary, basic elements of survey practice. However, this section is silent on the survey response rate achieved, which is another critical survey attribute – that is, out of all people approached to do the survey, what proportion responded. Since the survey did not use a probability-based sampling frame, it is unlikely to be a reliable reflection of Australian smoking prevalence (and its overestimated smoking prevalence figures show that in each of the surveys), but since it did not report survey response rates, readers cannot know if it is even a true reflection of Australian online panel members.

The relatively large numbers used in the survey and the use of questions consistent with those used in the NDSHS, cannot make up for the failure to use a probability-based sampling frame from which to select a sample in the first place, and the lack of information on survey response rate.

As noted at the outset, the aim of the legislation that introduced plain packaging with larger graphic health warnings was to weaken the appeal of smoking and strengthen knowledge of health effects: it did not involve any immediate call to action. Its effect is likely to be a longer-term one, enhancing the effects of campaigns and tax increases in discouraging youth smoking uptake and prompting quit attempts and thereby contributing to the decline in the prevalence of smoking over the longer term. But even if the aim had been to prompt an immediate drop in prevalence, the Philip Morris study was not sufficiently powered to find one.

While survey samples of around the 5000 mark are adequate to detect large changes in attitudes and behaviour, this number is nowhere near large enough to detect the very small changes in prevalence in any country that might be expected year to year. The NDSHS with a sample of 24,000 Australians is large enough to pick up declines in prevalence of smoking of 1% to 2%, the sorts of drops that might be feasible over a three-year period. To pick up a 0.5% decline in prevalence (a decline of the sort of magnitude that might be expected over a 12-month period) would require a sample size of over 90,000 respondents. The follow-up surveys of just over 5000 respondents used in the London Economics reports would be able to detect any decline in prevalence over a one-year period only if that decline were larger than 2% points – a drop in relative terms that would be unprecedented in tobacco control history.

Table 7.1: Sample sizes required to detect various declines in prevalence

At a starting daily prevalence of ...	... to detect, at alpha = 0.05 and power of 0.80, (two-sided test) a decline of ...			
	2.0%	1.5%	1.0%	0.5%
20%	6,039	10,844	24,641	99,519
17.5%	5,406	9,728	22,149	89,630

Source: http://www.stat.ubc.ca/~rollin/stats/ssize/b2.html

Governments are understandably eager for information about the impact of plain packaging. Well-designed studies on changes in attitudes and beliefs will be highly instructive. But given the likely mode of effect of this policy, it is likely to be many years before an impact on the decline in prevalence can be accurately assessed.

Never say die

On the day after the Chantler report (76) was released, BATA issued a press release (361) declaring:

> Since plain packaging was introduced, industry volumes had actually grown for the first time in over a decade while the decline in the number of people smoking had dropped by over half.
>
> From 2008 to 2012 smoking incidence, or the number of people smoking, was declining at an average rate of -3.3% a year. Since plain packaging was introduced, that decline rate slowed to -1.4%,' Mr McIntyre said. 'Over the five years in the lead-up to the introduction of plain packaging, total tobacco industry volumes were declining at an average rate of -4.1%.
>
> Subsequently, since plain packs were introduced on 1 December 2012, industry volumes have actually grown for the first time in a long time to +0.3%. 'Further, the number of cigarettes smoked on a daily basis declined at a rate of -1.9% in the five years leading up

to plain packaging, while it slowed to -1.4% after green packs hit shelves.

The long-term decline of people giving up smoking at a fairly consistent rate and also smoking less has changed for the worse.

So here was BATA, a company normally breathless with excitement in being able to report growth in market volume to its investors, reporting the trifecta of a bounce-back in growth (the first 'in a long time') a slowing in the decline in the number of cigarettes being smoked each day, and an apparent halt in smoking cessation and attributing this growth to the introduction of plain packs. Recipients of this press release were supposed to understand that BATA was *really unhappy* about all this renewed growth and that they would have preferred the pre-plain packs days when each of these basic indicators were heading south for the company.

BATA's press release was issued in spite of the Chantler report saying of their data on the alleged 0.3% growth in market volume:

This data is [sic] likely to be affected by transitional impacts. For example, retailers returned a significant quantity of tobacco stock in branded packaging during the first half of 2013 which was subsequently destroyed rather than smoked. Stockpiling in anticipation of pre-announced tax increases will also have affected the data.

Data on volumes at the final point of sale, which is less affected by these transitional impacts, shows consumption has fallen since the introduction of plain packaging. Cigarette sales in grocery stores fell by around 0.9% in 2013 according to the Retail World trade magazine. It is noteworthy that the population over 15 years of age increased by 1.5% in 2013.

Chantler's comments about old non-compliant stock being dumped or sent back to the manufacturers were supported by remarks made by Jeff Rogut in comments made to the same Philip Morris organised meeting in London in 2013 mentioned earlier. He told the meeting:

There was an enormous amount of work for retailers to clear out the old stock. Some stock was taken back and some retailers chose to dump the stock. So the small retailers were really acting as the implementers of government policy.

Implementers of government policy? Well, yes. That would be in the same way that dairy companies are 'implementers' of government policy on pasteurisation, and petrol companies on lead-free petrol policy. What a burdensome thing it is to be a retailer! Plain packaging was the fourth time since 1973 that Australian retailers had been required to change all tobacco stock over to packs with newly legislated health warnings. Any retailer who was unaware that it would be illegal to sell the old branded packs after 1 December 2012 would have had to have been in a deep coma. They had 12 months' high profile notice about the impending changeover. Rogut failed to note whether the supplying manufacturers were still off-loading their old stock to retailers too close to the date after which it would be illegal to sell it. And if retailers were silly enough to overstock the soon-to-be illegal fully branded packs, those in the meeting were presumably supposed to all agree that this was yet another catastrophe to be heaped on the towering plain packaging debacle.

Impact of plain packaging on children

Most analysts of the likely impact of plain packaging believe that its main impact will be on children over the next generations – the primary intent of the legislation as outlined from the outset by Nicola Roxon. Just as no Australian child aged born since 1992 has ever seen a local tobacco advertisement or tobacco-sponsored sporting event, no child growing up after December 2012 will ever see carcinogenic tobacco products packaged in carefully market researched attractive boxes. Smoking rates among youth today are the lowest ever recorded. Plain packs are expected to preserve and continue that downward momentum, starving the industry of new generations of new smokers as older smokers quit and die early.

Australia has been very successful in reducing smoking by children and young people aged under 18 years. Data from 2011 show that only 3.6% of 12–17 year olds are 'committed smokers' (ie. smoked on three or more days in past week), the lowest on record. (362) Moreover, total underage tobacco consumption by secondary school students was only just over 100 million cigarettes in 2011 (based on average reported weekly consumption of 17.16 cigarettes per week for the 44,683 children 12–15 years and 22.66 cigarettes per week for the 57,328 students aged 16 and 17 who were estimated to be smoking at least weekly). (362) This represents less than 0.5% of the total 22 billion cigarettes (manufactured cigarettes or equivalent roll-your-own cigarettes or cigars) that were subject to excise and customs duty in the same year. (363)

This context is critical for any discussion about what plain packaging might do to total demand for cigarettes among children, the main target of the policy, both now and into the future. Even if plain packaging was to cause an immediate fall in tobacco use of 5% (which would catapult the policy into the vanguard of proximally impactful strategies), the problems in being able to detect this effect using available or any conceivable data set are insurmountable.

It would not be possible to use customs and excise clearance data on apparent tobacco consumption to make claims about what proportion of any changes were attributable to changes in consumption by young smokers because those survey-based data are of course not matched in any way to customs and excise data on who is consuming the cigarettes released into the market by local manufacturers or importers. Instead estimates of the amount being consumed by different population segments are estimated by applying survey data extrapolations to total apparent consumption (customs and excise) data.

If we hypothesised that plain packs might cause what would be a remarkable and possibly unprecedented *additional* 5% (relative) decline in the proportion of under 18 year olds being committed smokers (smoking on three or more times per week) in a year after the introduction of plain packaging, we would need to conduct a before and after study capable of detecting a 5% shift from the current 3.6% down to 3.42%.

To detect with a significance level of 5% and a power of 80%, we would need to survey 164,087 children (364) in *each* of two separate surveys, before and after the introduction of plain packaging to detect such a difference. Such an undertaking is completely out of the ballpark of any study of smoking prevalence ever conducted in Australia. The national Australian Secondary Schools Alcohol and Drugs study of children's drug use (including smoking) samples just under 25,000 children nationally. (362)

University of Zurich report

In March 2014, the industry made yet another attempt to convince the world that plain packs had been a flop. This time, they focused on the impact on children via a Philip Morris-commissioned report from two researchers at the University of Zurich. (365). This report used 13 years of data on 14–17 year olds self-reported smoking included in monthly door-to-door cross-sectional surveys.

It is interesting to note here that Philip Morris has purchased data on youth smoking despite frequent public statements about its disinterest in the youth market. The report's authors concluded that there was no evidence of any impact on youth smoking prevalence for the 12 months from December 2012.

However, despite enthusing that their data were 'reliable cigarette market data', they also noted about the youth data that:

> Since the monthly sample sizes are rather small, ranging mostly between 200 and 350, and since the minors included in the sample change from month to month, it is expected that the monthly observed prevalence is rather unstable over time. This is indeed the case.

Again, Cancer Council Victoria quickly threw withering sunlight on this tobacco industry-commissioned report's many problems (366), commencing by noting:

> The report is seriously flawed conceptually. It is based on the straw man principle that plain packaging could be expected to immediately lead to a detectable reduction in adolescent smoking prevalence. No other tobacco control intervention has achieved that and neither is this the expectation of governments or credible researchers.

Many other problems were identified in the report.

The survey of adolescents was completed at home, when many parents would be present. This could lead to under-reporting of smoking.

and

The small monthly sample size prohibits any credible analysis of change over a short period of time. The authors describe the sample as being between 200 to 350 adolescents per month, (although they neglect to point out the sample size in the last several years has been reduced to closer to 200 per month). The authors' entire analysis is based on the fact that they have been able to fit a trend line to the measure of smoking over the 13-year period examined. This is not a test of plain packaging but a simple description of how much on average smoking prevalence has declined over the 13-year period. It would be truly concerning if any ongoing survey in Australia could not yield this basic descriptive parameter, since there has been such a large gradual decline smoking over this 13 year period due to the aforementioned ongoing tobacco control policies and program efforts. (366)

The day of reckoning

17 July 2014 is unlikely to be a date that the global tobacco industry will ever forget. At 1am Canberra time an embargo was lifted on a set of numbers that drove a stake deep into the heart of Big Tobacco's continuing best efforts to deny that plain tobacco packaging had made any impact on Australians' smoking.

The AIHW released the results of its latest national survey of drug, alcohol and tobacco use, involving 23,855 people. (194) These surveys have been conducted every three years since 1991, when 24.3% of Australians aged 14 and over smoked on a daily basis. In November 2013, this figure had almost halved to 12.8%. With another 3% smoking less than daily, Australia's 15.8% was now the lowest daily rate in the world, with Canada in second place with 16.2%. (367) Sweden is in world's first place on daily smoking (11%) but with another 10% smoking less than daily, its 21% total smoking rate (368) places it well behind Australia,

Canada, the USA and England (see Figure 7.1). Moreover, the percentage fall in Australia between 2010 and 2013 was a record 15.2%. The average percentage decline across the nine triennial surveys since 1991 had been 6.5%, with the previous biggest fall being 11%. (Figure 7.2)

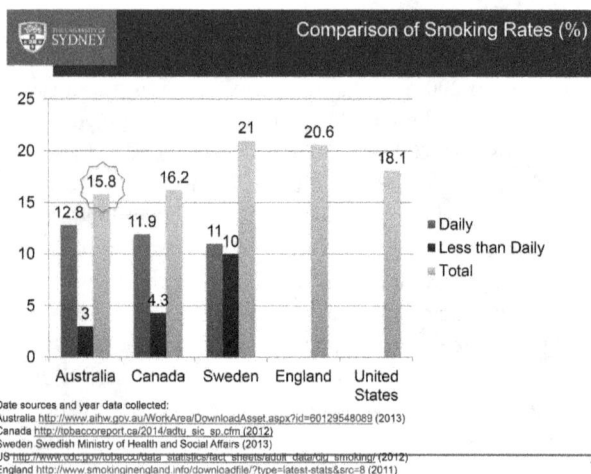

Figure 7.1 Smoking prevalence in Australia, Canada, USA, England and Sweden, latest available data

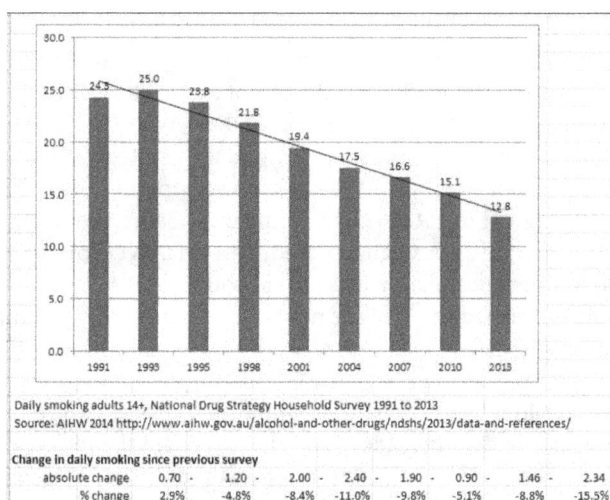

Daily smoking adults 14+, National Drug Strategy Household Survey 1991 to 2013
Source: AIHW 2014 http://www.aihw.gov.au/alcohol-and-other-drugs/ndshs/2013/data-and-references/

Change in daily smoking since previous survey								
absolute change	0.70 -	1.20 -	2.00 -	2.40 -	1.90 -	0.90 -	1.46 -	2.34
% change	2.9%	-4.8%	-8.4%	-11.0%	-9.8%	-5.1%	-8.8%	-15.5%

Figure 7.2 Daily smoking, adults 14+, Australia 1991–2013

Interest naturally centred on whether the fall could be attributed to the introduction of plain packaging. Other than the routine twice-yearly consumer price index (CPI) tax increases in each of 2011, 2012 and 2013, bans on point of sales retail displays, a continuation of anti-smoking campaigning throughout the period in question, and measures like smokefree restaurants and pubs that have been in place for many years, the elephant-in-the-room explanatory variable was the implementation of plain packaging in December 2012. Together with almost continuous national news diet of debate about the policy throughout much of the three years in question, no other policy or program presented as a plausible candidate.

In the weeks before this data bombshell exploded, the Murdoch-owned newspaper *The Australian* had run a major campaign involving three front page stories and whole pages led by IPA-affiliated journalists and contributors (369). They drew on internal tobacco industry data that was never made available for public scrutiny. This mystery data purported to claim a 0.3% *increase* in consumption following the introduction of plain packs. The treasury quietly released tobacco customs and excise data showing a fall of 3.4% in 2013 relative to 2012 when tobacco plain packaging was introduced. There had been a larger fall between 2010–2011, but that was an exceptional year which saw an un-precedented 25% increase in tobacco tax introduced at the beginning of May 2010. (66) The Australian Bureau of Statistics also released data on expenditure on tobacco for the December 2012 ($3.508b) and the March 2013 ($3.405b) quarters, showing that the introduction of plain packaging was followed by a 2.9% fall in consumption.

The timing of *The Australian*'s campaign coincided with a final consultation period in England preceding a final decision on a stated intention to introduce plain packs in that country.

17 July unleashed some of the most desperate straw-clutching from the industry and its blogosphere errand boys I have ever seen. Imperial Tobacco and Philip Morris opened the batting, claiming there was no change in the long-term downward trend. BAT issued a press release containing at least two lies. Like Imperial, they said the fall was 'in line with historical trends'. (370) It wasn't. It was the biggest percentage fall *ever* recorded since the surveys commenced. Next, they highlighted the impact of the 2010 tax rise. There had been a 25% tobacco tax increase in early May 2010, but the first five months impact of that rise coincided with the data collection period (29 April – 14 September 2010) for the *previous* AIHW survey, published in 2011.

Then they referred to the December 2013 12.5% tax rise as an in-fluence. But data collection for the 2011–2013 AIHW report occurred between 31 July 2013 and 1 December 2013, the day an extra 12.5% tobacco tax was introduced. It could therefore have not influenced the data showing the fall.

They also explained that the 12.8% prevalence figure was a fudge because it was only daily smokers. It didn't include 'casual' smokers, whom we were told would lift the true 'incidence figure' to 16.4%. (And note here that BAT apparently didn't know the basic difference be-tween incidence and prevalence.) But they couldn't even get that right. The AIHW data showed 12.8% daily, 1.4% weekly, and 1.6% less than weekly, making 15.8%. Pathetically, here was BAT desperate to claim as their own those who admit to smoking a cigarette once in a blue moon. Note that the prevalence of those who smoked at any frequency (daily, weekly and less than weekly) fell by 12.2% between 2010 and 2013, another record fall, while the average three-yearly declines over the previous 20 years was just 6.8%.

Then they whined that because the data included the 12–17 year age group (where only 3.4% smoked daily), this would have artificially deflated the 'true' figure. This ignores that the 14 years and over figure had been standard in every year since the surveys commenced in 1991, and that between the 2010 and 2013 surveys, smoking fell in every age group above 18 years.

However, a tiny ray of hope remained. A tobacco-loving English blogger noticed that in the 12–17 year age group (the principal target of plain packaging legislation) the percentage of daily smokers actually rose from 2.5% to 3.4%. The jubilant blogger took the trouble to construct a bold graph that emphasised this massive uplift. But he failed to tell his readers that for five of 10 data cells which made up the figures, the standard error was more than 50% ('too unreliable for general use') and another two cells with lower standard errors 'should be used with caution').

Citi, the global market investment advisors, were in no doubt about the meaning of the data, saying it provided 'the best data' to support the British government's imminent decision to legislate plain packs and that the data would 'substantially undermine' the tobacco industry's argument that there was no good evidence that plain packaging would achieve its stated aims. (371)

This is not likely to be the last round of denials from Big Tobacco. But their hollow denials of impact have now become little more than laugh-a-minute spectator sport.

'My cigarettes now taste lousy'

One night I had friends over to dinner and decanted a bottle of $15 Australian shiraz into an empty bottle of very expensive French Chateau Margaux that I'd been given as a gift. As I brought it to the table, I spoke about our friendship and how I wanted them to share this special wine. As people took their first careful sips, no one was rapturous, but all said the wine was truly wonderful and commented about its mouth feel, how easily it slid down the throat and how you could 'taste the French soil' in French wines. When I quickly revealed the hoax there was long conversation about many experiences with expectations priming experience.

Those studying placebo and nocebo effects in medicine are very fa-miliar with this phenomenon, as is the marketing industry. A study of the influence of pricing on perceptions of the taste of wine shows that my dinner experience was not a one-off example. (372) Those studied reported that a bottle of wine selling at $90 was experienced as more satisfying than exactly the same bottle where the subjects were told the price was $10.

But brain scans showed this phenomenon was not just people say-ing the $90 wine tasted better, their brain activity showed they really experienced it. Adam Ferrier, a psychologist working in advertising de-scribed it this way:

> The subjects' medial orbitofrontal cortex, an area of the brain strongly associated with experiencing pleasure, lit up like a Christ-mas tree when the subjects tasted the $90 bottle. This is despite, and this is the really interesting bit, the areas of the brain responsible for experiencing taste (the insula cortex, the ventroposterior medial nu-cleus of the thalamus, or the parabrachial nucleus of the pons) did not light up any differently between the tastes tests of the $10 v $90 bottle. Therefore, even though the taste part of the brain recorded no difference between the bottles, the pleasure part of the brain did. (373)

From 1 October 2012 it was illegal for old 'branded' packs to be man-ufactured in Australia, and for such branded packs to be imported. From this date until 1 December 2012, tobacco retailers could sell both branded and plain packs. Compliant plain packs began appearing in shops from early September and immediately reports began coming in. Shortly afterwards, a colleague dropped by my office and said she'd been to her hairdresser on the weekend and the woman in her 20s who had cut her hair, knowing she worked in health, had told her that she had finally decided to quit: she couldn't bear the thought of being seen with one of those ugly new packs.

Mike Daube similarly told us:

> So I stopped off at the local supermarket to buy a few plain packs and a young woman – she would have been about 20 – who didn't know me from a hole in the ground, behind the counter, opened the

shelves behind her, gave me some packs, pointed to them and said: 'That made me give up'. That was within days and I thought that's nice – we do the research, but it's actually nice to get that personal story.

Anecdotes like this may not be worth much in isolation, but when they move from a trickle to a stream, it's often a sign of things that will be validated in formal population-wide surveys down the track.

Soon after plain packs came on the market, I took three calls in the space of a week where the callers asked if there had been some sort of tobacco formula change that had accompanied the switch to plain packs. 'My usual brand tastes really different – far worse' was the drift of the comments. Other colleagues were getting these calls too, and they were also going to the office of the new health minister, Tanya Plibersek. She told the *New York Times:*

Of course there was no reformulation of the product. It was just that people being confronted with the ugly packaging made the psychological leap to disgusting taste ... the best short-term indication I have that it's working is the flood of calls we had in the days after the introduction of plain packaging accusing the government of changing the taste of cigarettes. (374)

This phenomenon was entirely expected. People in marketing have long understood that packaging can prime expectations. In first days after implementation of the legislation, Adam Ferrier wrote:

This experience has been found to relate to packaging and its contribution to taste in numerous studies, across numerous categories. Packaging strongly influences the taste of something as the brain is looking for cues to help create its story of tastiness (or not).

When tasting a cigarette, all advertising contributes to the taste of that cigarette. People used to see 'advertising' as the stuff that belonged on TV. However, marketers today know that every little thing they do is a form of promotion for the brand. Packaging, shelf wobblers, websites, the cars the sales team drive, the sales team – they are all marketing, and they are all forms of advertising. And of all of them, packaging is arguably the most important contributor to the brand for three reasons; (a) it's on 24-hours a day, (b) it's experienced at point of purchase, (c) it was completely under the marketers control. This was especially true for cigarette manufacturers who had other advertising levers pulled from them years ago.

Cigarette packaging – with its bright colours and symbols of freedom and power – was a cue that this product tasted nice. It made the cigarette more enjoyable. Now these images have been replaced with images of disease and an unpleasant olive green (itself a colour associated with sour taste). There are few cues left that suggest the product will 'taste' nice. Consumers will begin to taste, you guessed it, smoke!

If this is the hallmark of a nanny state, then as the son of a smoker who died of cancer way too young I happily say 'Goo goo ga ga. Keep looking after us.' (373)

8
The future

The global history of tobacco control is a history of vanguard nations taking what, at the time, seemed like bold, sometimes radical steps. These always attracted derision at the time from the tobacco industry, but sometimes also from the public, the media and politicians.

But there are many examples of pioneering initiatives first introduced by single nations or states then being adopted by large numbers of other nations in subsequent years. The most obvious examples are restrictions and bans on tobacco advertising, smokefree workplaces and public places like restaurants and bars, and most recently, graphic health warnings on packs. In the face of huge opposition from the tobacco industry, Canada was the first nation to introduce graphic health warnings in 2001. By October 2012, this had increased to 63 nations. (205)

Plain packaging is also a good candidate for the continuing history of domino effects because, as a regulatory measure, it is relatively inexpensive for governments to implement, as all packaging costs are borne by the tobacco industry. Government costs consist of any that may be involved in defending their plain packaging legislation and its implementation, and any surveillance costs post-implementation. Note that the High Court of Australia ordered that the tobacco companies bringing the case against plain packaging should pay all costs involved in the action.

Brand names – the last bastion

Plain packaging eviscerates, but does not drive a fatal stake through, the still-beating heart of tobacco industry marketing. The one big opportunity remaining for the industry to brand its deadly products with associations designed to distract its customers from their concerns about health remains with opportunities to name brands in beguiling new ways.

The Australian legislation is silent on any limitations on what companies can call their brands. Variant names are limited in being required to refer to (72):

> ... the name used to distinguish that kind of tobacco product from other tobacco products that are supplied under the same brand, business or company name, by reference to one or more of the following:
> (a) containing or not containing menthol;
> (b) being otherwise differently flavoured;
> (c) purporting to differ in strength;
> (d) having or not having filter tips or imitation cork tips;
> (e) being of different length or mass.

Here, the industry has considerable latitude to make claims about particular words like 'smooth' as referring to flavour, rather than to the characteristics of users. But when it comes to words used to name brands, the Act is an open door for introducing creative brand names. Already one company, Imperial Tobacco, introduced a new brand name to its *Peter Stuyvesant* brand. '*Peter Stuyvesant + Loosie*' (see Figure 8.1) was a gimmick innovation that provided one extra cigarette in a pack of 20s and thereby allowed the company to introduce a brand name change while flagging an apparent premium offer of an extra cigarette.

There would be nothing in the Act stopping the company introducing new variations on the core brand name by for example introducing variations like 'Peter Stuyvesant – Post Sex' or 'Peter Stuyvesant – Foreplay', using words from teenage argot ('Peter Stuyvesant – Totally Sick'), or in ways that would attract particular subcultures 'Peter Stuyvesant – Goths', political orientations 'Peter Stuyvesant – Liberals', sporting allusions 'Peter Stuyvesant – Gold Medals' and so on.

Figure 8.1 Imperial Tobacco's newly named brand 'Peter Stuyvesant + Loosie'.

Plain packaging beyond Australia

There has been great international interest in what Australia has done. Nicola Roxon told us:

> DFAT [the Department of Foreign Affairs and Trade], that often sticks very much to its foreign affairs diplomacy, . . . was a bit taken

aback how many requests in different countries they were getting for packets and information and advice on how it had happened, and most of that started post the High Court decision.

As we finish this book, some 20 months after Australia made it illegal to sell tobacco products in fully branded packs, three nations – New Zealand, Ireland and the United Kingdom – are well advanced in their parliamentary processes to introduce plain packaging. Another seven nations (Finland, Turkey, South Africa, Chile, Brazil, France and India) have made statements or have seen developments which portend implementation.

New Zealand

In April 2012 the New Zealand government agreed in principle to introduce plain packaging reforms that were in alignment with Australia's, pending the outcome of a public consultation process. The public consultation closed in October 2012 and Cabinet considered a report on the consultation in February 2013. The government decided to proceed with plain packaging legislation and a bill was lodged in the New Zealand parliament in December 2013.

The Smoke-free Environments (Tobacco Products and Packaging) Amendment Bill (375) had its first reading in the New Zealand parliament in February 2014. New Zealand associate health minister, Tariana Turia, introduced the bill by stating that 'when tobacco manufacturers push tobacco, they are not simply selling a stick of nicotine; they are selling status, social acceptance and adventure.' (376) The bill received overwhelming support with the exception of one dissenting MP from a minor conservative party.

Following the positive first reading results, the bill was referred to the Health Select Committee for public consultation. The committee received more than 17,000 written submissions, the bulk of which were made up of form letters and postcards solicited through a campaign organised by the three major tobacco companies operating in New Zealand. The committee held public hearings in April 2014 and is expected to provide a final report in August 2014. (377)

New Zealand prime minister John Key has repeatedly stated that the bill will not be sent to the governor general for royal assent until the WTO challenges against the Australian plain pack laws are settled.

United Kingdom

In April 2014, the Chantler report on plain packaging concluded that plain packaging would assist in reducing smoking by young people in particular. The British minister for public health, Jane Ellison commended the report in the House of Commons, saying:

> In light of this report and the responses to the previous consultation in 2012, I am therefore currently minded to proceed with introducing regulations to provide for standardised packaging. I intend to publish the draft regulations, so that it is crystal clear what is intended, alongside a final, short consultation, in which I will ask, in particular, for views on anything new since the last full public consultation that is relevant to a final decision on this policy. I will announce the details about the content and timing of that very shortly, but would invite those with an interest to start considering any responses they might wish to make now. The House will understand that I want to move forward as swiftly as possible. (378)

The UK has seen intense advocacy for plain packs since 2008. We are grateful to ASH UK for providing the timeline below on how the UK arrived at the ministerial statement of intent cited above. We set it out in detail below to give readers a sense of the time and various stages that are involved from an initial proposal through to the time when legislation is introduced. Throughout this protracted process the tobacco industry seeks to delay and defeat every step.

Table 8.1: Plain packs in the United Kingdom

31 May 2008	The UK Labour government (Labour) consults on a new strategy for tobacco control, including plain packaging. (379)
30 October 2008	ASH (UK) publishes *Beyond smoking kills* to mark the 10th anniversary of the white paper *Smoking kills* and set an agenda for action for the decade to come. (380) The report recommends plain packaging and is endorsed by 100 health organisations including Cancer Research UK and the British Heart Foundation.
25 June 2009	An amendment on standard packaging is tabled to the Health Bill by backbenchers in the Lords and the Commons.
1 February 2010	UK government launches a new tobacco strategy, *A smokefree future: a tobacco control plan for England*, which includes the possible introduction of standardised packaging. (381) There is opposition within government so a commitment to proceed is not possible, but says 'The government believes that the evidence base regarding "plain packaging" needs to be carefully examined. Therefore, the government will encourage research to further our understanding of the links between packaging and consumption, especially by young people. The government will also seek views on, and give weight to, the legal implications of restrictions on packaging for intellectual property rights and freedom of trade.' BAT says that the government will face a 'huge fight' from the tobacco industry if it moves ahead with the plans. Imperial Tobacco calls the proposal a 'counterfeiter's charter'.
6 May 2010	New coalition government (led by Conservative Party) formed following UK general election.
24 September 2010	The European Commission launches a public consultation;on a proposal to revise Directive 2001/37/EC which covers health warnings, limits on toxic constituents, etc., for tobacco products. The

	consultation includes a proposal for plain packaging.
20 November 2010	Following meeting with Australian health minister Nicola Roxon at an international health ministers event, UK health secretary, Andrew Lansley, announces he is investigating the viability of introducing standardised packaging, saying: 'It's wrong that children are being attracted to smoke by glitzy designs on packets.' (382)
30 November 2010	Publication of *Healthy lives, healthy people*, a public health white paper stating that the government will consider forcing tobacco companies to adopt plain packaging to reduce the attraction of smoking and the number of young people taking up smoking.
1 December 2010	European Union launches a public consultation on the introduction of plain packaging in its revised tobacco products directive.
9 March 2011	UK government publishes *Healthy lives, healthy people: a tobacco control plan for England* in which it commits itself to consult within the year on putting tobacco products in plain packaging.
17 January 2012	*Plain packs protect* campaign, spearheaded by Smokefree SouthWest, is launched.
13 April 2012	The UK government launches a public consultation which seeks people's views on whether or not standardised packaging should be adopted, or whether a different option should be considered.
17 April 2012	Northern Ireland health minister gives his support to standard packs.
15 May 2012	The Tobacco Retailers' Alliance launches anti-plain packaging postcard campaign.
1 June 2012	Pro-smoking activists threaten and harass health campaigners, reports *The Guardian*. (383)

15 June 2012	Packaging companies form a group to fight the UK government's proposals for plain packaging of tobacco products. The nameless group includes Weidenhammer Packaging Group, Payne, Parkside Flexibles Group, Chesapeake and the API Group.
18 June 2012	Following lobbying from the Tobacco Retailers' Alliance, the consultation documents are made available in Urdu, Gujarati and Tamil and the closing date for the consultation is extended.
20 June 2012	Philip Morris releases reports alleging the systematic review of the evidence is flawed and plain packaging will make counterfeiting easier.
3 July 2012	The Tobacco Retailers Alliance delivers 2,500 *No to plain packs* postcards signed by staff in independent shops across the UK to the department of health.
6 July 2012	JTI launches £2m advertising campaign against standardised packaging.
19 July 2012	Unite The Union claims plain packaging would 'inevitably' lead to 25% job losses in the print industry.
4 August 2012	The National Federation of Retail Newsagents asks its 16,000 members to sign a petition against standard packs.
8 August 2012	FOREST presents a 235,000-strong petition in opposition to plain packaging to the government.
10 August 2012	End of UK consultation.
20 September 2012	Department of health director of promotion announces that South Africa is exploring cigarette plain packaging and will issue a report on its feasibility by the end of this year.

28 September 2012	JTI launches second phase of campaign against plain packaging in the UK.
23 November 2012	A report by Luk Joossens, commissioned by Cancer Research UK, finds that, contrary to industry claims, standardised packs are unlikely to cause extra counterfeiting.
7 February 2013	Ian Paisley Jr MP delivers an open letter signed by 73 fellow MPs who oppose standardised packaging to health secretary Jeremy Hunt.
14 February 2013	Launch of the Smokefree Action Coalition's *The clock is ticking* campaign to lobby MPs, and marking six months since the end of the consultation.
5 March 2013	*The Guardian* reports that the government is planning to legislate for plain cigarette packaging within the year. The next day, a spokesman for the prime minister denies the news, stating that 'no decisions have yet been taken'.
13 March 2013	The Advertising Standards Authority rules that adverts against standard packs run by Japan Tobacco's Gallaher last year were 'misleading'.
15 March 2013	The Scottish Liberal Democrats give full support to standardised packaging after passing a motion of confidence in support of legislation at their conference.
27 March 2013	Scottish public health minister announces the Scottish government's support for standard packaging.
8 April 2013	JTI rolls out phase three of its anti-plain packaging campaign.
17 April 2013	Responding to a question in parliament on standardised packaging, health minister says that the government is currently taking a 'careful look' at all the evidence submitted as part of the department of health's public consultation.

19 April 2013	Public health minister Anna Soubry says she is 'persuaded' by the evidence on standardised packaging.
3 May 2013	News that UK government is to abandon standard packaging plans surfaces among accusations that the chief Tory strategist, Australian Lynton Crosby, is behind the move due to his links with the tobacco industry. (384) It subsequently emerges that his firm, Crosby Textor, is in the pay of Philip Morris.
8 May 2013	On the morning of the Queen's Speech, which sets out the government's legislative agenda, the health secretary says that no decision has been made regarding standard packs, adding that 'just because something is not in the Queen's Speech, doesn't mean the government cannot bring it forward as law.'
28 May 2013	The Irish government announces its intention to ban cigarette pack branding.
21 July 2013	A summary report on the consultation is published, together with a written ministerial statement, in which the secretary of state for health says that the government 'has decided to wait until the emerging impact of the decision in Australia can be measured before we make a final decision on this policy in England'. (385)
18 November 2013	A cross-party group of peers tables an amendment to the Children and Families Bill to introduce standardised tobacco packaging at report stage. This is a crucial step, as the government knew that the amendment was likely to pass in the Lords and may well pass in the Commons.
28 November 2013	Facing possible defeat in the House of Lords over the amendment, the government announces it will introduce its own amendment to the Children and Families Bill to give the secretary of state for health the power to introduce standardised packaging through regulations, while at the same time launching a review of the public health evidence

headed up by eminent paediatrician, Sir Cyril Chantler. The amendment passed without dissent in the Lords.

10 February 2014	Amendments to the Children and Families Bill are passed in the Commons 453 for and 24 against – this is a whipped vote but this is a government which has faced significant rebellions and only a tiny minority voted against. (386) The opponents, in forcing a vote, have been very helpful in clarifying the level of support. Standardised packaging covers the whole of the UK.
13 March 2014	The Children and Families Bill becomes law after receiving royal assent.
3 April 2014	Paediatrician Sir Cyril Chantler publishes his report in which he concludes that standardised packaging would have a positive impact on public health.
27 June 2014	Draft regulations on standardised packaging published for public consulation.
7 August 2014	Closing date for submissions.

Ireland

In May 2013 the Irish government, under the leadership of health minister Dr James Reilly, announced it was planning new regulations on tobacco plain packaging, with a planned implementation date in 2014. Reilly is an unwavering advocate of plain packaging of tobacco products, and has stated he his prepared for a legal challenge from the tobacco industry. (387) The tobacco industry and its allies have perpetuated the same myths as they did in Australia that the reforms violate intellectual property law, will lead to increased smuggling and won't reduce smoking.

In April 2014, the Irish Health Committee presented its report on plain packaging. The recommendations cover almost identical ground to that covered by the Australian legislation. (388) Specific to plain packaging reforms, the report also recommends: (389)

- the standardisation of the size of tobacco packaging
- the inner packaging of tobacco products to be the same colour as the outside surface
- a separate and distinct definition for brand, company and business name so as to prevent tobacco manufacturers from promoting brand variants to the status of brands
- the maximum length/number of characters in brand and variant names.

The bill passed the second stage of its passage through the Irish Senate (Seanad) in June 2014 (390). It seems possible that Ireland may be the second nation after Australia to implement plain packaging.

Early developments in other nations

Since the Australian plain packaging bill passed into law, I have undertaken three WHO multi-country consultancies focused exclusively on plain packaging. One was held in Brunei Durassalam in January 2012, where representatives from 11 nations were present, including several nations not from the south-east Asian region. Another was in Ankara, Turkey, in September 2012, where some 42 nations from the European and Eastern Mediterranean region were present. A third was held in Noumea, New Caledonia, in March 2013, where government representatives from all Pacific island nations attended a South Pacific Commission meeting. A pan-African meeting has also been held in Capetown, South Africa.

Brunei Darussalam, which has very strong tobacco control, is known to have plain packaging under active consideration and has a leader with extreme wealth who would not be disturbed by legal threats.

There is intense interest in India about plain packaging. (295) A national meeting was held on the issue in 2012, with a report published in June 2012. In September 2013, a special session on the issue was included in the Tobacco Endgame Conference in New Delhi, and Indian legal scholars have begun publishing papers on the concept. (391) Indian MP Baijayant 'Jay' Panda introduced a private member's bill on plain packaging in December 2012, but it did not progress.

In July 2014 the High Court of Uttar Pradesh, after being petitioned by an NGO, recommended that the government of India introduce plain packaging. (392)

There is some momentum in France toward plain packing with a report, in May 2014, that the health minister Marisol Touraine would introduce a bill in June for plain packaging. In late September Touraine announced that the policy would be implemented from the beginning of 2016. (393)

South Africa's health minister Aaron Motsoaledi announced in July 2014 that his nation planned to introduce plain packs from 2015 and was unlikely to wait for the decision of the WTO case with Australia. (394) Turkey also announced at the same time that it would rapidly progress the introduction of the measure from the start of 2015. (395) Chile's Senate Health Committee endorsed a comprehensive set of tobacco control proposals in July 2014, which included plain packaging.

Finland's action plan for tobacco control includes a plain packaging proposal. (396) Brazil's Anvisa, the country's equivalent of the US Food and Drug Administration, announced in June 2014 that it would be recommending plain packaging. Anvisa was the agency responsible for Brazil's globally historic ban on all tobacco flavourings, so it has a track record of getting tobacco legislation implemented.

So as of August 2014, nine nations besides Australia have either introduced legislation, are on the cusp of it or have announced their intentions to do so. The global plain pack domino spectacle looks to have commenced.

As we have seen, the tobacco industry has already shown its interest in using international trade treaties to attempt to stop domestic tobacco control policies and legislation that threaten its interests. Fooks and Gilmore (397) have recently reviewed efforts by Philip Morris International to influence the United States Trade Representative to use the multinational TPP for such a purpose. There is virtually no transparency about how the TPP is being negotiated, and other than leaked drafts, no formal access to what has been already decided. Their paper concludes:

[Philip Morris International's] formal request to the [United States Trade Representative] that the TPP be used to extend IP rights, harmonise the process of regulatory formation, and provide a comprehensive system of ISDS [Investor-State Dispute Settlement] reflects the contents of leaked drafts of the TPP agreement. These suggest the TPP will extend IP protection to trademark use, strengthen corporate influence in regulatory formation and provide tobacco companies with extensive powers to litigate against governments directly. Although the extension of IP protection is subject to exceptions for measures aimed at promoting public health, the precise scope of these exceptions is unclear. Consequently, all three measures are likely to increase the tobacco industry's policy influence and to deter governments from introducing plain packaging, albeit in different ways.

First, by increasing litigation risk for legislating states, the extension of IP protection to trademark use will increase tobacco companies' power to present the costs associated with plain packaging and other policies affecting pack design as prohibitively expensive.

Likewise, proposals such as regulatory review, stakeholder consultation and the use of impact assessments provide the industry with a range of tools to access and feed information into health policymaking. Combined with the TPP's proposal for states to provide access to 'supporting documentation' relating to regulatory measures, analyses and data, which may exacerbate existing information asymmetries between states and multinational corporations, these reforms are likely to facilitate challenges to regulatory innovation under international law. By underpinning these measures with ISDS, which increases the economic costs associated with litigation and institutionally embeds uncertainty in treaty interpretation, the TPP provides a powerful new toolbox for the industry in preventing the introduction of plain packaging and other innovative health measures.

Finally, the lack of transparency in the TPP negotiations illustrates the limitations inherent in the state-centric nature of article 5.3 of the WHO FCTC. Article 5.3 aims to limit tobacco industry involvement in health policy by, among other things, requiring parties to the convention to make interactions between the tobacco industry and public officials as transparent as possible. The USA is a non-party to the convention and is, therefore, under no obligation to make public any involvement of tobacco companies, either directly or through third parties, in TPP policymaking. This enables the tobacco industry to undermine APEC [Asia-Pacific Economic Cooperation] states' efforts to implement article 5.3 and influence health policy remotely through TPP negotiations.

There has been considerable expression of concern about whether the TPP could be used to thwart other nations covered by the TPP from doing what Australia has on plain packaging, and even whether the current government might be persuaded to sacrifice Australia's plain packaging laws on the altar of its wider concerns to see the TPP adopted.

Encouragingly here, Australia's trade minister Andrew Robb has twice gone out of his way to emphasise that the Australian government's negotiations in the TPP would not see plain packaging somehow sacrificed to the wider terms of the treaty being developed. In a strongly worded letter to *The Age* newspaper he wrote:

> Australia is a world leader in tobacco control. It is incorrect for an 'observer' at the recent Trans-Pacific Partnership talks in Singapore to suggest Australia is blocking the right of other TPP parties to follow Australia's lead. My primary focus in the TPP is to advance Australia's national interest, not compromise it. The Australian government has made it clear it will not accept an outcome that undermines our right to regulate for public health, including on tobacco control. Under existing international trade obligations, Australia has the right to implement tobacco control measures, such as plain packaging for tobacco products, in the interests of public health. Australia is very happy to consider any proposal in the TPP that confirms this right. Ultimately, Australia will only sign up to a TPP deal that includes appropriate safeguards for public health. (398)

And again later he was reported in the *Financial Review*, saying: 'The plain packaging measure was introduced by the previous government from a legitimate public health standpoint.' (399)

In January 2014, the British retail trade publication *The Grocer* reported that Imperial Tobacco's chief in Australia, Melvin Ruigrok, was moving to the UK to help his company 'gear up for an escalation in the fight against plain packaging'. The article reported an Imperial spokesman explaining that: 'Melvin brings with him first-hand experience, having successfully led Australia through display bans and plain pack legislation, experience that will be essential as the UK market works through these very same regulatory pressure.' (400)

'Successfully led Australia through . . . plain pack legislation' . . . In the film *Monty Python and the Holy Grail*, there's a famous scene where King Arthur fights the Black Knight (see https://www.youtube.com/watch?v=ikssfUhAlgg). Quickly losing two arms, the Black Knight considers the loss 'only a flesh wound'. Down two arms and a leg, he declares he's invincible. When King Arthur lops off his other leg, the Knight says 'right, we'll call it a draw'. Stan Shatenstein, a long-time analyst of tobacco control argues that, like the Black Knight, the industry's complete Australian humiliation is already being spun as a 'success' because so far, no other country has yet implemented plain packaging.

The history of tobacco control is a history of global dominoes tumbling first slowly, but then very, very quickly. As this book goes to press, there is keen interest to see whether Ireland or the United Kingdom becomes the second nation to legislate on plain packaging. Australia, in being the first nation has hopefully unleashed a virulent, high contagious and deadly agent that should cause immense damage to the tobacco industry over the next decades. In 1985 Hugh Cullman, vice chairman of Philip Morris Companies Inc told an international tobacco industry meeting in Denmark: 'As one of our Australian colleagues puts it, a sneeze in one country today cause international pneumonia tomorrow!' (401)

Let us hope that plain packaging becomes as highly contagious as all other platforms of comprehensive tobacco control have over the past three to four decades, and that it proves to be highly resistant to any 'treatments' with which the global tobacco industry tries to dowse it.

References

1. Doll R, Hill AB. Smoking and carcinoma of the lung; preliminary report. Br Med J. 1950;2 (4682):739–48.
2. Wynder EL, Graham EA. Tobacco smoking as a possible etiologic factor in bronchiogenic carcinoma; a study of 684 proved cases. J Am Med Assoc. 1950;143 (4):329–36.
3. The Cancer Council Australia. The price of tobacco products in Australia. Table 13.3.2. 2014. Available from: http://www.tobaccoinaustralia.org.au/chapter-13-taxation/ 13-3-the-price-of-tobacco-products-in-australia.
4. Durkin S, Brennan E, Wakefield M. Mass media campaigns to promote smoking cessation among adults: an integrative review. Tobacco Control. 2012;21 (2):127–38.
5. King B, Borland R. What was "light" and "mild" is now "smooth" and "fine": new labelling of Australian cigarettes. Tobacco Control. 2005;14 (3):214–5.
6. Chapman S, Carter SM. "Avoid health warnings on all tobacco products for just as long as we can": a history of Australian

tobacco industry efforts to avoid, delay and dilute health warnings on cigarettes. Tobacco Control. 2003;12 (Suppl 3):iii13–22.

7. Commonwealth of Australia. Official Commmittee Hansard. House of Representatives. Standing Committee on Health and Ageing. Tobacco Plain Packaging Bill 2011, Trade Marks Amendment (Tobacco Plain Packaging) Bill 2011. 2011. Available from: http://tiny.cc/fzxrox.

8. Webb WH (Philip Morris). Status of the Marlboro Development Programme. 7 Dec 1984. Available from: http://legacy.library.ucsf.edu/tid/gmr98e00.

9. Ochsner A. Bronchogenic carcinoma: a largely preventable lesion assuming epidemic proportions. Chest. 1971;59:358–9.

10. Proctor RN. Tobacco and the global lung cancer epidemic. Nature Reviews Cancer. 2001;1 (1):82–6.

11. Djordjevic MV, Stellman SD, Zang E. Doses of nicotine and lung carcinogens delivered to cigarette smokers. J Natl Cancer Inst. 2000;92 (2):106–11.

12. National Cancer Institute USA. Harms of smoking and health benefits of quitting. 1 Dec 2011. Available from: http://www.cancer.gov/cancertopics/factsheet/Tobacco/Cessation.

13. Doll R, Peto R, Boreham J, Sutherland I. Mortality in relation to smoking: 50 years' observations on male British doctors. BMJ. 2004;328 (7455):1519.

14. Shatenstein S, Chapman S. The banality of tobacco deaths. Tobacco Control. 2002;11 (1):1–2.

15. Chapman S, Wong WL, Smith W. Self-exempting beliefs about smoking and health: differences between smokers and ex-smokers. Am J Public Health. 1993;83 (2):215–9.

16. Oakes W, Chapman S, Borland R, Balmford J, Trotter L. "Bulletproof skeptics in life's jungle": which self-exempting beliefs

about smoking most predict lack of progression towards quitting? Preventive Medicine. 2004;39 (4):776–82.

17. Cancer Research UK. Oral Cancer Risk Factors. Tobacco. Smoking. 2013. Available from: http://tiny.cc/rxxrox.

18. Cancer Australia. What is head and neck cancer? Incidence and mortality. 2014. Available from: http://canceraustralia.gov.au/ affected-cancer/cancer-types/head-neck-cancers.

19. Australian Medical Assoociation. Doctor delivers $1.2 billion blow to tobacco – and counting. Australian Medicine. 2014. Available from: http://tiny.cc/shyrox.

20. Tully R. Plain Packs History. 1994. Available from: http://legacy.library.ucsf.edu/tid/jxd28a99.

21. Sweanor DT. Effective beats dramatic: a commentary on Australia's plain packaging of cigarettes. Drug Alcohol Rev. 2011;30 (6):683–4.

22. Centre for Behavioural Research in Cancer. Health warnings and contents labelling on tobacco products. Review, research and recommendations prepared for the Ministerial Council on Drug Strategy Tobacco Task Force on tobacco health warnings and contents labelling in Australia. Melbourne: Centre for Behavioural Research in Cancer, Anti-Cancer Council of Victoria, 1992.

23. Beede P, Lawson R. The effect of plain packages on the perception of cigarette health warnings. Public Health. 1992;106 (4):315–22.

24. Carr-Gregg M. Mandatory plain packaging for tobacco products. World Health Forum. 1992;13 (2–3):204–5.

25. Carr-Gregg MR, Gray AJ. "Generic" packaging--a possible solution to the marketing of tobacco to young people. Med J Aust. 1990;153 (11–12):685–6.

26. Beede P, Lawson R. Brand image attraction: the promotional impact of cigarette packaging. NZ Fam Physician. 1991;18:175–7.

27. Goldberg M, Kindra G, Lefebvre J, Tribu L, Liefeld J, Madill-Marshall J. When packages can't speak: possible impacts of plain and generic packaging of tobacco products. Legacy Tobacco Documents, University of California, San Francisco; 1995. Available from: http://legacy.library.ucsf.edu/tid/rce50d00.

28. Goldberg ME, Liefeld J, Madill J, Vredenburg H. The effect of plain packaging on response to health warnings. Am J Public Health. 1999;89 (9):1434–5.

29. Laugesen M. Tobacco promotion through product packaging. Toxic Substances Board (New Zealand). 1989. Available from: http://legacy.library.ucsf.edu/tid/uqs48a99/.

30. Durston B, Jamrozik K, editors. Conference Resolutions. Seventh World Conference on Tobacco and Health; 1990; Perth.

31. British American Tobacco. Generic Packaging Meeting 22/9/93: Reference Documents. 22 Sept 1993. Available from: http://legacy.library.ucsf.edu/tid/msq47a99/.

32. Riordan M. Message. Private and confidential. Sydney: WD & HO Wills; 26 April 1994. Available from: http://tiny.cc/pnyrox.

33. Philip Morris. PMI corporate affairs weekly highlights by region. 3 Jan 1994. Available from: http://tiny.cc/gf2rox.

34. Harvey A. Doctors' plan to put cigarettes in plain packs fails. 24 July 1995. Available from: http://tiny.cc/ii2rox.

35. Australian Government. Government response to the Report of the Senate Community Reference Committee. The Tobacco Industry and the Costs of Tobacco-related Illness. 1997. Available from: http://legacy.library.ucsf.edu/tid/jer01d00/pdf.

36. Voon T, Mitchell AD, Liberman J, Ayres G, editors. Public health and the plain packaging of cigarettes. Legal issues. Cheltenham, UK: Edward Elgar; 2012.

37. Kelton MH, Jr., Givel MS. Public policy implications of tobacco industry smuggling through Native American reservations into Canada. Int J Health Serv. 2008;38 (3):471–87.

38. Luik J, editor. Plain Packaging and the Marketing of Cigarettes. Oxfordshire: Admap Publications; 1998.

39. Physicians for Smoke-Free Canada. Packaging Phoney Intellectual Property Claims. 2009. Available from: http://tiny.cc/yp2rox.

40. Physicians for Smoke-free Canada. The plot against plain packaging. 2008. Available from: http://www.smoke-free.ca/pdf_1/ plotagainstplainpackaging-apr1%27.pdf.

41. Cunningham R, Kyle K. The case for plain packaging. Tobacco Control. 1995;4 (1):80–6.

42. Wakefield M, Letcher T. My pack is cuter than your pack. Tobacco Control. 2002;11 (2):154–6.

43. Wakefield M, Morley C, Horan JK, Cummings KM. The cigarette pack as image: new evidence from tobacco industry documents. Tobacco Control. 2002;11 (Suppl 1):I73–80.

44. McGrady B. TRIPS and trademarks: the case of tobacco. World Trade Review. 2004;3 (1):53–82.

45. World Health Organization. Third session of the Conference of the Parties to the WHO FCTC. Geneva: WHO. Available from: http://www.who.int/fctc/cop/sessions/third_session_cop/en/.

46. World Health Organization. Guidelines for implementation of Article 11 of the WHO Framework Convention on Tobacco Control (Packaging and labelling of tobacco products) 2011. Available from: http://tiny.cc/zr5rox.

47. World Health Organization. Guidelines for implementation of Article 13 of the WHO Framework Convention on Tobacco Control (Tobacco advertising, promotion and sponsorship) 2008. Available from: http://www.who.int/fctc/guidelines/article_13.pdf.

48. Cancer Research UK. Briefing: tobacco packaging and labelling. 2005. Available from: http://tiny.cc/5t5rox.

49. Freeman B, Gartner C, Hall W, Chapman S. Forecasting future tobacco control policy: where to next? Aust N Z J Public Health. 2010;34 (5):447–50.

50. Chapman S, Freeman B. Regulating the tobacco retail environment: beyond reducing sales to minors. Tobacco Control. 2009;18 (6):496–501.

51. Gartner CE, Barendregt JJ, Hall WD. Multiple genetic tests for susceptibility to smoking do not outperform simple family history. Addiction. 2009;104 (1):118–26.

52. Gartner CE, Hall WD, Chapman S, Freeman B. Should the health community promote smokeless tobacco (snus) as a harm reduction measure? PLoS Med. 2007;4 (7):e185.

53. Chapman S. The case for a smoker's license. PLoS Med. 2012;9 (11):e1001342.

54. Freeman B, Chapman S, Rimmer M. The case for the plain packaging of tobacco products. 2007. Available from: http://www.acosh.org/resources/GenericPackaging.pdf.

55. Scottish Government. Scotland's Future Is Smoke-Free: A Smoking Prevention Action Plan. May 2008. Available from: http://www.scotland.gov.uk/Resource/Doc/223415/0060163.pdf.

56. UK Department of Health. Consultation on the future of tobacco control. 31 May 2008. Available from: http://tiny.cc/bx5rox.

57. Baker J, Hayes L. Approval for plain packaging of cigarettes and plain cigarettes, recall of the Alliance of Australian Retailers advertising campaign, and approval for an increase in Graphic Health Warning size. Melbourne: Centre for Behavioural Research in Cancer, Cancer Council Victoria, 2011.

58. Morgan Stanley Research Europe. Tobacco: Late to the Party. London: Morgan Stanley Research; 2007.

59. Rossel S. "Little hope in appealing to natural justice." TJI interview with Adam Spielman. 2 Sept 2008. Available from: http://tiny.cc/ 0z5rox.

60. Spielman A. Anti-tobacco plans for England should not upset investors. London: Citi; 1 Feb 2010.

61. Hedley D. Legisation against the tobacco industry. Euromonitor. 17 Nov 2010. Available from: http://tiny.cc/l85rox.

62. Pierce JP, Dwyer T, Frape G, Chapman S, Chamberlain A, Burke N. Evaluation of the Sydney" Quit. For Life" anti-smoking campaign. Part 1. Achievement of intermediate goals. Med J Aust. 1986;144 (7):341–4.

63. Cancer Council Western Australia. The progress of tobacco control in Western Australia: achievements, challengesand hopes for the future. Perth: Cancer Council Western Australia; 2008. Available from: http://www.cancerwa.asn.au/resources/ 2009-OrderForm-Progress-of-tobacco-control-in-WA.pdf.

64. Farouque F. A straight shooter. The Age. 13 Apr 2012. Available from: http://tiny.cc/8d6rox.

65. Connors E. Where there's smoke. Australian Financial Review. 29 Jul 2011. Available from: http://tiny.cc/1h6rox.

66. Commonwealth of Australia. The Treasury. Post implementation review: 25 per cent tobacco excise increase. Feb 2013. Available from: http://tiny.cc/4j6rox.

67. Freeman B, Chapman S, Rimmer M. The case for the plain packaging of tobacco products. Addiction. 2008;103 (4):580–90.

68. National Preventative Health Taskforce. Australia: the healthiest country by 2020. A discussion paper. 2008. Available from: http://tiny.cc/cl6rox.

69. National Preventative Health Taskforce. Submissions received. 2009. Available from: http://tiny.cc/tn6rox.

70. Lateline ABC-TV (Australia). Cigarette packaging decision may set world standard: expert. Australian Broadcasting Corporation. 10 June 2009. Available from: http://www.abc.net.au/lateline/content/2008/s2594912.htm.

71. Associated Press. Aussies crackdown on cigarette packaging. 2010. Available from: http://www.youtube.com/watch?v=-5UB2jSpN8o.

72. Australian Government. Tobacco Plain Packaging Act 2011. 2011. Available from: http://www.comlaw.gov.au/Details/C2011A00148

73. Australian Government. Department of Health. Health warnings. 2012. Available from: http://www.health.gov.au/internet/main/publishing.nsf/content/tobacco-warn.

74. Commonwealth of Australia. Tobacco Advertising Prohibition Act 1992. Commonwealth Consolidated Acts; 1992. Available from: http://www.austlii.edu.au/au/legis/cth/consol_act/tapa1992314/.

75. WHO Framework Convention on Tobacco Control Convention Secretariat. Parties to the WHO Framework Convention on Tobacco Control. 2013. Available from: http://www.who.int/fctc/signatories_parties/en/.

76. Chantler C. Standardised packaging of tobacco. Report of the independent review undertaken by Sir Cyril Chantler. April 2014. Available from: http://www.kcl.ac.uk/health/10035-TSO-2901853-Chantler-Review-ACCESSIBLE.PDF.

77. Australian Government Department of Prime Minister and Cabinet. Transcript of joint doorstop Commonwealth Parliamentary Offices Sydney. 29 April 2010. Available from: http://pmtranscripts.dpmc.gov.au/browse.php?did=17256.

78. Australian Government Department of Health and Ageing. Consultation Paper. Tobacco Plain Packaging Bill 2011 Exposure Draft. 2011. Available from: http://tiny.cc/2vfqox.

79. GfK bluemoon. Market research to determine effective plain packaging of tobacco products. 2011. Available from: http://tiny.cc/do8rox.

80. Stark J. Seeing red over olive ciggie packs. The Age (Melbourne). 8 May 2011. Available from: http://www.theage.com.au/national/seeing-red-over-olive-ciggie-packs-20110507-1edg1.html.

81. Underwood RL. The communicative power of product packaging: creating brand identity via lived and mediated experience. Journal of Marketing Theory & Practice. 2003;11 (1):62.

82. Underwood RL, Ozanne J. Is your package an effective communicator? A normative framework for increasing the communicative competence of packaging. Journal of Marketing Communication. 1998;4:207–20.

83. Palmer A. The Product. Principles of Marketing. Oxford: Oxford University Press/Books; 2000. p. 215–38.

84. Lambat I. Top dogs. What it takes to enter into the league of global bestsellers – and how to remain there. Tobacco Reporter. 2007 (February):40–4.

85. CNN Money. 10 most valuable global brands. 2013. Available from: http://tiny.cc/fu8rox.

86. Krugman DM, Quinn WH, Sung Y, Morrison M. Understanding the role of cigarette promotion and youth smoking in a changing marketing environment. Journal of health communication. 2005;10 (3):261–78.

87. Wen CP, Chen T, Tsai YY, Tsai SP, Chung WS, Cheng TY, et al. Are marketing campaigns in Taiwan by foreign tobacco companies targeting young smokers? Tobacco Control. 2005;14 (Suppl 1):i38–44.

88. Assunta M, Chapman S. Industry sponsored youth smoking prevention programme in Malaysia: a case study in duplicity. Tobacco Control. 2004;13 Suppl 2:ii37–42.

89. Carter SM. From legitimate consumers to public relations pawns: the tobacco industry and young Australians. Tobacco Control. 2003;12 Suppl 3:iii71–8.

90. Chaloupka FJ, Cummings KM, Morley CP, Horan JK. Tax, price and cigarette smoking: evidence from the tobacco documents and implications for tobacco company marketing strategies. Tobacco Control. 2002;11 Suppl 1:I62–72.

91. Cummings KM, Morley CP, Horan JK, Steger C, Leavell NR. Marketing to America's youth: evidence from corporate documents. Tobacco Control. 2002;11 (Suppl 1):I5–17.

92. Pollay RW. Targeting youth and concerned smokers: evidence from Canadian tobacco industry documents. Tobacco Control. 2000;9 (2):136–47.

93. Perry CL. The tobacco industry and underage youth smoking: tobacco industry documents from the Minnesota litigation. Archives of Pediatrics & Adolescent Medicine. 1999;153 (9):935–41.

94. Anon. Opportunities in packaging innovation. Philip Morris; 1992. Available from: http://legacy.library.ucsf.edu/tid/hwe36e00.

95. British American Tobacco. The vanishing media. 1979. Available from: http://tobaccodocuments.org/health_canada/03300624.pdf.

96. Scheffels J. A difference that makes a difference: young adult smokers' accounts of cigarette brands and package design. Tobacco Control. 2008;17 (2):118–22.

97. Weeks C. Tobacco marketers get more creative as restrictions grow. Ottawa Citizen. 13 Nov 2006.

98. Conjuring pack appeal. World Tobacco. 2004 (200):35–40.

99. Accu-pac provides extra pack. World Tobacco. 2005 (208):55.

100. Cork A. A matter of image. World Tobacco. 2004 (203):2.

101. Eindhoven G. Elegant packs promote image, defend property rights. World Tobacco. 1999 (170):16–8.

102. Rommel C. The final warning. World Tobacco. 2006 (210):16–8.

103. Health Canada Tobacco Control Programme. A Proposal to Regulate the Display and Promotion of Tobacco and Tobacco-Related Products at Retail. Ottawa: Health Canada, 2006.

104. Philip Morris Limited. Marketing new products in a restrictive environment. Philip Morris international meeting, Naples, Florida. 1990. Available from: http://legacy.library.ucsf.edu/tid/yhs55e00/pdf

105. Hedley D. Packaging, the last chance marketing saloon. 2010. Available from: http://www.tobaccojournal.com/Packaging_the_last_chance_marketing_saloon.49910.0.html.

106. Anon. Leveraging good looks and novelty value. Tobacco Journal International. 2009. Available from: http://www.tobaccojournal.com/Leveraging_good_looks_and_novelty_value.49604.0.html.

107. Pollay RW. Export "A" ads are extremely expert, eh? Tobacco Control. 2001;10 (1):71–4.

108. Henningfield JE, Benowitz NL, Slade J, Houston TP, Davis RM, Deitchman SD. Reducing the addictiveness of cigarettes. Tobacco Control. 1998;7 (3):281–93.

109. Barbeau EM, Leavy-Sperounis A, Balbach ED. Smoking, social class, and gender: what can public health learn from the tobacco industry about disparities in smoking? Tobacco Control. 2004;13 (2):115–20.

110. Poland BD, Cohen JE, Ashley MJ, Adlaf E, Ferrence R, Pederson LL, et al. Heterogeneity among smokers and non-smokers in attitudes and behaviour regarding smoking and smoking restrictions. Tobacco Control. 2000;9 (4):364–71.

111. Ferraro R, Bettman J, Chartrand TL. The power of strangers: The effect of incidental consumer brand encounters on brand choice. Journal of Consumer Research. 2009;35:729–41.

112. Rootman I, Flay B. A study on youth smoking: plain packaging, health warnings, event marketing and price reductions. Toronto: University of Toronto, University of Illinois at Chicago, York University, Ontario, Tobacco Research Unit, Addiction Research Foundation, 1995.

113. Hoek J. An evaluation of regulatory responses governing the use of tobacco descriptors. New Zealand: Massey University, 2006.

114. Cavalcante TM. Labelling and packaging in Brazil. World Health Organisation, (no year).

115. Brown and Williamson Tobacco Corporation. Untitled (Speech notes of a Brown and Williamson employee.) Media release. San Francisco: Legacy Tobacco Documents Library University of California; 1985. Available from: http://legacy.library.ucsf.edu/tid/knn70f00.

116. Cetron MJ WB. The future of the tobacco industries: tobacco and confectinary marketing and distribution (Volume 1). Forecasting International Ltd. 20 May 1985. Available from: http://legacy.library.ucsf.edu/tid/ckd65e00/pdf.

117. Trachtenberg JA. Here's one tough cowboy. Forbes. 1987;139 (108).

118. Anthony S. Analysing Australia's cigarette packaging regulations. 2010. Available from: http://tiny.cc/7b9rox.

119. KOOL new look. World Tobacco. 2002 (188):6.

120. Joy R. Brand identity becomes brand experience. World Tobacco. 2001 (184):10.

121. Joy R. Packs will carry the message. World Tobacco. 2003 (197):61–2.

122. Mawditt N. Putting pack opportunities into the frame. World Tobacco. 2006 (212):36–7.

123. Anon. A new level in foil. World Tobacco. 2006 (215):82.

124. Simpson D. Hong Kong: Marlboro tries it on (the pack). Tobacco Control. 2002;11 (3):171.

125. Slade J. The pack as advertisement. Tobacco Control. 1997;6:169–70.

126. Zimmel S. Graphic expansion of pack printing. World Tobacco. 2003;194:39.

127. Blum A. Cigarette cards-irony in propaganda. Tobacco Control. 1995;1995 (2):117–18.

128. Chapman S. Australia: British American tobacco "addresses" youth smoking. Tobacco Control. 2007;16 (1):2–3.

129. Anon. Cigarette split pack defeated. The Daily Telegraph. 2006.

130. Hammond D. Canada: a new angle on packs. Tobacco Control. 2006;15 (3):150.

131. Tobacco Journal International. Barezzi Award goes to Imperial Canada. 2006. Available from: http://tiny.cc/sd9rox.

132. Bennets J. Protest over smoke tin. The Press. 2006.

133. KT&G releases new cigarettes. 14 Dec 2006. Available from: http://www.djtimes.co.kr/news/articleView.html?idxno=28832.

134. Jung JM, Kellaris JJ. Cross-national differences in proneness to scarcity effects: The moderating roles of familiarity, uncertainty avoidance, and need for cognitive closure. Psychology and Marketing. 2004;21 (9):739–53.

135. Wayne K. An eye for packaging design. World Tobacco. 2006 (212):35.

136. Beirne M. RJR Gets Over the 'Hump' With Camel No. 9 for Women. Brandweek. 2007;48 (7):6.

137. Yahoo! Answers. Camel No. 9 cigarettes? 2007. Available from: http://tiny.cc/qh9rox.

138. Lucky. Smoking and straightening. 2007. Available from: http://web.archive.org/web/20070215123222/ http://lucky.vox.com/.

139. Freeman B, Chapman S. Open source marketing: Camel cigarette brand marketing in the "Web 2.0" world. Tobacco Control. 2009;18 (3):212–7.

140. Moodie C, Hastings GB. Making the pack the hero, tobacco industry response to marketing restrictions in the UK: findings from a long-term audit. International Journal of Mental Health and Addiction. 2011;9 (1):24–38.

141. Ford A, Moodie C, Hastings G. The role of packaging for consumer products: understanding the move towards 'plain' tobacco packaging. Addiction Research and Theory. 2012;20 (4):339–47.

142. Moodie C, Hastings G. Tobacco packaging as promotion. Tobacco Control. 2010;19 (2):168–70.

143. Ford A. The packaging of tobacco products. Stirling: Centre for Tobacco Control Research; 2012. Available from: http://tiny.cc/ s99rox.

144. Hammond D. Plain packaging regulations for tobacco products: the impact of standardizing the color and design of cigarette packs. Salud Publica Mex. 2010;52 (Suppl. 2):226–32.

145. Beede P, Lawson R, Shephard M. The promotional impact of cigarette packaging: a study of adolescent responses to cigarette plain-packs. Launceston, Australia: University of Otago, 1990.

146. Centre for Health Promotion. Effects of plain packaging on the image of tobacco products among youth. Toronto: University of Toronto, 1993.

147. Madill-Marshall J, Goldberg M, Gorn G. Two experiments assessing the visual and semantic images associated with current and plain cigarette packaging. Advertising and Consumer Research. 1996;23 (267–8).

148. Northrup D, Pollard J. Plain packaging and other tobacco issues: a survey of grade 7 and grade 9 Ontario students. Institute for Social Research Newsletter; 1995. Available from: http://tiny.cc/icasox.

149. RBJ Health Management Associates. Impact of plain packaging of tobacco on youth perceptions and behaviour. Report of study 1. Toronto, Ontario, Canada: RBJ Health Management Associates, 1993.

150. Hammond D, Parkinson C. The impact of cigarette package design on perceptions of risk. Journal of Public Health (Oxford). 2009;31 (3):345–53.

151. Doxey J, Hammond D. Deadly in pink: the impact of cigarette packaging among young women. Tobacco Control. 2011;20 (5):353–60.

152. Hammond D, Doxey J, Daniel S, Bansal-Travers M. Impact of female-oriented cigarette packaging in the United States. Nicotine Tobacco Research. 2011;13 (7):579–88.

153. Donovan R. Smokers' and non-smokers' reactions to standard packaging of cigarettes. Perth, Australia: University of Western Australia. 1993.

154. Wakefield M, Germain D, Durkin S. How does increasingly plainer cigarette packaging influence adult smokers' perceptions about brand image? An experimental study. Tobacco Control. 2008;17 (6):416–21.

155. Germain D, Wakefield MA, Durkin SJ. Adolescents' perceptions of cigarette brand image: does plain packaging make a difference? Journal of Adolescent Health. 2009;46 (4):385–92.

156. Wakefield M, Germain D, Durkin S, Hammond D, Goldberg M, Borland R. Effects of increasing size of health warnings on plain vs branded packs. Society for Research in Nicotine and Tobacco 17th Annual Meeting. 2011. Available from: http://www.srnt.org/conferences/past/index.cfm.

157. Hammond D, Dockrell M, Arnott D, Lee A, McNeill A. Cigarette pack design and perceptions of risk among UK adults and youth. Eur J Public Health. 2009;19 (6):631–7.

158. Hoek J, Wong C, Gendall P, Louviere J, Cong K. Effects of dissuasive packaging on young adult smokers. Tobacco Control. 2011;20:183–8.

159. Mutti S, Hammond D, Borland R, Cummings MK, O'Connor RJ, Fong GT. Beyond light and mild: cigarette brand descriptors and perceptions of risk in the International Tobacco Control (ITC) Four Country Survey. Addiction. 2011;106 (6):1166–75.

160. Centre for Behavioural Research in Cancer. Paper 13: Adolescents' reactions to cigarette packs modified to increase extent and impact of health warnings. Health warnings and product labelling on tobacco products. Melbourne: Anti-Cancer Council of Victoria; 1992.

161. Hammond D, Fong G, Borland R, Cummings KM, McNeill A, Driezen P. Text and graphic warnings on cigarette packages: findings from the international tobacco control four country study. American Journal of Preventive Medicine. 2007;32 (3):202–9.

162. Pollay RW, Dewhirst T. A Premiere example of the illusion of harm reduction cigarettes in the 1990s. Tobacco Control. 2003;12 (3):322–32.

163. Hammond D. Standardized packaging of tobacco products: evidence review. Irish Department of Health. 2014. Available from: http://health.gov.ie/blog/publications/ standardised-packaging-d-hammond/.

164. Freeman B. Tobacco plain packaging legislation: a content analysis of commentary posted on Australian online news. Tobacco Control. 2011;20 (5):361–6.

165. Ling PM, Glantz SA. Tobacco industry research on smoking cessation. Recapturing young adults and other recent quitters. J Gen Intern Med. 2004;19 (5 Pt 1):419–26.

166. Hopkinson N. Tobacco lobbyist gives the game away – branded tobacco packaging is more appealing to children. Twitter. @COPdoc. 2014. Available from: https://twitter.com/COPDdoc/ status/449564125056622593/photo/1.

167. Cornford FM. Microcosmographica Academica. London: Bowes and Bowes; 1908.

168. Smith GCS, Pell JP. Parachute use to prevent death and major trauma related to gravitational challenge: systematic review of randomised controlled trials. BMJ. 2003;327 (7429):1459–61.

169. Gittins R. Under fire, big tobacco rolls out the poor little stupid nation argument. Sydney Morning Herald. 30 May 2011. Available from: http://tiny.cc/g9asox.

170. Quit Victoria, Cancer Council Victoria. Plain packaging of tobacco products: a review of the evidence. 2011. Available from: http://www.cancervic.org.au/downloads/mini_sites/Plain-facts/ TCUCCVEvOverview_FINALAUG122011.pdf.

171. Hammond D. Tobacco labelling and packaging toolkit. A guide to FCTC Article 11. 2009. Available from: http://www.tobaccolabels.ca/toolkit/.

172. Moodie C, Stead M, Bauld L, McNeill A, et al. Plain tobacco packaging: a systematic review. 2011. Available from: http://tiny.cc/nhbsox.

173. Heydari G, Tafti SF, Telischi F, Joossens L, Hosseini M, Masjedi M, et al. Prevalence of smuggled and foreign cigarette use in Tehran, 2009. Tobacco Control. 2010;19 (5):380–2.

174. Tobacco Tactics. Will O'Reilly. 17 Mar 2014. Available from: http://www.tobaccotactics.org/index.php/ Will_O%E2%80%99Reilly.

175. O'Reilly W. Smuggling will be easier. Wigan Today. 9 Dec 2013. Available from: http://www.wigantoday.net/news/letters/ smuggling-will-be-easier-1-6304350.

176. PricewaterhouseCoopers. Research report on the illegal tobacco market. Document tabled as part of a formal submission (no. 46) made by British American Tobacco Australia in relation to the Inquiry into Tobacco Smoking in New South Wales in 2006. 2005. Available from: http://tiny.cc/eobsox.

177. PricewaterhouseCoopers. Illegal tobacco trade: costing Australia millions. Strategies to curb the supply and use of illegal tobacco products. Report prepared for British American Tobacco Australia (BATA). 2007. Available from: http://tiny.cc/8wbsox.

178. PricewaterhouseCoopers. Australia's illegal tobacco market: counting the cost of Australia's black market. February 2010. Available from: http://tiny.cc/5ybsox.

179. Deloitte. Illicit trade of tobacco in Australia. 2011. Available from:http://www.bata.com.au/group/sites/bat_7wykg8.nsf/vwPagesWebLive/DO7WZEX6/$FILE/medMD8EHAKD.pdf?openelement.

180. Deloitte. Illicit trade of tobacco in Australia: an update 2011. June 2011.

181. Deloitte. Illicit tobacco trade atlas. 2011. Available from: http://www.illegaltobacco.com.au/.

182. Deloitte. Illicit trade of tobacco in Australia: report for 2011. May 2012. Available from: http://www.bata.com.au/group/sites/bat_7wykg8.nsf/vwPagesWebLive/DO8RG8JK/$FILE/medMD8TWTX9.pdf?openelement.

183. Deloitte. Illicit trade of tobacco in Australia:Update for 2012: a report prepared for British American Tobacco Australia Limited, Philip Morris Limited and Imperial Tobacco Australia Limited. Dec 2012. Available from: http://www.bata.com.au/group/sites/bat_7wykg8.nsf/vwPagesWebLive/DO9879X3/$FILE/medMD99T566.pdf?openelement.

184. KPMG. Illicit tobacco in Australia. 2013 Half Year Report. October 2013. Available from: http://www.ecta.org/IMG/pdf/kpmg_report_on_illicit_trade_australia_4_nov_2013.pdf.

185. KPMG. Illicit tobacco in Australia. 2013 full year report. 2014. Available from: http://tiny.cc/z1bsox.

186. Commonwealth of Australia. Tobacco Plain Packaging Bill 2011, Trade Marks Amendment (Tobacco Plain Packaging) Bill 2011. Available from: http://tiny.cc/f6csox.

187. Australian Institute of Health and Welfare (AIHW). 2010 National Drug Strategy Household Survey report. Tobacco smoking-related behaviours. 2011. Available from: http://www.aihw.gov.au/WorkArea/ DownloadAsset.aspx?id=10737421314.

188. Quit Victoria. A critique: Illicit trade of tobacco in Australia: Report for 2011: a report prepared for British American Tobacco Australia Limited, Philip Morris Limited and Imperial Tobacco Australia Limited, May 2012. 2012. Available from: http://www.cancervic.org.au/downloads/mini_sites/Plain-facts/ CritiqueDeloitte_May_2012_Update_-_Public_copy.pdf

189. Quit Victoria. Cancer Council Victoria. Analysis of KPMG LLP report on use of illicit tobacco in Australia. March 2014. Available from: http://www.cancervic.org.au/downloads/mini_sites/ Plain-facts/analysis-kpmg-llp-report-illicit-tobacco-aust-2013.pdf.

190. Siahpush M, Heller G, Singh G. Lower levels of occupation, income and education are strongly associated with a longer smoking duration: multivariate results from the 2001 Australian National Drug Strategy Survey. Public Health. 2005;119 (12):1105–10.

191. Transparency International. Corruption perceptions index 2013. 2013. Available from: http://www.transparency.org/cpi2013/ results.

192. Morgan Stanley Europe. Imperial Tobacco. London: Morgan Stanley; 2 Feb 2010.

193. Chenoweth N. Tobacco companies' $2.2b payday. Australian Financial Review. 2 Jul 2014. Available from: http://tiny.cc/q8csox.

194. Australian Institute of Health and Welfare. National Drugs Strategy Household Surveys (NDSHS). Highlights from the 2013

survey. Canberra: AIHW; 17 Jul 2014. Available from:
http://www.aihw.gov.au/alcohol-and-other-drugs/ndshs/.

195. Zacher M, Bayly M, Brennan E, Dono J, Miller C, Durkin S, et al.
Personal tobacco pack display before and after the introduction of
plain packaging with larger pictorial health warnings in Australia:
an observational study of outdoor cafe strips. Addiction. 2014;109
(4):653–62.

196. Chapman S. One hundred and fifty ways the nanny state is good
for us. The Conversation. 1 Jul 2013. Available from:
https://theconversation.com/
one-hundred-and-fifty-ways-the-nanny-state-is-good-for-us-15587.

197. Deloitte. Alliance of Australian Retailers. Potential impact on
retailers from the introduction of plain tobacco packaging. Feb
2011. Available from: https://www.australianretailers.com.au/
downloads/pdf/deloitte/2011_01_31_AAR_Plain_Packaging2.pdf.

198. Alliance of Australian Retailers. Submission to Department of
Health and Ageing. 6 Jun 2011. Available from:
http://webarchive.nla.gov.au/gov/20140211231857/
http://www.yourhealth.gov.au/internet/yourhealth/publishing.nsf/
Content/plainpack-tobacco-subs-a.

199. Deloitte Australia. Alliance of Australian Retailers. Plain
packaging and channel shift. June 2011. Available from:
http://web.archive.org/web/20140308205854/
https://www.australianretailers.com.au/downloads/pdf/deloitte/
Potential_impact_of_channel_shift.pdf.

200. Hawke A. Adjournment – taxation speeches. Alex Hawke MP
website. 5 Jul 2011. Available from: http://www.alexhawke.com.au/
content/5711-adjournment-taxation.

201. Australian Retailers' Association. Retailers facing duplication of tobacco laws – State display bans make plain packaging pointless. 7 Apr 2011. Available from: http://tiny.cc/zgdsox.

202. Wakefield M, Bayly M, Scollo M. Product retrieval time in small tobacco retail outlets before and after the Australian plain packaging policy: real-world study. Tobacco Control. 2013;23 (1):70–6.

203. Chapman S. Plain cigarette packs: how long does it take to find in shop? 2012. Available from: http://tiny.cc/yttrox.

204. Metherell M. Alcohol industry upset over link to plain pack ads. Sydney Morning Herald. 29 Jun 2011.

205. Canadian Cancer Society. Cigarette Package Health Warnings. 2012. Available from: http://global.tobaccofreekids.org/files/pdfs/en/WL_status_report_en.pdf.

206. Parascandola M. Lessons from the history of tobacco harm reduction: The National Cancer Institute's Smoking and Health Program and the "less hazardous cigarette". Nicotine Tobacco Research. 2005;7 (5):779–89.

207. Merritt C. The law blows Our Bill's cover. Weekend Australian. 28 Jul 2012.

208. Snowdon C. You really didn't see this coming. Velvet Glove, Iron First. 20 Dec 2012. Available from: http://velvetgloveironfist.blogspot.com.au/2012/12/you-really-didnt-see-this-coming.html.

209. International Tobacco Control Policy Evaluation Project. FCTC Article 11Tobacco Warning Labels. Evidence and Recommendations from the ITC project. 2009. Available from: http://www.itcproject.org/files/ITC_Tobacco_Labels_Bro_V3.pdf.

210. Glantz SA, Slade J, Bero LA, Hanauer P, Barnes DE, editors. The Cigarette Papers. California, US: University of California Press; 1998.

211. Wikipedia. Tobacco Master Settlement Agreement. 2014. Available from: http://en.wikipedia.org/wiki/Tobacco_Master_Settlement_Agreement.

212. Philip Morris Corporate Affairs Department. Australia: smoking and health strategy some recent developments in Australia. February 1978. Available from: http://legacy.library.ucsf.edu/tid/loh24e00/pdf.

213. Benson S. Coles pulls out of pro-cigarette campaign. Daily Telegraph (Sydney). 11 Aug 2010. Available from: http://www.dailytelegraph.com.au/archive/news/coles-pulls-out-of-pro-cigarette-campaign/story-e6frez7r-1225903660384.

214. Benson S. Woolies pulls plug over ads. The Daily Telegraph (Sydney). 13 Aug 2010. Available from: http://www.dailytelegraph.com.au/woolies-pulls-plug-over-ads/story-fn5zm695-1225904675110.

215. Buchanan M, McKenny L. Unlikely alliance. Sydney Morning Herald. 5 Aug 2010. Available from: http://tiny.cc/mmdsox.

216. Anon. Small stores hit by tobacco laws. Northern Territory News. 9 Mar 2011.

217. Lateline ABC-TV (Australia). The tobacco files. 10 Sept 2010. Available from: http://www.abc.net.au/lateline/content/2010/s3008987.htm.

218. Lateline ABC-TV (Australia). Big Tobacco slammed over ads. Australian Broadcasting Corporation. 11 Aug 2010. Available from: http://www.abc.net.au/lateline/content/2010/s2980489.htm.

219. Nico J. Cigarettes in plain packets "unfair". Midland Reporter (Australia). 15 March 2011. Available from: http://midland.inmycommunity.com.au/news-and-views/ local-news/Cigarettes-in-plain-packets-unfair/7586161/.

220. Carter SM. Cooperation and control: the Tobacco Institute of Australia. Tobacco Control. 2003;12 Suppl 3:iii54–60.

221. Carter SM, Chapman S. Smoking, disease, and obdurate denial: the Australian tobacco industry in the 1980s. Tobacco Control. 2003;12 Suppl 3:iii23–30.

222. Evans H. Big tobacco in denial. Pressure Point. ABC TV. 1984. Available from: https://www.youtube.com/ watch?v=__XpbLUOJxM.

223. Cadzow J. Hi ho hi ho it's off to work we go. Sydney Morning Herald (Good Weekend). 27 Sept 2008.

224. British American Tobacco. Campaign questions expensive plain packaging experiment. Media release. 2011. Available from: http://www.bata.com.au/group/sites/bat_7wykg8.nsf/ vwPagesWebLive/DO7WZEX6/$FILE/ medMD8GX5XH.pdf?openelement.

225. Johnson S. British American Tobacco boss David Crow tells children not to smoke. Herald Sun (Melbourne). 20 May 2011. Available from: http://tiny.cc/rrptox.

226. Carlton M. Tobacco claim all smoke and mirrors. Sydney Morning Herald. 21 May 2011. Available from: http://www.smh.com.au/federal-politics/political-opinion/ tobacco-claim-all-smoke-and-mirrors-20110520-1ewn2.html.

227. Australian Government. Department of Health and Ageing. Public consultation on the exposure draft of the Tobacco Plain Packaging Bill 2011: Summary of submissions. 2012. Available from: http://webarchive.nla.gov.au/gov/20140211193845/

http://www.yourhealth.gov.au/internet/yourhealth/publishing.nsf/
Content/plainpack-tobacco#.VDMkDPlTbza.

228. American Legislative Exchange Council (ALEC). Letter to
Australian Cabinet: Resolution urging the Obama administration
to protect intellectual property rights and oppose plain packaging
initiatives proposed by trading partners worldwide. 7 Oct 2010.
Available from: http://archive.treasury.gov.au/documents/2086/
PDF/Document_3.pdf.

229. Landman A. ALEC and the tobacco industry. Center for Media
and Democracy; 2011. Available from: http://www.prwatch.org/
news/2011/07/10787/alec-and-tobacco-industry.

230. Drape J. Big tobacco "abusing" FOI process: govt. Sydney
Morning Herald. 19 Oct 2011. Available from:
http://news.smh.com.au/breaking-news-national/
big-tobacco-abusing-foi-process-govt-20111019-1m7g1.html.

231. Commonwealth of Australia. Official Committee Hansard.
Community Affairs Legislation Committee – 15/02/2012 –
Estimates. 2012.

232. Hunt E. Tobacco companies lose appeal in fight against plain
packaging. Herald Sun. 23 Aug 2011. Available from:
http://www.heraldsun.com.au/archive/news/
tobacco-companies-lose-appeal-in-fight-against-plain-packaging/
story-fn7x8me2-1226120278669.

233. Australian Government, Department of Health and Ageing.
Important changes to the sale of tobacco products in Australia.
Resources for retailers and other suppliers of tobacco products.
2014. Available from: http://health.gov.au/internet/main/
publishing.nsf/Content/tpp-resources.

234. Seitam C. Plain packaging will hit sales hard, and big tobacco is worried. Sydney Morning Herald. 20 Apr 2011. Available from: http://tiny.cc/dmntox.

235. Menzies House. Home. 2014. Available from: http://www.menzieshouse.com.au/.

236. Fong GT, Hammond D, Laux FL, Zanna MP, Cummings KM, Borland R, et al. The near-universal experience of regret among smokers in four countries: findings from the International Tobacco Control Policy Evaluation Survey. Nicotine Tobacco Research. 2004;6 (Suppl 3):S341-51.

237. Farley SM, Coady MH, Mandel-Ricci J, Waddell EN, Chan C, Kilgore EA, et al. Public opinions on tax and retail-based tobacco control strategies. Tobacco Control. 2013.

238. Australian Electoral Commission. Election 2013. Virtual Tally Room. The Official Electon Results. 2014. Available from: http://results.aec.gov.au/17496/Website/SenateStateFirstPrefs-17496-NSW.htm.

239. Freeman B, Chapman S, Storey P. Banning smoking in cars carrying children: an analytical history of a public health advocacy campaign. Aust N Z J Public Health. 2008;32 (1):60-5.

240. National Preventative Health Taskforce. Technical Report No. 2. Tobacco control in Australia: making smoking history. Canberra: Commonwealth of Australia 2008.

241. WHO Framework Convention on Tobacco Control (FCTC). Conference of the Parties to the WHO Framework Convention on Tobacco Control. Third session. Durban, South Africa, 17-22 November 2008. Decisions. 16 Feb 2009. Available from: http://www.smoke-free.ca/plain-packaging/documents/2008/FCTC_COP3_DIV3-en.pdf.

242. National Preventative Health Taskforce. Consultations. 24 Jul 2009. Available from: http://www.preventativehealth.org.au/internet/preventativehealth/publishing.nsf/Content/engagement-and-consultation-1lp.

243. National Preventative Health Taskforce. Australia: the healthiest country by 2020. National Preventative Health Strategy – the roadmap for action. 2009. Available from: http://www.preventativehealth.org.au/internet/preventativehealth/publishing.nsf/Content/nphs-roadmap-toc.

244. Rudd K. Anti-smoking action. Australian Government. Department of Prime Minister and Cabinet. OM Transcripts. 29 Apr 2010. Available from: http://pmtranscripts.dpmc.gov.au/browse.php?did=17255.

245. World Trade Organization. Notification G/TBT/N/AUS/67. 8 Apr 2011. Available from: http://docsonline.wto.org/imrd/directdoc.asp?DDFDocuments/t/G/Tbtn11/AUS67.doc.

246. Australian Government. Department of Health and Ageing. Submissions to the Public Consultation on the exposure draft of the Tobacco Plain Packaging Bill 2011 (April – June 2011). 2011. Available from: http://webarchive.nla.gov.au/gov/20140211193845/http://www.yourhealth.gov.au/internet/yourhealth/publishing.nsf/Content/plainpack-tobacco.

247. World Trade Organization. Members debate cigarette plain-packaging's impact on trademark rights. WTO News. 7 Jun 2011. Available from: http://www.wto.org/english/news_e/news11_e/trip_07jun11_e.htm.

248. Commonwealth of Australia. House of Representatives. Official Hansard No. 18. Monday, 21 November. 2011. Available from: http://tiny.cc/2aesox.

249. Philip Morris International. Philip Morris Asia Files Lawsuit Against The Australian Government Over Plain Packaging. 2011. Available from: http://www.pmi.com/eng/media_center/press_releases/Pages/201111211453.aspx.

250. Parliament of Australia. Bills of previous Parliaments. Tobacco Plain Packaging Bill 2011. 2011. Available from: http://parlinfo.aph.gov.au/parlInfo/search/display/display.w3p;query=Id%3A%22legislation%2Fbillhome%2Fr4613%22.

251. Parliament of Australia. House Standing Committee on Health and Ageing. Committee activities (inquiries and reports). Inquiry into Tobacco Plain Packaging. 2011. Available from: http://www.aph.gov.au/Parliamentary_Business/Committees/House_of_Representatives_Committees?url=haa/./billtobaccopackage/report.htm.

252. Parliament of Australia. House Standing Committee on Health and Ageing. Committee activities (inquiries and reports). Inquiry into Tobacco Plain Packaging. Submissions. 2011. Available from: http://www.aph.gov.au/Parliamentary_Business/Committees/House_of_Representatives_Committees?url=haa/./billtobaccopackage/subs.htm.

253. Parliament of Australia. House Standing Committee on Health and Ageing. Committee activities (inquiries and reports). Inquiry into Tobacco Plain Packaging. Schedule of public hearings, programs and transcripts. 2011. Available from: http://www.aph.gov.au/Parliamentary_Business/Committees/House_of_Representatives_Committees?url=haa/./billtobaccopackage/hearings.htm.

254. Parliament of Australia. Trade Marks Amendment (Tobacco Plain Packaging) Bill 2011 [Provisions]. Information about the Inquiry. 2011. Available from: http://www.aph.gov.au/

Parliamentary_Business/Committees/Senate/
Legal_and_Constitutional_Affairs/Completed inquiries/2010-13/
trademarksamendment/info.

255. Parliament of Australia. House Standing Committee on Health
and Ageing. Committee activities (inquiries and reports). Inquiry
into Tobacco Plain Packaging. Report. 2011. Available from:
http://www.aph.gov.au/Parliamentary_Business/Committees/
House_of_Representatives_Committees?url=haa/./billtobaccopackage/
report.htm.

256. Parliament of Australia. Trade Marks Amendment (Tobacco Plain
Packaging) Bill 2011 [Provisions]. Submissions received by the
Committee. 2011. Available from: http://www.aph.gov.au/
Parliamentary_Business/Committees/Senate/
Legal_and_Constitutional_Affairs/Completed inquiries/2010-13/
trademarksamendment/submissions.

257. Parliament of Australia. Trade Marks Amendment (Tobacco Plain
Packaging) Bill 2011. Public Hearings and Transcripts. 2011.
Available from: http://www.aph.gov.au/Parliamentary_Business/
Committees/Senate/Legal_and_Constitutional_Affairs/Completed
inquiries/2010-13/trademarksamendment/hearings/index.

258. ABC News. Roxon delays push for plain packaging. 2 November
2011. Available from: http://www.abc.net.au/news/2011-11-02/
roxon-delays-push-for-plain-package-cigarettes/3614794.

259. Chapman S, Wakefield M. Tobacco control advocacy in Australia:
reflections on 30 years of progress. Health Education & Behavior.
2001;28 (3):274–89.

260. Christofides N, Chapman S, Dominello A. The new pariahs:
discourse on the tobacco industry in the Sydney press, 1993–97.
Aust N Z J Public Health. 1999;23 (3):233–9.

261. Campbell D. Crumbs cried little tobacco as nanny state bit into its gingerbread house. Sydney Morning Herald. 28 Jun 2011. Available from: http://tiny.cc/5desox.

262. Chapman S. Why the tobacco industry fears plain packaging. Med J Aust. 2011;195 (5).

263. Chapman S. Pack in the smoking. New Scientist. 2011;210 (2810):22–3.

264. Chapman S. The tobacco industry is terrified of plain packs. BMJ. 2012;344.

265. Chapman S. Big tobacco and plain packaging. Living Ethics: Newsletter of the St James Ethics Centre. 2012 (89):13.

266. Chapman S. Academic bloodsport at Melbourne Univsersity. Crikey. 3 June 2010. Available from: http://www.crikey.com.au/2010/06/03/academic-blood-sport-at-melbourne-university/.

267. Chapman S. Big Tobacco losing ground on plain packs but homing in on world's poor. The Conversation. 28 Feb 2013. Available from: http://tiny.cc/2jntox.

268. Chapman S. Big Tobacco crashes at first legal hurdle on plain packaging. The Conversation. 15 Aug 2012. Available from: http://theconversation.com/big-tobacco-crashes-at-first-legal-hurdle-on-plain-packaging-8807.

269. Chapman S. BAT's ad campaign against plain packs: pull the other one. Crikey. 30 May 2011. Available from: http://tiny.cc/miesox.

270. Chapman S. Whiff of desperation as tobacco lobby loses its puff over packaging. Sydney Morning Herald. 8 Jan 2013. Available from: http://tiny.cc/jmesox.

271. Chapman S. Projecting the impact of plain packets isn't so simple. ABC The Drum. 18 Jul 2012. Available from: http://www.abc.net.au/unleashed/4138730.html.

272. Chapman S. Plain tobacco packs awaken a sleeping tobacco industry. Huffington Post. 7 May 2012. Available from: http://www.huffingtonpost.co.uk/simon-chapman/plain-tobacco-packs_b_1499203.html.

273. Chapman S. Tobacco boss's struggle with arithmetic. Crikey. 11 Aug 2011. Available from: http://www.crikey.com.au/2011/08/11/tobacco-bosss-struggle-with-arithmetic/.

274. Chapman S. Why is Deloitte's name on junk tobacco research? ABC The Drum. 6 Jul 2011. Available from: http://www.abc.net.au/unleashed/2783400.html.

275. Chapman S. Dodgy data enlisted in the propaganda war against plain packaging of cigarettes. Croakey. 28 Jun 2011. Available from: http://tiny.cc/1nesox.

276. Chapman S. Factoids and legal bollocks in war against plain packaging. Crikey. 9 Jun 2011. Available from: http://www.crikey.com.au/2011/06/09/factoids-and-legal-bollocks-in-war-against-plain-packaging/.

277. Chapman S. Tobacco lobby's plain-pack threat not based on reality. Crikey. 17 May 2011. Available from: http://www.crikey.com.au/2011/05/17/tobacco-lobbys-plain-pack-threat-not-based-on-reality/.

278. Chapman S. Ignore big tobacco's absurd fight against plain packaging. New Scientist. 2 May 2011. Available from: http://www.newscientist.com/article/mg21028100.100.

279. Chapman S. Plain packs: tobacco industry bares its butts to bluff Rudd. Crikey. 5 Mar 2010. Available from: http://www.crikey.com.au/2010/03/05/plain-packs-tobacco-industry-bares-its-butts-to-bluff-rudd/.

280. Chapman S, Freeman B. From brand to bland—the demise of cigarette packaging. BMJ. 2011;343.

281. Chapman S, Freeman B. Message is as plain as the packaging. Newcastle Herald. 1 Sep 2010.
282. Daube M. In praise of Australia's best minister for prevention. The Conversation. 6 Jul 2012. Available from: http://theconversation.com/in-praise-of-australias-best-minister-for-prevention-8051.
283. Daube M. World-first plain packaging for tobacco products a step closer to becoming law. The Conversation. 25 Aug 2011. Available from: http://tiny.cc/hpesox.
284. Davison M. Smoke and mirrors: Big Tobacco's last gasp legal challenge to plain packaging. The Conversation. 17 May 2011. Available from: http://tiny.cc/lqesox.
285. Davison M. Big Tobacco vs Australia: Philip Morris scores an own goal. The Conversation. 19 Jan 2012. Available from: http://theconversation.com/big-tobacco-vs-australia-philip-morris-scores-an-own-goal-4967.
286. Davison M. Big tobacco's huff and puff is just hot air. Sydney Morning Herald. 4 May 2010. Available from: http://www.smh.com.au/federal-politics/society-and-culture/big-tobaccos-huff-and-puff-is-just-hot-air-20100503-u3p0.html.
287. Davison M. Plain packaging bill to extinguish some tobacco trade marks. ABC The Drum. 15 Apr 2011. Available from: http://www.abc.net.au/unleashed/56666.html.
288. Day M. I have more faith in people than tobacco lobbyists. The Conversation. 20 Sept 2013. Available from: http://theconversation.com/i-have-more-faith-in-people-than-tobacco-lobbyists-18307.
289. Evans S. Big Tobacco's looming High Court challenge to plain packaging law. The Conversation. 2 Nov 2011. Available from: http://tiny.cc/sintox.

290. Faunce T. An affront to the rule of law: international tribunals to decide on plain packaging. The Conversation. 28 Aug 2012.

291. Freeman B. The evidence is in – plain cigarette packs turn young smokers off. The Conversation. 24 May 2011. Available from: http://theconversation.com/ the-evidence-is-in-plain-cigarette-packs-turn-young-smokers-off-1443.

292. Freedman M. In praise of nannies. Sydney Morning Herald. 18 Jul 2011. Available from: http://www.smh.com.au/federal-politics/ society-and-culture/in-praise-of-nannies-20110718-1hkqo.html.

293. Gittins R. Big tobacco – what have they been smoking? Sydney Morning Herald. 22 Aug 2012. Available from: http://www.smh.com.au/federal-politics/political-opinion/ big-tobacco--what-have-they-been-smoking-20120821-24kmt.html.

294. Greenland S. Spluttering on: why big tobacco just can't butt out on plain packaging. The Conversation. 8 Jun 2011. Available from: http://tiny.cc/wresox.

295. Grills N. Plain tobacco packaging in India: a giant leap for global public health. The Conversation. 5 Sept 2012. Available from: http://tiny.cc/qsesox.

296. Grogan P. A few plain facts amid the smoke and mirrors. The Punch. 20 Apr 2011.

297. Harrison P. Plain cigarette packaging will change smoking . . . slowly. The Conversation. 11 Apr 2011. Available from: http://theconversation.com/ plain-cigarette-packaging-will-change-smoking-slowly-737.

298. Hill D. Tobacco industry has much to fear. Sydney Morning Herald. 4 Jul 2011. Available from: http://www.smh.com.au/ federal-politics/political-opinion/ tobacco-industry-has-much-to-fear-20110407-1d63x.html.

299. Irvine J. It's plain to see what's behind the smokescreen. Sydney Morning Herald. 20 May 2011. Available from: http://tiny.cc/ugntox.

300. Leeder S. Plain packaging wraps up a big year for health legislation in 2011. The Conversation. 29 Nov 2011. Available from: http://tiny.cc/qfntox.

301. MacKenzie R. Why bilateral investment treaties are the last refuge of Big Tobacco. The Conversation. 16 Aug 2012. Available from: http://tiny.cc/gentox.

302. McLeod C. Tobacco PR push runs out of puff as retailers play victim. The Conversation. 20 Apr 2011. Available from: http://theconversation.com/tobacco-pr-push-runs-out-of-puff-as-retailers-play-victim-742.

303. Moodie R. Nanny knows best: Why Big Tobacco's attack on Mary Poppins ought to backfire. The Conversation. 20 Jun 2011. Available from: http://tiny.cc/juesox.

304. O'Shea B. Package deal. The West Australian (The Wire). 30 Jun 2011.

305. Rattan R. Big Tobacco's death-defying campaign on plain packaging. The Conversation. 17 May 2011. Available from: http://theconversation.com/big-tobaccos-death-defying-campaign-on-plain-packaging-1314.

306. Rimmer M. The High Court and the Marlboro Man: the plain packaging decision. The Conversation. 18 Oct 2012. Available from: http://tiny.cc/3cntox.

307. Rimmer M. The Olive Revolution: Australia's plain packaging leads the world. The Conversation. 15 Aug 2012. Available from: http://theconversation.com/the-olive-revolution-australias-plain-packaging-leads-the-world-8856.

308. Rimmer M. Big Tobacco's box fetish: plain packaging at the High Court. The Conversation. 20 Apr 2012. Available from: http://theconversation.com/ big-tobaccos-box-fetish-plain-packaging-at-the-high-court-6518.

309. Rimmer M. Tobacco's mad men threaten public health. The Conversation. 22 Sept 2011. Available from: http://theconversation.com/ tobaccos-mad-men-threaten-public-health-3450.

310. D R. Big Tobacco v Australia: Philip Morris jumps the gun on legal challenge. The Conversation. 27 Jun 2011. Available from: http://tiny.cc/lwesox.

311. Tienhaara K. Government wins first battle in plain packaging war. The Conversation. 15 Aug 2012. Available from: http://theconversation.com/ government-wins-first-battle-in-plain-packaging-war-8855.

312. Vieceli J. It's poo brown and olive green as cigarette packs lose their magic colours. The Conversation. 14 Apr 2011. Available from: http://tiny.cc/lxesox.

313. Voon T. Australia's plain tobacco packaging law at the WTO. The Conversation. May 2013. Available from: http://theconversation.com/ australias-plain-tobacco-packaging-law-at-the-wto-14043.

314. Bajzert L. If the government steals brands from the tobacco companies, what's next? Mumbrella. 11 May 2011. Available from: http://tiny.cc/tyesox.

315. Berg C. Plain packs pointless when smoke gets in our eyes. Sydney Morning Herald. 17 Apr 2011. Available from: http://tiny.cc/l3mtox.

316. Novak J. Simon Chapman is blowing smoke on smoking. ABC The Drum. 25 May 2011. Available from: http://www.abc.net.au/unleashed/2730672.html.

317. Wilson T. Trademark rights to extinguish plain packaging bill? ABC The Drum. 11 Apr 2011. Available from: http://www.abc.net.au/unleashed/55680.html.

318. Durkin SJ, Germain D, Wakefield M. Adult's perceptions about whether tobacco companies tell the truth in relation to issues about smoking. Tobacco Control. 2005;14 (6):429–30.

319. Wakefield M, Miller C, Woodward S. Community perceptions about the tobacco industry and tobacco control funding. Aust N Z J Public Health. 1999;23 (3):240–4.

320. The Wirthlin Group. Australian Corporate Image Study. General public and opinion leaders. April 1993. Available from: http://legacy.library.ucsf.edu/tid/pti19e00/pdf.

321. Chapman S. The news on smoking: newspaper coverage of smoking and health in Australia, 1987–88. Am J Public Health. 1989;79 (10):1419–21.

322. Durrant R, Wakefield M, McLeod K, Clegg-Smith K, Chapman S. Tobacco in the news: an analysis of newspaper coverage of tobacco issues in Australia, 2001. Tobacco Control. 2003;12 (suppl 2):ii75-ii81.

323. Champion D, Chapman S. Framing pub smoking bans: an analysis of Australian print news media coverage, March 1996–March 2003. Journal of Epidemiology and Community Health. 2005;59 (8):679–84.

324. Anon. Labor has numbers to pass new smoking law. Herald Sun (Melbourne). 25 May 2011. Available from: http://www.heraldsun.com.au/news/breaking-news/

government-has-numbers-to-pass-new-smoking-laws/
story-e6frf7jx-1226062544714.

325. Houston C. Big Tobacco 'scaremongering'. The Age (Melbourne).
22 May 2011. Available from: http://www.theage.com.au/national/
big-tobacco-lobby-scaremongering-20110521-1ey4n.html.

326. Grattan M. Leadership lacking as Libs squabble over smoking. 27
May 2011. Available from: http://tiny.cc/qbntox.

327. Chapman S. Civil disobedience and tobacco control: the case of
BUGA UP. Billboard Utilising Graffitists Against Unhealthy
Promotions. Tobacco Control. 1996;5 (3):179–85.

328. Hockley C. Libs yield on smokes packaging. Adelaide Advertiser.
1 Jun 2011.

329. Woodley N. Tobacco giants launch High Court challenge. ABC
The World Today. 17 Apr 2012. Available from:
http://www.abc.net.au/worldtoday/content/2012/s3479228.htm.

330. Berkovic N. Legal experts back Canberra. The Australian. 30
April 2010. Available from: http://www.theaustralian.com.au/
archive/politics/legal-experts-back-canberra/
story-e6frgczf-1225860371872.

331. Wilson T. Plain packaging may require up to $3.4 billion taxpayer
gift annually to big tobacco and film companies. IPA. 26 Apr 2010.
Available from: http://ipa.org.au/library/publication/
1272344059_document_governing_in_ignorance_-_26042010.pdf.

332. Wilson T. Plain packaging ploy likely to go up in smoke. The
Australian. 30 Apr 2010. Available from:
http://www.theaustralian.com.au/opinion/
plain-packaging-ploy-likely-to-go-up-in-smoke/
story-e6frg6zo-1225860365444.

333. Wilson T. Governing in ignorance: Australian governments
legislating, without understanding, intellectual property.

Melbourne: Institute of Public Affairs; May 2010. Available from: http://tiny.cc/d9mtox.

334. ABC Media Watch. Smoking out the spin. 10 May 2010. Available from: http://www.abc.net.au/mediawatch/transcripts/s2895480.htm.

335. Swan J. Institute opposing plain packaging funded by tobacco company. Sydney Morning Herald. News and Features. Page 3. 31 May. 2012. Available from:http://tiny.cc/81esox.

336. Kerr C. Taxpaper may take wrap rap on cigarettes. The Australian. 16 Sept 2010.

337. Millson S. Group Head of Corporate Affairs for BAT, second letter to Deborah Arnott, ASH UK, 18 June. 2013.

338. High Court of Australia. JT International SA v Commonwealth of Australia [2012] HCA 43. 5 Oct 2012. Available from: http://www.austlii.edu.au/au/cases/cth/HCA/2012/43.html.

339. McCabe Centre for Law and Cancer. High Court finds Australia's world first plain packaging constitutional. 2014. Available from: http://www.mccabecentre.org/focus-areas/tobacco/.

340. Liberman J. Plainly constitutional: the upholding of plain tobacco packaging by the High Court of Australia. Am J Law & Med. 2013;39:361–81. Available from: http://www.mccabecentre.org/downloads/Liberman_plainly_constitutional_FINAL.pdf

341. Elliot T. Tim Wilson: freedom figher. Sydney Morning Herald (Good Weekend). 22 Feb 2014. Available from: http://www.smh.com.au/lifestyle/tim-wilson-freedom-fighter-20140217-32umq.html.

342. Dispute Settlement Body, WTO. Australia – certain measures concerning trademarks and other plain packaging requirements applicable to tobacco products and packaging. 2014. Available from: http://tiny.cc/h3esox.

343. Australian Government, Department of Foreign Affairs and Trading. Honduras. Australia's trade and investment relationship with Honduras. 2013. Available from: http://www.dfat.gov.au/geo/fs/hond.pdf.

344. Australian Government, Department of Foreign Affairs and Trading. Ukraine. Australia's trade and investment relationship with Ukraine. 2013. Available from: http://www.dfat.gov.au/geo/fs/ukra.pdf.

345. Martin A. Philip Morris Leads Plain Packs Battle in Global Trade Arena. Bloomberg News. 2013. Available from: http://www.bloomberg.com/news/2013-08-22/philip-morris-leads-plain-packs-battle-in-global-trade-arena.html.

346. Davison M. The legitimacy of plain packaging under international intellectual property law: why there is no right to use a trademark under either the Paris convention or the trips agreement. In: Mitchell A, Voon T, Liberman J, editors. Public Health and Plain Packaging of Cigarettes: Legal Issues. Cheltenham: Edward Elgar; 2012.

347. Voon TS. Flexibilities in WTO Law to Support Tobacco Control Regulation. American Journal of Law and Medicine. 2013;39 (2–3).

348. McCabe Centre for Law & Cancer. Dispute in the World Trade Organization 2014. Available from: http://www.mccabecentre.org/focus-areas/tobacco/dispute-in-the-world-trade-organization.

349. Chapman S, Alpers P, Agho K, Jones M. Australia's 1996 gun law reforms: faster falls in firearm deaths, firearm suicides, and a decade without mass shootings. Injury Prevention. 2006;12 (6):365–72.

350. Commonwealth of Australia Attorney Generals' Department. Investor-state arbitration – tobacco plain packaging. 2014.

Available from: http://www.ag.gov.au/internationalrelations/
internationallaw/pages/tobaccoplainpackaging.aspx.

351. Robinson AA. Notice of claim under the Australia 'Hong King
agreement for the promotion and protection of investments. 2011
Available from: http://www.ag.gov.au/Internationalrelations/
InternationalLaw/Documents/Philip Morris Asia Limited Notice
of Claim 27 June 2011.pdf.

352. United Nations Commission on International Trade Law
(UNCITRAL). UNCITRAL Arbitration Rules. 2010. Available
from: http://www.uncitral.org/uncitral/en/uncitral_texts/
arbitration/2010Arbitration_rules.html.

353. Permanent Court of Arbitration. Philip Morris Asia Limited
(Hong Kong) v. The Commonwealth of Australia. 2012. Available
from: http://www.pca-cpa.org/showpage.asp?pag_id=1494.

354. Permanent Court of Arbitration. Philip Morris Asia Limited
(Hong Kong) v. The Commonwealth of Australia. Procedural
Order No.5 Regarding Confidentiality. 30 November. 2012.
Available from: http://www.pca-cpa.org/showfile.asp?fil_id=2064

355. National Cancer Institute. The Role of the Media in Promoting
and Controlling Tobacco Use. Tobacco Control Monograph No.
19. Bethesda, MD: U.S.: Department of Health and Human
Services, National Institutes of Health, National Cancer Institute;
2008.

356. Intergovernmental Committee on Drugs Standing Committee on
Tobacco. The National Tobacco Strategy 2012–2018. 2012.
Available from: http://www.nationaldrugstrategy.gov.au/internet/
drugstrategy/publishing.nsf/Content/
D4E3727950BDBAE4CA257AE70003730C/$File/National
Tobacco Strategy 2012-2018.pdf.

357. Snowdon C. That plain packaging study. Velvet glove, Iron Fist. 2013. Available from: http://velvetgloveironfist.blogspot.com.au/ 2013/07/that-plain-packaging-study.html.

358. Winstanley M, White V, Germain D, Zacher M. Tobacco in Australia. 1.3 Prevalence of smoking. 2011. Available from: http://www.tobaccoinaustralia.org.au/chapter-1-prevalence/ 1-3-prevalence-of-smoking-adults.

359. Imperial Tobacco Merchant Cantos. Imperial Tobacco – half year 2013 results. Available from: http://video.merchantcantos.com/ media/202678/imperial_tobacco_half_year_results_transcript.pdf.

360. Rogut J. Plain crazy. 7 May 2013. Available from: http://www.asiantrader.biz/features/PLAIN+CRAZY/1330.

361. British American Tobacco Australia. Industry volumes up, illegal tobacco up, while the number of people quitting halves. 4 Apr 2014. Available from: http://www.bata.com.au/group/sites/ bat_7wykg8.nsf/vwPagesWebLive/DO9FC38M/$FILE/ medMD9HTTCS.pdf?openelement.

362. White V, Bariola E. Tobacco use among Australian secondary students in 2011. In Australian secondary school students' use of tobacco, alcohol, and over-the-counter and illicit substances in 2011. Drug Strategy Branch Australian Government Department of Health and Ageing. 2012. Available from: http://www.nationaldrugstrategy.gov.au/internet/drugstrategy/ Publishing.nsf/content/school11

363. Scollo M. Table 2.2.5 Chapter 2. Trends in tobacco consumption, in Tobacco in Australia: facts and issues. Melbourne, Australia. 2013. Available from: http://www.tobaccoinaustralia.org.au/ chapter-2-consumption/ 2-2-dutiable-tobacco-products-as-an-estimate-of-to.

364. Select Statistical Services. Sample size calculator: comparing two proportions. 2014. Available from: http://www.select-statistics.co.uk/ sample-size-calculator-two-proportions.

365. Kaul A, Wolf M. The (Possible) Effect of Plain Packaging on the Smoking Prevalence of Minors in Australia: A Trend Analysis. Department of Economics. University of Zurich. March 2014. Available from: http://www.econ.uzh.ch/static/wp/econwp149.pdf.

366. Cancer Council of Victoria. Comments on Kaul & Wolf "The (possible) effect of plain packaging on the smoking prevalence of minors in Australia: a trend analysis". 26 March 2014. Available from: http://www.cancervic.org.au/downloads/tobacco_control/ 2013/Cancer_Council_Victoria_comments_on_Kaul_Wolf.pdf.

367. Propel Centre for Population Health Impact. Tobacco Use in Canada – Patterns and Trends 2014. Waterloo, Canada. 2014. Available from: http://tobaccoreport.ca/2014/adtu_sic_sp.cfm.

368. World Health Organization. Reporting Instrument of the WHO Framework Convention on Tobacco Control. Sweden. 2014. Available from: http://www.who.int/fctc/reporting/party_reports/ swe/en/.

369. Daube M, Chapman S. The Australian's dissembling campaign on tobacco plain packaging. Med J Aust. 2014;4:1.

370. British American Tobacco Australasia. Smoking rates underestimated. Media Release. 17 July 2014. Available from: http://www.bata.com.au/group/sites/bat_7wykg8.nsf/ vwPagesWebLive/DO9FC38M/$FILE/ medMD9M4AFJ.pdf?openelement.

371. Citi Research Equities. Tobacco- Australia data provides ammunition for plain packaging elsewhere. 17 Jul 2014. Available only to subscribers.

372. Plassmann H, O'Doherty J, Shiv B, Rangel A. Marketing actions can modulate neural representations of experienced pleasantness. Proceedings of the National Academy of Sciences. 2008;105 (3):1050–4.

373. Ferrier A. Smoke and mirrors in cigarette marketing. ABC The Drum. 3 Dec 2012. Available from: http://www.abc.net.au/news/ 2012-11-30/smokers-believe-plain-pack-cigarettes-taste-worse/ 4400748.

374. Siegel M. Law spoils tobacco's taste, Australians say. New Tork Times. 10 Jul 2013. Available from: http://www.nytimes.com/ 2013/07/11/business/global/ law-spoils-tobaccos-taste-australians-say.html?_r=0.

375. Parliamentary Counsel Office. New Zealand Legislation. Smoke-free Environments (Tobacco Plain Packaging) Amendment Bill. 2014 [cited 2014 22 April]. Available from: http://www.legislation.govt.nz/bill/government/2013/0186/latest/ DLM5821008.html?src=qs.

376. New Zealand Parliament. Hansard. Smoke-free Environments (Tobacco Plain Packaging) Amendment Bill — First Reading. 11 Februray. 2014. Available from: http://www.parliament.nz/en-nz/ pb/debates/debates/50HansD_20140211_00000028/ smoke-free-environments-tobacco-plain-packaging-amendment.

377. New Zealand Parliament. Select committee details. Health. 2014. Available from: http://www.parliament.nz/en-nz/pb/sc/details/ health/00DBHOH_BBSC_SCHE_1/ business-before-the-health-committee.

378. Ellison J. Oral statement to the House of Commons on publication of Sir Cyril Chantler report on standardised packaging of tobacco products. 3 Apr 2014. Available from:

http://www.gov.uk/government/speeches/
chantler-report-on-standardised-packaging-of-tobacco-products.

379. Department of Health, NHS, UK. Consultation on the future of tobacco control. 2008. Available from: http://webarchive.nationalarchives.gov.uk/+/www.dh.gov.uk/en/ consultations/liveconsultations/dh_085120.

380. ASH UK. Beyond Smoking Kills. 2008. Available from: http://ash.org.uk/current-policy-issues/beyond-smoking-kills.

381. Department of Health, NHS, UK. A smokefree future: a comprehensive tobacco control strategy for England. 2010. Available from: http://webarchive.nationalarchives.gov.uk/ 20100509080731/www.dh.gov.uk/en/Publicationsandstatistics/ Publications/PublicationsPolicyAndGuidance/DH_111749.

382. BBC News. Health. Make cigarette packaging plain, government urges. 21 November 2010. Available from: http://www.bbc.co.uk/ news/health-11796903.

383. Campbell D, Meikle J. Pro-smoking activists threaten and harass health campaigners. The Guardian. News. Society. Smoking. 2 Jun 2012. Available from: http://www.theguardian.com/society/2012/ jun/01/pro-smoking-activists-health-campaigners.

384. ASH UK. Media Brefing. Standardised Packaging of Cigarettes. Has the Government Caved in to Tobacco Lobbying? 2013. Available from: http://www.smokefreeaction.org.uk/files/docs/ PPmediabrief20130503.pdf.

385. Department of Health, UK. Press release. Consultation on standardised packaging of tobacco products. 21 July 2013. Available from: http://www.gov.uk/government/news/ consultation-on-standardised-packaging-of-tobacco-products.

386. The Public Whip. Children and Families Bill — Prohibition on Purchasing Tobacco for a Child and Regulation of Tobacco

Products. 10 February. 2014. Available from:
http://www.publicwhip.org.uk/
division.php?date=2014-02-10&number=208.

387. Rimmer M. Ireland, Plain Packaging, and the Olive Revolution.
2014. Available from: http://infojustice.org/archives/32484.

388. House of the Oireachtas. Reports of the Joint Committee on
Health and Children. 3 April 2014 – Report on the General
Scheme of the Public Health (Standardised Packaging of Tobacco)
Bill 2013. 2014. Available from: http://www.oireachtas.ie/
parliament/oireachtasbusiness/committees_list/
health-and-children/reports/.

389. Houses of the Oireachtas. Press releases. Health Committee
publishes report on tobacco plain packaging Bill. 2014. Available
from: http://www.oireachtas.ie/parliament/mediazone/
pressreleases/name-21484-en.html.

390. Government of Ireland. Public Health (Standardised Packaging of
Tobacco) Bill 2014, Bill Number 54 of 2014, introduced in the
Seanad (Senate) June 11, 2014. Second Stage in the Seanad
approved June 17, 2014. 2014. Available from:
http://www.oireachtas.ie/
viewdoc.asp?DocID=26331&&CatID=59.

391. Anderson A. The legality of plain packaging under international
law. Economic and Political Weekly. 2014;49 (11):21–4.

392. Times HCH. UP court recommends plain packaging for
cigarettes. Hindustan Times. 25 Jul 2014. Available from:
http://tiny.cc/30mtox.

393. Anon. France moves towards plain cigarette packaging and e-cig
ban. France 24. 30 May 2014. Available from: http://tiny.cc/
c6mtox.

394. Roelf W. S.Africa plans plain cigarette packaging by 2015 – minister. Reuters. 24 Jul 2014. Available from: http://www.reuters.com/article/2014/07/24/safrica-tobacco-idUSL6N0PZ4FZ20140724.

395. Anon. Sigara yasaginda yeni yol haritasi! Htekonomi. 25 Jul 2014

396. Government of Finland. Action plan to make the country smoke-free by 2040. June 2014. Available from: http://www.who.int/fctc/implementation/news/news_Fin/en/.

397. Fooks G, Gilmore AB. International trade law, plain packaging and tobacco industry political activity: the Trans-Pacific Partnership. Tobacco Control. 2014;23:e1 doi:10.1136/tobaccocontrol-2012–050869

398. Robb A. Standing firm in talks (letter). 16 Dec 2013. Available from: http://www.theage.com.au/comment/the-age-letters/casual-destruction-of-priceless-qualities-20131215-2zf6q.html.

399. Kehoe J. Packaging laws under fire. Australian Financial Review. 31 Jan 2014.

400. Hegarty R. Melvin Ruigrok takes charge at Imperial Tobacco UK as plain packs legislation looms. The Grocer (UK). 26 Jan 2014. Available from: http://tiny.cc/t6esox.

401. Cullman H. Chairman's Remarks. INFOTAB Workshop.Copenhagen, Denmark. 1985. Available from: http://legacy.library.ucsf.edu/tid/tdy88e00.

Index

Index

www.ingramcontent.com/pod-product-compliance
Lightning Source LLC
Chambersburg PA
CBHW062205270326
41930CB00009B/1650